D1823498

True Emotions

Consciousness & Emotion Book Series

Consciousness & Emotion Book Series publishes original works on this topic, in philosophy, psychology and the neurosciences. The series emphasizes thoughtful analysis of the implications of both empirical and experiential (e.g., clinical psychological) approaches to emotion. It will include topical works by scientists who are interested in the implications of their empirical findings for an understanding of emotion and consciousness and their interrelations.

For an overview of all books published in this series, please see
http://benjamins.com/catalog/ceb

Editors

Ralph D. Ellis
Clark Atlanta University

Peter Zachar
Auburn University Montgomery

Editorial Board

Carl M. Anderson
McLean Hospital, Harvard University
School of Medicine, Cambridge, MA

Bill Faw
Brewton Parker College,
Mt. Vernon, GA

Eugene T. Gendlin
University of Chicago

Jaak Panksepp
Bowling Green State University, OH

Maxim I. Stamenov
Bulgarian Academy of Sciences

Douglas F. Watt
Quincy Hospital, Boston, MA

Advisory Editors

Bernard J. Baars
Wright Institute, Berkeley, CA

Thomas C. Dalton
California Polytechnic Institute,
San Luis Obispo, CA

Nicholas Georgalis
East Carolina University, Greenville,
NC

George Graham
Georgia State University

Valerie Gray Hardcastle
Virginia Polytechnic Institute,
Blacksburg, VA

Alfred W. Kaszniak
University of Arizona, Tucson, AZ

Alfred R. Mele
Florida State University,
Talahassee, FL

Natika Newton
Nassau County Community College,
New York

Martin Peper
University of Marburg, Germany

Edward Ragsdale
New York, NY

Howard Shevrin
University of Michigan,
Ann Arbor, MI

Lynn Stephens
University of Alabama,
Birmingham, AL

Kathleen Wider
University of Michigan, Dearborn, MI

Volume 9

True Emotions
by Mikko Salmela

True Emotions

Mikko Salmela
University of Helsinki

John Benjamins Publishing Company
Amsterdam / Philadelphia

The paper used in this publication meets the minimum requirements of the American National Standard for Information Sciences – Permanence of Paper for Printed Library Materials, ANSI z39.48-1984.

Library of Congress Cataloging-in-Publication Data

Salmela, Mikko, 1967-
True Emotions / Mikko Salmela.
     p.   cm. (Consciousness & Emotion Book Series, ISSN 2352-099X ; v. 9)
Includes bibliographical references and index.
1. Emotions. I. Title.
BF531.S25   2014
152.4--dc23   2014016853
ISBN 978 90 272 4159 7   (Hb ; alk. paper)
ISBN 978 90 272 6981 2   (Eb)

© 2014 – John Benjamins B.V.
No part of this book may be reproduced in any form, by print, photoprint, microfilm, or any other means, without written permission from the publisher.

John Benjamins Publishing Co. · P.O. Box 36224 · 1020 ME Amsterdam · The Netherlands
John Benjamins North America · P.O. Box 27519 · Philadelphia PA 19118-0519 · USA

Table of contents

Acknowledgements

This book has been in the making for a long time. Its first ideas about emotional authenticity began to take shape during my post-doc year 2001–2002 at the University of Texas at Austin where I had the privilege of developing my thoughts in discussions with Robert C. Solomon (1942–2007), a pioneer of the "emotional turn". Another stimulating philosophical companion was Verena Mayer who hosted my Alexander von Humboldt fellowship at the University of Munich 2006–2007 and again for a shorter period in the fall 2009.

Various other individuals have also given valuable feedback on my texts at various points of writing this volume and the articles that are included in it. These people include, in alphabetical order, Åsa Carlson, Louis C. Charland, Julien A. Deonna, Kristin Klamm-Doneen, Rick Anthony Furtak, Felicitas Kraemer, Robert Roberts, and Fabrice Teroni. Moreover, an anonymous reviewer for the Consciousness & Emotion Book Series suggested for my penultimate manuscript several helpful amendments on the neurophysiological implementation of human emotions. The remaining shortcomings are of course solely my own. I am also grateful to Ralph Ellis, the Co-Editor of the Consciousness & Emotion Book Series, whose kind support I have been able to rely on. Finally, my deepest gratitude goes to my wife Liisa Lampi for her ceaseless support on my personal journey towards emotional authenticity.

Three chapters of the volume are revised versions of my previously published articles. These articles are "What is emotional authenticity?" (*Journal for the Theory of Social Behaviour* 35, 2005, 209–230); "True emotions," (*The Philosophical Quarterly* 56, 2006, 382–405); and "Authenticity and Occupational Emotions" (in M. Salmela and V. Mayer (Eds): *Emotions, Ethics, and Authenticity. Consciousness and Emotion Book Series*, Vol. 5, pp. 133–151, Amsterdam: John Benjamins). Also sections from my article "Can emotion be modelled on perception?" *Dialectica* 65 (2011), 1–29, are used in Chapter 2. I am grateful to Wiley and John Benjamins for permission to reprint this material in the present volume.

CHAPTER 1

Introduction

Emotion research is a diverse field of interdisciplinary scholarship that has emerged from the so called "emotional turn" in the sciences and humanities since the 1970s. This turn brought with it a fresh interest in the nature of emotions and their various roles in individual and social behaviour. Philosophers rediscovered the intentionality of emotions as evaluative representations of objects that motivate the subject of emotion to act in accordance with the emotional evaluation. Yet this cognitive account that goes back to Ancient philosophy has been contested by feeling theorists who draw their inspiration from David Hume and, even more so, William James. In the meanwhile, psychologists studied, among other things, the various components of emotion – facial expressions, appraisal processes, action tendencies, physiological and hormonal changes, and subjective experiences – debating the causal relations of these components and their contingent or necessary role in human emotions and thus joining the philosophical debate on the cognitive or noncognitive nature of emotions. In this debate, social psychologists and sociologists have generally taken the former side as they have emphasized the influence of social processes, structures, and norms on the emotions of individuals on the one hand, and the constitutive role of emotions in binding people to sociocultural structures and long-lasting relations – either amicable or antagonistic – on the other hand. Neuroscientists joined the "emotional turn" only in the 1990s, but they have compensated this later start with impressive findings on how the brain processes and implements emotions. Finally, the findings of historians indicate that the properties, functions, and mechanisms that other researchers have ascribed to emotions are more or less timeless as there have been emotional regimes and communities that set norms for emotions and their expression in past societies as well.

In an important sense, the "emotional turn" has then been a matter of turning the philosophical and scientific gaze to affective phenomena that have always been there even if their research has been neglected until recently. Yet it seems obvious that a concurrent multidisciplinary interest in emotions is not a coincidence but manifests a long and extensive cultural transition in which emotions and other affective phenomena have become more important to individuals; more cherished and trusted in building and maintaining evaluative meanings and attitudes about the self, the others, and the world. Love has replaced other arrangements as the ideal basis of marriage and family life, especially in Western culture but also else-where through its global influence. Happiness, fun, excitement, enthusiasm, feel-ings of togetherness and other rewarding affective experiences are also sought in other domains of life, such as work, hobbies, social life, and other recreational ac-tivities, both in the short and the long run. In this pursuit of happiness, we have come to rely on therapies whose common denominator is the focus on emotions and their regulation. The therapeutic narratives hold the promise of guiding the clients of therapy from suffering caused by interrupted "self-realization" to more "authentic" and "healthy" emotions. Yet by regarding emotions as something that people must continuously manage and control in order to successfully navigate the precarious social world of contemporary capitalism, therapies tend to end up re-ducing the ideal of authenticity into conforming to existing social roles and their situational norms of appropriateness, as the sociologist Eva Illouz observes in her insightful study *Saving the Modern Soul* (2008). Accordingly, sociologists and phi-losophers are pessimistic about the possibility of giving any plausible standards to such ideals as emotional authenticity whose debased and truncated forms pervade contemporary popular culture.

Even so, this pessimism is disturbing given that we live in a culture in which individuals rely on their emotions in making significant choices about their lives as well as in forming evaluative attitudes towards the world. The naïve rhetoric of authenticity should not blind us to the fact that authenticity is an influential cul-tural ideal, whether or not we like this. Therefore, it may be more commendable to follow the example of Charles Taylor who in his *Ethics of Authenticity* (1991) took the ideal of authenticity seriously and proposed a robust philosophical ac-count of authenticity in ethics as an alternative to simple subjectivism. In a like manner, I believe that the therapeutic travesties of authenticity have not removed the relevance of questions about the authenticity and appropriateness of emo-tions, including the question about the nature of emotions as states that are ca-pable of being evaluated in terms of authenticity or appropriateness in the first place. These problems about the nature, authenticity, and appropriateness of emo-tions associate with three meanings of "true" in the context of emotions: what emotions really or *truly are*; what does it mean for an emotion to be *true to the self*; and what does it mean for an emotion to be *true to the world*? – thus the seem-ingly arrogant title of this book, *True Emotions*. All these problems are theoretical but they have important ramifications beyond the scope of philosophical emotion theory as I hope to show. This introductory chapter introduces the problems that are associated with these three meanings of "true emotion" and motivates their choice to the spotlight of this study, thereby laying out the synopsis for the rest of the book.

What emotions truly are?

There is a wide agreement among emotion researchers, both empirical and philosophical, that the function of emotions is to evaluate perceived changes in the environment for their significance to the subject's concerns and to motivate adaptive responding to the situation. Each emotion type serves this general function of emotions in its own specific domain. Thus, the function of fear is to detect threats and dangers to the subject and to motivate fight or flight in response to danger. Likewise, the function of anger is to detect transgressions, offences, or slights against the subject and to motivate revenge or retaliation – either actual or symbolic – against the perpetrator. Or, the function of guilt is to detect one's own transgressions against others and to motivate submissive and apologizing behaviour towards the victim or victims. Moreover, emotion types are largely individuated on the basis of those evaluations and behaviours – both expressive and purposive – that they involve either on the basis of evolutionary hard-wiring or cultural learning or, as is often the case, through a combination of the two, namely culturally influenced evolutionary action readiness. Special-purpose mechanisms that operate on logical processing of information can be built into robots as well. However, robots cannot respond by 'gut appraisals', nor can their evaluative states be inherently affective in the same way as emotions. Feelings of emotion face both inwards and outwards: they emerge from the body's changing action readiness but they can also infuse our intentional representations of particular objects in the world in typical emotional experiences.

In spite of rapprochement in the big picture, emotion theorists still disagree on the more precise nature of emotions. Paul Griffiths reinvigorated this debate with his provocatively titled book *What Emotions Really Are* (1997). There he claimed that emotions do not constitute a natural kind but fall into two or three importantly dissimilar subtypes – evolutionarily primitive affect programmes, cognitively complex emotions, and disclaimed actions (socially sustained pretences)[1] – that have little in common with each other. The main problem is that the causal mechanisms of different types of emotion do not coincide, allowing reliable projections of properties, functions, and explanatory principles from individual instances to all responses that we call "emotions" in vernacular language or even in science.

---

1.   Griffiths introduces disclaimed actions as the third main type of emotion in his book *What Emotions Really Are*. These are emotions experienced and enacted in transitory social roles that are functional either for the individual or for society or both. In order to serve their functions, these emotions are interpreted as passive and involuntary even if they did not exist without the relevant social roles as James Averill (1982) remarks. Griffiths later focuses on the distinction between affect programs and complex emotions to which he possibly includes disclaimed actions.

To illustrate, fear of a terrorist attack against one's home town is significantly dissimilar from fear of falling from a steep cliff. The former fear normally responds to information about the extremely small likelihood of such an attack, whereas the information that one is safe may not help to alleviate the latter fear when one is standing on the edge of a cliff. Fear of falling from cliffs is a disposition that evolution has built into our biological constitution because this response helped our ancestors to survive and reproduce while their less fearful contemporaries perished. Even if all fears are sensitive to dangers, dangers may be dissimilar in different cases, indicating that evolutionarily early and late fears have somewhat dissimilar functions in our mental and behavioural economy. Moreover, the persistence of evolutionarily early fears in spite of contrary information suggests that these emotions operate on at least partially different neural pathways than culturally learned fears in the human brain.

However, instead of closing the debate on the nature of emotions, Griffiths' rejection of "emotion" as a plausible scientific category inspired a wave of new theories that sought to bring emotions back into a single explanatory frame. As the result of this development, disagreements between traditionally opposite approaches have become more sophisticated and subtle, which has contributed to a rapprochement in emotion theory as all theories now must accommodate – in one way or another – the intentional aboutness, affective phenomenology, evaluative function, motivational force, and rational justifiability of human emotions. Even so, it is important to emphasize that the rapprochement is limited to the set of those *properties* of emotion that any plausible theory must explain. Different theories of emotion still diverge from each other in their ways of accommodating these properties even if their disagreements are more difficult to detect behind a wide consensus on the properties that require explanation. One such disagreement is whether emotion involves cognition always, sometimes, or never. Cognitive theories of emotion are plausible only if human emotions always rather than merely sometimes involve cognitions; mere causation or regulation by cognition is insufficient unless cognitions are also constituents of emotion, as Clore and Ortony (2000) point out. Otherwise emotions are either noncognitive, or they divide between two main types, cognitive and noncognitive, as Griffiths argued.

Cognitive theories suggest that emotions are always cognitive because they can serve their evaluative function only if they involve appraisals or evaluative judgments of their particular objects in their content that can be explicated in terms of conceptually structured propositional attitudes. Cognitivists emphasize that the content of all emotions need not be constituted of concepts; otherwise the theory could not accommodate such emotions as fear of flying that we feel in spite of contrary evaluative judgments about the situation, or the emotions of prelinguistic infants and higher animals who do not possess semantic concepts in the first place.[2] However, cognitivists maintain that the content of emotion is nevertheless conceptually explicable even in those cases where it is not constituted of concepts (Nussbaum, 2001; Roberts, 2003).

In contrast, noncognitive theories deny that emotions must involve concepts in order to serve their evaluative function. Ascribing concepts to all human emotions is metaphorical at best and misleading at worst. Cognitive appraisals may contingently elicit and regulate emotions but they are never constituents of emotion. Moreover, the content of emotion can be explicated in functional terms that emphasize a reliable causal co-occurrence between emotions and those things – dangers, losses, offences, and so on – that emotions represent in their content (Prinz, 2004). Or the content of emotion is nonconceptual, constituted of fast, automatic, and highly modular appraisals that occur at a subpersonal and subdoxastic level of information processing which is distinct from cognition proper (Robinson, 2005).

In order to adjudicate the dispute about the role of cognition in emotion, we must clarify what we mean by cognition. A well-known debate in the 1980s between psychologists Robert Zajonc (1923–2008) and Richard Lazarus (1922–2002) addressed this question (for a review, see Schorr, 2001). In his studies on subliminal perception, Zajonc (1980) found that we can form likings and aversions to objects on the basis of mere exposure to them, without conscious awareness of exposure and recognition of the object. This phenomenon is known as "the mere exposure effect". From these empirical results Zajonc concluded that feeling precedes cognition, or, "preferences need no inferences". Moreover, Zajonc claimed that affect constitutes an information processing system that is functionally and neuroanatomically independent from conscious thinking as there are separate brain structures, neural pathways, and neurotransmitters for cognition and affect. This neurophysiological evidence explains why emotions can be recalcitrant and outlast changes of beliefs and appraisals.

Lazarus (1982, 1984) admitted Zajonc's empirical points but maintained that they do not undermine appraisal theory if we understand the notion of cognition in a broad sense. Thus he argued that in emotion, cognition always mediates the relationship between person and environment. Information processing cannot

---

2.   Here and in what follows, "concept" is understood as referring to semantic, linguistic concepts. I acknowledge that it is possible to ascribe psychological categories that functionally resemble concepts in mediating distinct behavioural responses to equally distinct perceived events to even nonlinguistic animals. In the Representational Theory of Mind, such categories are conventionally called "concepts". However, I believe that it is useful to distinguish concepts of this kind from semantic concepts as there are logical differences between the two. I will return to this topic in the next chapter when discussing differences between conceptual and nonconceptual content.

constitute relational meaning without some kind of evaluation of the information for its relevance to the subject's well-being. However, cognitive activity in appraisal does not imply deliberate reflection, rationality, or awareness. Moreover, Lazarus argued that mere feelings and preferences created through exposure effect are not yet emotions. Nevertheless, all processes of meaning generation are cognitive. An appraisal may operate at different levels of complexity, from the most primitive and inborn to the most symbolic and experience-based. Therefore, cognitive appraisal is always involved in emotion, even in creatures phylogenetically more primitive than humans.

The debate resolved in a consensus that the proper question concerns the correct definition of cognition, as Leventhal and Scherer (1987) pointed out. If cognition requires conscious reflection and thought, as Zajonc proposed, all emotions clearly do not require cognitive mental states as their necessary causes or constituents. Yet if every kind of receiving and processing information for its significance to the subject's concerns counts as cognition, as Lazarus suggested, all emotions come out as cognitive. Zajonc (1984) rejected the latter view of cognition as overly inclusive, because it blurs distinctions between cognition, perception, and sensation. However, no significant progress from these positions on cognition has taken place in emotion theory since the days of the Zajonc-Lazarus debate. Instead, a new dividing line between cognitive and noncognitive theories of emotion has emerged regarding their preferred views of cognition. Cognitive theorists of emotion typically favour broad functional accounts of cognition, whereas noncognitive theorists prefer narrow neuroanatomical, mechanism- or code-based accounts, or several of them (Moors, 2007). Thus, Martha Nussbaum (2001, p. 129) defends "a multifaceted notion of cognitive interpretation or seeing-as, accompanied by a flexible notion of intentionality that allows us to ascribe to a creature more or less precise, vaguer or more demarcated, ways of intending an object and marking it as salient." In contrast, Jesse Prinz (2004, p. 46) argues that "a cognitive act is an act of generating a thought under top-down control." These characterizations of cognition by leading representatives of cognitive and noncognitive theories of emotion in philosophy display no headway from the respective positions of Lazarus and Zajonc.

In this situation, it would be convenient to embrace and defend one account of cognition and examine whether or not emotions come out as cognitive or noncognitive from that perspective. Indeed, this straightforward strategy has been popular both among philosophers and affective scientists. Unfortunately, it is not a very informative strategy because the different concepts of cognition operate at different levels of analysis, as Agnes Moors (2007) remarks in her useful taxonomy and review of definitions of cognition. It shows that arguments for cognitive or noncognitive views of cognition at one level do not solve the question once and for all at other levels of analysis. Individual authors typically downplay this problem by resorting to their favourite conception of cognition. Yet the fact that these conceptions operate at different levels of analysis reduces the force and appeal of this argumentative strategy.

Therefore, I suggest that we must confront and answer the question about the role of cognition in emotion at different levels of analysis. Following David Marr's (1982) classic analysis of vision that Moors utilizes in her taxonomy as well, the relevant levels of analysis are functional, algorithmic, and implementational. Of these three levels, the first and the second are relevant from a philosophical point of view. At the first level, the question is whether or not the process that leads from the intake of perceptual or conceptual information to the triggering of an emotional response always involves cognition. At the second level, the mechanisms and forms of representation involved in the processing of input into output come under focus. Examples of mechanisms are rule-based and associative processes, whereas forms of representation include conceptual and nonconceptual representations. The third level of analysis concerns the physiological and neural implementation of emotional processes in the brain. Accordingly, this level of analysis belongs to the domains of biological psychology and affective neuroscience.

In what follows, I shall focus on the role of cognition at the first two levels of analysis, functional and algorithmic, that already on disciplinary grounds belong to philosophical and psychological theorizing on emotions. Empirical evidence on the implementation of emotions in the human brain and elsewhere in the body is obviously important as well. Therefore, I include discussion on the neurophysiology of emotions in some sections to support my discussion at the other levels of analysis. Even so, questions about the role of cognition in emotion can never be solved by studying merely the brain. The basic reason is that we cannot identify the phenomena whose implementation in the brain we should study without reference to our experience. Indeed, an initial identification of "emotion" on the basis of phenomenological and conceptual investigation must precede any empirical study of emotion because otherwise we would not know what to study and how to demarcate "emotion" from other mental and bodily states with which it mixes and mingles all the time. Moreover, we cannot drop phenomenological and conceptual research even after emotion has been tentatively identified, because emotions are not purely physiological phenomena whose study could be handed over to natural science in the same way as the study of chemical substances. Instead, emotions have features such as experience and intentionality, a place in complex webs of meaning, and susceptibility to rational standards of warrant that resist scientific treatment (Roberts, 2003; Döring, 2007). For all these reasons, I discuss cognition in emotion at the level of implementation only in connection with the other two levels of analysis in Chapter 2.

However, this examination can only provide us with a typology of those representations and processes that figure in human emotions. Depending on one's preferred theory, emotions may last from seconds to minutes or even days. Few jokes amuse us longer than a few seconds, whereas grief at the loss of a significant other may last for weeks or months, even years. Time is an important factor because the longer emotions last, the more obviously they involve many types of representations and processes that interact with each other in producing and reinforcing emotions. Thus if emotions typically last from 0.5 to 4 seconds as affect programme theorists such as Richard Levenson (1988) suggest, appraisals are capable of serving as mere triggers of highly stereotypic emotional responses. Instead, if emotions are taken to last longer, from seconds to minutes or hours, appraisal can be understood as a process that constantly updates information about the emotion-eliciting situation in relation to one's active goals as well as to feedback from the body and the world, modifying the emotional response accordingly. The theoretical question is where to draw the line between an emotion and its regulation and where does cognition fit in in this divide.

Emotion regulation is a process that extends beyond the generation of an emotional response and continues until its termination (Gross, 1998). This means that processes of emotion generation and emotion regulation overlap and intertwine during an emotion. Different theoretical approaches disagree on whether generation and regulation should be conceptualized as separate processes or as complementary aspects of a single process of emotion. Thus noncognitive theories prefer to define emotion in terms of processes and representations that figure in emotion generation, whereas cognitive theories maintain that generative and regulatory processes intertwine, giving all post-infantile human emotions a cognitive imprint (Gross & Barrett, 2011). Even so, the role of regulation in emotion has not been problematized in theoretical debates between noncognitive and cognitive theories on the nature of emotions (with the exception of Robinson, 2005). This is unfortunate because empirical research can offer evidence which helps us to adjudicate which approach – the narrow noncognitive or the broad cognitive – to the role of regulatory processes in emotion is correct. This question on the role of cognition in the dynamics of emotion will occupy me in Chapter 3.

What is emotional authenticity?

The second main theme of the book is emotional authenticity. Authenticity is an elusive ideal. "To thine own self be true", advised Polonius his son Laertes in *Hamlet*. Yet it is not obvious what it means to be true to one's self. On the one hand, emotions are promising candidates for providing a standard of our true self as they often seem to identify our cares and values more reliably than evaluative beliefs. We may pay lip service to several values but if violations against them do not elicit any anger or sadness in us, our commitment to those values seems superficial at best. However, in this case, we face the question what grounds the authenticity of emotions themselves? Emotions are thoroughly infused with biological endowments, social and cultural norms, and contingent facts of our individual biographies. All these elements come together in Ronald de Sousa's notion of *paradigm scenario*, which involves two elements: "first, a situation type providing the characteristic *objects* of the specific emotion-type, and second, a set of characteristic or 'normal' responses to the situation, where normality is first a biological matter and then very quickly becomes a cultural one" (de Sousa, 1987, p. 182). Yet if my emotions are more or less fixed re-enactments of primal paradigm scenarios whose defining elements, formation process, and endorsement have been largely beyond my influence, why should those emotions be inalienable to the *present* me? Arguably emotions do not deserve the status of authenticity merely because they happen to be there, but only by virtue of conforming to some canon of value or rationality that we avow.

This brief discussion highlights two divergent intuitions about emotional authenticity. On the one hand, emotional authenticity seems to amount to spontaneity in one's emotions as they unfold and sincerity in their expression to oneself and others. Yet, on the other hand, authenticity seems more problematic than this. We sometimes find our spontaneous emotions curious or even unintelligible, and identify ourselves more readily with those emotions that emerge only later, after conscious reflection of the emotion-eliciting situation and our response to it. Feelings of insecurity, shame, or self-blame for instance may take us by surprise in social situations in which we do not recognize any reasons for those emotions. Our personal history may help us to explain the occurrence of those emotions but such understanding need not bring with it endorsement of those emotions as our authentic responses to the situation. These points suggest that spontaneity is not sufficient for the authenticity of emotions. However, spontaneity may not be necessary for authenticity either, because some emotions that emerge through conscious regulation rather than spontaneously may nevertheless qualify as authentic. Examples abound in our everyday lives where we skilfully adjust our emotions to social feeling rules that vary from situation to situation and from one social role to another. Discussion on emotional authenticity in other walks of life supports the impression that the notion of authenticity is shot through with paradoxes.

Inauthenticity has been associated with emotional labour more or less by definition ever since the concept was introduced by Arlie Hochschild in her modern sociological classic, *The Managed Heart* (1983). Hochschild argued that service workers such as flight attendants, debt collectors, and nurses alienate from their real emotions when they have to manage their emotions to meet the display and feeling rules of their occupational roles. If the expressed and experienced emotion do not match each other, the worker feels alienated by the emotional dissonance. Yet successful emotion management in a work role distorts one's spontaneous emotions and thereby engenders alienation from one's 'real' self as well. Other negative effects of emotional labour are mediated, in part, by the experience of emotional dissonance or by the sense of inauthenticity that are often defined interchangeably. These effects include emotional exhaustion and job dissatisfaction, stress and distress, depression, drug and alcohol abuse, absenteeism and turnovers, and other health problems. Even so, there is evidence that emotion management in a work role may in some conditions facilitate job satisfaction, self-efficacy, self-expression, and feelings of personal accomplishment – even experiences of authenticity. These are paradoxical results because emotional labour associates then with both authenticity and inauthenticity, which suggests that there is something wrong with the concept of authenticity in this discourse.

Other discourses in which the paradox of emotional authenticity emerges include gender studies and clinical psychology. Feminist researchers have argued that women's 'outlaw' emotions such as anger, resentment, and fear, which emerge spontaneously and resist rational reconceptualization, are indispensable as symptoms of oppression (M Griffiths, 1997; Jaggar, 1997). Accordingly, outlaw emotions may give rise to conscious insights into the sexist, racist, and other oppressive frameworks and thus pave the way to emancipation from those frameworks. Nevertheless, many outlaw emotions are rejected in the process of emancipation from oppressive frameworks. The problem is, then, which emotions are authentic: the recalcitrant emotions that were eliminated in the process of emancipation, or the new emotions, such as pride, joy, and self-confidence, that are acquired in the same process? An analogue problem emerges in psychotherapeutic practices in which attention to the client's sincere emotions is an indispensable key to an accurate diagnosis of his problems. However, since these emotions are often part of the disorder, they become moderated or eliminated along the process of recovery. The question is, then, which set of emotions is authentic: the pre-treatment one or the one emerging along with a successful treatment? Intuitively, we tend to answer that both types of emotions qualify as authentic, albeit in a different sense.

The challenge is to follow the lead of this intuition into explicating the different meanings of emotional authenticity, psychological and normative. This theoretical task will occupy me in Chapter 4. There I shall distinguish between two senses of emotional authenticity, the sincerity view and the integrity view. In Chapter 6 I apply this theoretical divide to the discourse in which the paradox of emotional authenticity has been particularly salient, namely emotion management at work. I argue that my distinction between two senses of authenticity allows us to remove the paradox of authenticity from emotions experienced in a work role. In addition, it explicates the conditions, both internal and external, on which occupational emotions may qualify as authentic in the normative sense.

What is emotional truth?

While the problem of emotional authenticity concerns emotions that are true to the self, an opposite problem focuses on the relation of emotions to their objects in the world. The latter problem is usually identified as that of the appropriateness of emotions. The idea that emotions can be appropriate, correct, or rationally warranted responses to their particular objects returned to the philosophical centre stage together with the rise of cognitive theories of emotion in the 1980s. Indeed, the ability of cognitive theories to accommodate and explicate the intentionality and rationality of emotions was a major asset of these theories in comparison to their traditional rivals, noncognitive feeling theories and behaviourism, which had no room for such idea.

The problem of emotional appropriateness was alien to feeling theories that identified emotions in terms of noncognitive sensations such as thrills, twinges, pangs, throbs, wrenches, or itches that are not intentional states in the first place. Bodily sensations may have a certain location, as when we feel "butterflies in the stomach", but they are not about anything else. Behaviourism rendered emotions as dispositions of distinct response patterns that tend to occur in a law-like manner in certain stimulus situations. An angry person, for instance, is disposed to shout aloud, pound tables, slam doors, pick fights and so on, and the emotion of anger is defined as the disposition to enact behaviours of this kind in certain stimulus situations. Unfortunately, the intentionality and appropriateness of emotions evade behaviourism as well. The account of emotions as stimulus-response pairs does not allow us to problematize the appropriateness of emotional responses to their eliciting situations because the latter are identified merely in terms of their causal role in triggering emotional responses.

Cognitive theories amended these views by ascribing to emotions an intentional, evaluative content that is directed at particular objects of emotion. The appropriateness of an emotion depends then on the fittingness of the emotional response to its particular object. For this purpose, cognitive theorists introduced the notion of *formal object*, an evaluative property that each token emotion of the same type explicitly or implicitly ascribes to its particular object and that provides the standard of fittingness for individual emotions of that type (Kenny, 1963; de Sousa, 1987; Goldie, 2004; Teroni, 2007). Examples of formal objects are danger or threat for fear, loss for sorrow, insult or offence for anger, and shamefulness for shame. An individual emotion is appropriate if the particular object of emotion has the formal property that the emotional evaluation ascribes to it. Even if this conceptual framework for analysing emotional appropriateness is more congenial to cognitive than noncognitive theories of emotion, the latter theories have found ways of accommodating this framework as part of the recent rapprochement in emotion theory. Thus theorists on both sides of the divide have suggested that emotions are capable of "getting things right" or "getting the world right" in their evaluation of particular objects, or "tracking" the evaluative properties of those objects (D'Arms & Jacobson, 2000a; Roberts, 2003; Goldie, 2004). The challenge is then to specify the conditions in which emotions are capable of getting things or the world evaluatively right – if emotional truth of this kind is possible in the first place.

Sceptics on the possibility of emotional truth can be divided into two main groups. In the first group are theorists who reject the possibility that emotions can veridically represent or track evaluative properties in the first place. These theorists are noncognivists who doubt that emotions have an evaluative content in either an intrinsic or a derivative sense. William James's (1884) classic view of emotions as perceptions of bodily changes as they occur is such a view. Other noncognitivists argue that emotions can be evaluated in terms of their situational appropriateness only in so far as we have control over them. And since we do not have control over our emotions but only over their elicitors, emotions are strictly speaking arational – beyond rational evaluation – even if they have a content (Prinz, 2004). At most, emotions can be evaluated for their adaptiveness in relation to the subject's needs. However, since the majority of contemporary noncognivists accommodate the idea of emotional content, they are more likely to belong to the second group of sceptics who challenge truth as the standard of situational appropriateness for emotions rather than the idea that emotions have one. These theorists who also include some cognitivists prefer to compare emotions to sense perceptions whose standard of successful representation is correctness rather than truth. They support this view with arguments about logical similarities between emotions and perceptions on the one hand, and about logical differences between emotions and beliefs – paradigmatic cognitive states – on the other hand (Gunther, 2003; Döring, 2003, 2004, 2007, 2009). The truth-aptness of emotions depends on the whether they resemble beliefs more than perceptions. I shall focus on this milder type of scepticism about the idea of emotional truth in Chapter 5, in which I shall also defend emotional truth against rival standards of emotional appropriateness. The stronger scepticism will be dealt with in the preceding chapters on what emotions truly are.

If situationally appropriate emotions adequately represent particular objects in terms of the relevant formal objects, then these emotions may help us in tracking or determining those evaluative properties that the formal objects denote. This has been the aim of neosentimentalist theories in contemporary meta-ethics. The basic idea is that certain value properties and their concepts depend fundamentally on human sensibilities as these values can be analysed or identified in terms of appropriate or correct or warranted sentiments. Values of this kind include the properties of admirable, funny, offensive, embarrassing, envious, dangerous, and shameful, while the corresponding emotions are admiration, amusement, anger, embarrassment, envy, fear, and shame, respectively. Neosentimentalist theories disagree on whether emotions allow us to track values that exist independently of our responses, or whether emotional responses constitute and determine values. Even so, those theorists agree on the basic idea of analysing sentimental values in terms of appropriate emotions, which justifies their classification into the same approach.

Neosentimentalist theories of value have two main problems. The first problem concerns the relation between evaluative concepts and the associated emotional responses. It seems that in order to avoid a vicious circle, we must deny that emotional responses involve those evaluative concepts that we purport to analyse or explicate in terms of the relevant responses. For instance, if we claim that amusement contains the concept of being funny, we cannot analyse this concept in terms of amusement, because understanding this emotion already requires a grasp of the concept of being funny that is part of the emotion. Many sentimentalists have avoided this problem by adopting noncognitive or nonconceptual theories of emotion. However, since the plausibility of these theories must be judged on independent grounds, this solution cannot be taken for granted.

The other main problem of neosentimentalist theories concerns the difficulty of distinguishing between reasons that are relevant and irrelevant to the appropriateness or warrant of emotions. The problem is that several types of reasons – epistemic, axiological, moral, strategic, or all-things-considered reasons – may underlie our actual emotional responses. Yet when we ask, for instance, whether or not a particular joke is funny or a particular action is offensive, we are not interested in whether it is strategically beneficial for us to laugh at the joke or take offence at the action. It may sometimes be beneficial to be amused at bad jokes or take offence at minor incidents in order to gain advances in social interaction, but these emotional responses do not reliable track or determine the evaluative properties that these emotions ascribe to their particular objects. The task is then to explicate the conditions on which this kind of reliable tracking or determination of evaluative properties is possible.

In the concluding chapter of the volume (Chapter 7), I shall apply my account of emotional truth, presented in Chapter 5, to these two problems of neosentimentalist theories of value. I suggest that the circularity problem that focuses on the possibility of analysing value concepts in terms of appropriate emotional responses may indeed be unsolvable, because most human emotions have conceptual content – as I will argue in Chapters 2 and 3. However, this problem does not affect the metaphysical version of neosentimentalism, because it may still be possible to track or determine value properties by means of appropriate emotions that ascribe the same properties to particular objects and events, provided that we can solve the problem with the right kind of reasons for appropriate emotions. I shall argue that my account of emotional truth is capable of making headway towards solving this problem, thus contributing to the project of identifying sentimental values.

CHAPTER 2

Cognition in the structure of emotion

This chapter focuses on the content of human emotions from a structural point of view. The various elements of emotion identified in this discussion will figure in the next chapter's account on the dynamics of emotion. I divide my discussion on the role of cognition in emotion into these two approaches because even if almost all theorists pay lip service to the dynamic character of emotions, most of them – and philosophers in particular with the exception of Jenefer Robinson (2005) – have remained firmly on the structural side in their accounts of emotional content. However, both perspectives must be kept in sight if we want to understand what emotions truly are.

The question about the role of cognition in emotion can be put at two different levels of analysis, functional and algorithmic, identified in the introductory chapter. Existing theories of emotion seldom distinguish between these two levels, which makes it difficult to evaluate and compare their claims about the involvement of cognition in emotion. Therefore, I have decided to separate these two levels of analysis in order to put the cognitive claim into a more comprehensive test. Another issue at stake is the robustness of the cognitive claim. Emotions are cognitive in a less robust sense if they involve cognition at only one level of analysis than if they involve cognition at both functional and algorithmic levels of analysis. I shall suggest that something like this is the case: that cognition is always involved in emotion at the functional level of analysis, whereas emotions divide into two kinds, cognitive and noncognitive, at the algorithmic level of mechanisms and types of representation. However, this distinction makes sense only from the structural perspective that does not take into consideration the interaction and integration of different kinds of processes and representations that occur in actual human emotions. This *dynamic* approach to the role of cognition on emotion will be taken up in the next chapter in which I shall argue that even those post-infantile human emotions that are triggered by noncognitive representations and processes involve cognition at the later stages of appraisal and emotion regulation that should be seen as parts of emotion. Therefore, all post-infantile human emotions qualify as robustly cognitive also at the algorithmic level of analysis. This chapter will focus on building a typology of those representations and processes that figure in the dynamic account.

Cognition in emotion at the functional level of analysis

Functionalist theories of mind identify types of mental states by their causal roles in the information processing system of which those states are part. All token states that serve in the same causal role belong to the same type in the functional sense, independently of their internal structure. Thus mental states of the same type can be realized by different kinds of physical states. This principle of *multiple realizability* allows us to ascribe cognitive and motivational states to both humans and animals as well as to robots and fictitious aliens whose internal constitution differs significantly from ours insofar as their states of the same kind share similar causal role in relation to their sensory input, other mental states, and behavioural responses. No wonder then that the leading metaphor of a functionalist theory of the mind is software – a computational program that can operate in organisms with different kinds of hardware. Accordingly, functionalism is a prevalent approach to information processing in cognitive psychology, cognitive science, and artificial intelligence in addition to philosophy of mind where it is an influential paradigm (see e.g. Lycan, 1994).

If we take a functionalist perspective to cognition, what is the causal role of cognition in the mental economy in general and in emotions in particular? Fred Dretske (1981) ascribes cognitive mental states to all systems that are capable of converting perceptual information into structures with a semantic content. He regards perception as a process by means of which information is delivered within a rich matrix of information to the cognitive centres for their selective use. The process of successful conversion of *analogue* sensory information into *digital* semantic form constitutes the essence of cognitive activity and the results of this activity are structures with a semantic content. More precisely, the semantic content of a *token* internal state is defined by the kind of information to which internal states of that *type* are selectively sensitive. A type of internal state, in turn, constitutes a semantic structure whose content derives from the sort of situations that the structure was either biologically pre-wired or culturally developed to represent. Semantic structures qualify as cognitive insofar as it is their content that is causally efficacious in determining the system's response. This entails that the system displays flexibility by assigning "a *sameness of output* to *differences of input*" (Dretske, 1981, p. 183, original italics).

Human concepts are paradigm examples of semantic structures. However, Dretske maintains that we must assign semantic contents to higher animals' internal states as well if we want to explain their discriminatory responses. Both humans and animals have semantic structures for representing various kinds of emotionally relevant situations, for instance. We attack or flee from objects that we categorize as threatening and seek to avoid disgusting substances. Dretske notices the reluctance of some philosophers to assign cognitive structures to non-linguistic animals. Yet he argues that their specialized yet flexible response patterns compel us to assign them internal states and functional concepts with a specific cognitive content. After all, an internal state qualifies as a cognition when it functions in a cognitive role.

We can now see why emotions necessarily involve cognitions at the functional level of analysis. Emotions are not reflexes or fixed action patterns that activate automatically in certain stimulus situations. Emotional responses may have some reflex-like features insofar as they unfold in the manner of complex, coordinated, and automated affect programs (see e.g. Ekman, 1992, 1999; Levenson, 2003). Yet these responses are flexible both in terms of their eliciting situations and behavioural output. This indicates that emotions involve mental representations that mediate between perceptions of emotion-eliciting stimuli and emotional responses. These mental representations are cognitive in the functional sense as they causally function in the role of cognition.

On the one hand, emotions display sameness of output in relation to varieties of input. For instance, both rabbits and humans respond with fear – in proper circumstances – to perceptions of a snake or a wolf or a fast approaching truck. Since the physical properties of these objects are dissimilar, we must assume that there is an internal mechanism that represents those objects as somehow similar; as threatening or dangerous in the case of fear. The sameness of response presupposes sameness of mental representation at the functional level of analysis. On the other hand, there are changes in output in relation to the same input. To quote Agnes Moors (2007, p. 1241):

> First, repeated encounters with the same stimulus can lead to a change in response – e.g. faster, more positive (cf. mere exposure); less intense (cf. habituation); more intense (cf. sensitisation). Second, the same stimulus can lead to a change in response due to (repeated) co-occurrence with other stimuli (cf. classical and evaluative conditioning). Third, the same stimulus can lead to different responses depending on the varying internal states such as motivation.

All these changes in output require flexibility in internal representations of input; in their accessibility, or in their association or integration with other representations. For instance, fear responses can adjust to repeated encounters with threatening stimuli by becoming either more intense (e.g. PTSD) or less intense (e.g. unlearning phobias in therapy); threatening stimuli may associate with innocuous ones, transmitting fear responses also to the latter; and other activated goals can ward off fear in a dangerous situation. This kind of flexibility in the input and output of emotions – that anatomically is founded on connections between the basolateral nuclei of the amygdala and the orbitofrontal and anterior cingulate cortical areas (e.g. Pessoa, 2008; Pessoa & Adolphs, 2010; Rolls, 2013) – can be explained only if emotions involve mental representations (e.g. Moors, 2007; Smith & Ellsworth, 1985).

Both cognitive and noncognitive theorists agree on the role of mental representations in the elicitation of emotions. Thus, for instance, Jesse Prinz (2004) maintains that all mental states that elicit instances of a particular emotion type together constitute the calibration file of that emotion type. However, he rejects cognitivism by arguing that "there is no internal state that always plays the role of triggering a higher cognitive emotion. Different items in our calibration files play that role on different occasions" (Prinz, 2004, p. 101). For instance, the elicitation file of fear may contain perceptions of a snake or a pointing gun, as well as judgments like "That's poison!" or "I'm in danger!" Yet from a functional perspective, the heterogeneity in the elicitation files of emotions is superficial because it hides an underlying homogeneity at the causal level of analysis: all items of the same elicitation file represent the same core relational theme as they give rise to token emotions of the same type. Since these inner causes have an essential role in emotions, emotion always involves cognition.

The functional view of cognition is capable of accommodating emotions elicited at different levels of information processing within the same theoretical model. Accordingly, the functional account has been very popular among multi-level appraisal theories which maintain that emotions involve representations of different types in the appraisal of their eliciting stimuli. In accordance with popular dual-process models of cognition developed in social and cognitive psychology and cognitive science, most contemporary appraisal theories distinguish between two levels of processing; "one conscious, deliberate, and under volitional control, the other automatic, unconscious, and uncontrollable", as Richard Lazarus (1991, p. 153) proposed. The former types of representations or processes have been characterized in various theories as "propositional" (Teasdale & Barnard, 1993), "deliberative" (Ben-Ze'ev, 2000), "rule-based" (Clore & Ortony, 2000; Smith & Neumann, 2005), "conceptual" (Leventhal & Scherer, 1987); or "reasoning" (Smith & Kirby, 2001), whereas representations or processes of the latter type are termed "schematic" (Leventhal & Scherer, 1987; Ben-Ze'ev, 2000), "associative" (Clore & Ortony, 2000; Smith & Kirby, 2001; Smith & Neumann, 2005), or "implicational" (Teasdale & Barnard, 1993). Emotions involve other components besides appraisals as well, but the causal and constitutive role of appraisals at either or both levels of information processing renders emotions cognitive according to these theories. Louis Charland (1997) captures the strategy of multi-level accounts by subsuming different types of processes and representations into his explicitly functionalist "Representational Theory of Emotion", which distinguishes between "affective cognition" and "affective perception". In this early theory, Charland purports to synthesize both cognitive and noncognitive approaches in the philosophy of emotions by ascending to a higher level of description, that of representations, which are neutral in both epistemological and ontological terms.

The functional notion of representation has allowed multi-level appraisal theorists to maintain that mental representations at different levels of information processing have the same or similar evaluative content insofar as they elicit emotional responses of the same type. For instance, some fears are elicited quickly and effortlessly from perceptual stimuli, whereas others emerge only through slow and effortful understanding of conceptual information. It is obvious that representations of danger that have the same causal role in emotion elicitation emerge as the result of different types of processes in somewhat different areas of the human brain in these two kinds of fear. However, multi-level appraisal theories maintain that these differences do not significantly affect the nature of emotions. To quote Clore and Ortony (2000, p. 42), "the cognitive claim is that emotions are reactions to (or representations of) the personal meaning and significance of situations, not that emotions originate in the cerebral cortex". The recognition of personal meaning is automatic and nonconscious if it takes place in the subcortical pathway of the brain. However, from an informational and functional point of view it is still a *recognition*, and as such a kind of cognition, as Robert Solomon (2004, p. 79) points out.

In spite of their popularity, multi-level appraisal theories with their functional view of cognition have been subject to persistent criticism especially in philosophy. One of the most vehement critics of this approach has been Paul Griffiths (1997; 2004), who argues that functional similarities are shallow in comparison to homological similarities that are manifested at the level of causal mechanisms and physiological implementation. Appraisal theories are vulnerable to such criticism as they avoid commitments in these matters or provide only tentative hypotheses (Moors, 2009). Thus, Griffiths claims that instances of the same vernacular emotion type such as anger, fear, and sadness fall into two subtypes – affect program emotions and cognitively complex emotions – which have little in common. Affect programmes are phylogenetically ancient, informationally encapsulated, and reflex-like emotional responses that are homologous with the emotions of other vertebrates, and therefore, constitute a plausible natural kind. In contrast, complex emotions are culturally specific responses that operate on semantically structured representations of objects, events, or states of affairs, without possessing a distinct, emotion-specific physiology. Griffiths (1997, p. 16) concludes that "the two kinds of emotion have different phylogenies, different adaptive functions, different neuroscience, and different roles in human psychology, [and therefore t]he concept that groups them together has no discernible theoretical utility."

With these theoretical tools Griffiths attacks multi-level appraisal theories that purport to bridge the gap between affect programme emotions and complex emotions by maintaining that all instances of the same vernacular emotion type share the same or similar content. Griffiths argues that this view contradicts the hierarchical architecture of the emotional brain. Representations with the same content cannot operate at different levels of implementation. Further still, he suggests that there are several differences between low- and high-level appraisals. First of all, lower-level emotional appraisals involve action-oriented representations that unite the functions of belief and desire. This kind of "collapse of the attitudes" (Millikan) is typical of mental representations in simple organisms. Moreover, Griffiths argues that lower-level representations differ from higher-level ones in terms of their impoverished inferential role:

> First, low-level appraisal processes do not have access to most of what is represented elsewhere in the brain... Secondly, the processes of affective computing, as opposed to their final output, are not available for inspection by other cognitive subsystems.... Finally, the inferential principles used in affective computing are not truth-preserving, but heuristically survival-enhancing. (Griffiths 2004, p. 247)

Together these arguments suggest that theories based on functional accounts of cognition skate over important dissimilarities between different kinds of emotions and their eliciting appraisals, which therefore cannot have the same content even in terms of their causal-representational role. Even if emotions involve mental representations that function as inner causes of emotion, those representations and the ensuing emotional responses are too dissimilar to each other to ground an informative representational theory of the emotions in the manner suggested by Charland (1997). This conclusion leads to the next level of analysis where the question about the role of cognition in emotion is put in terms of mechanisms and formats of representation.

Cognition in emotion at the algorithmic level of analysis

Dissatisfaction with cognitive theories of emotion that invoke functionalist accounts of cognition has fuelled attempts to distinguish between cognitive and noncognitive processes and representations at other levels of analysis, typically at the algorithmic level that deals with mechanisms of information processing and formats of representation. Several theorists have suggested that we should distinguish between different kinds of representation in emotional content; indeed, this is a basic claim of multi-level appraisal theories. If we bracket these theorists' favourite functional account of cognition, the analyses of multi-level appraisal theories on the different mechanisms of information processing and modes of representation contribute directly to the discussion on the role and nature of cognition in emotion at the algorithmic level of analysis.

If causal role defines cognition (and other mental states) at the functional level of analysis, dual-process models of information processing provide a basis for a heuristic distinction between cognitive and noncognitive representations and processes at the algorithmic level of analysis. Representations can be divided into those with *conceptual* and *nonconceptual* content, respectively, whereas processes have been characterized in terms of two mutually opposite property clusters.[1] On the one hand, there are associative, heuristic, parallel, automatic, implicit, unconscious, fast, cognitively undemanding, and evolutionarily old processes that we share with other animals. On the other hand, there are distinctively human and evolutionarily new processes that are rule-based, analytic, serial, controlled, explicit, conscious, slow, and cognitively demanding (see e.g. Evans & Frankish, 2009). For the sake of simplicity and in agreement with many dual-process theorists, I refer to these two broad types of processes as *implicit* and *explicit* without assuming that all the other properties listed in the respective clusters go along with these notions.

The two distinctions between conceptual and nonconceptual content on the one hand and between implicit and explicit processes on the other hand yield four possible combinations of processes and representational contents. These combinations are (1) *explicit processing with conceptual content*; (2) *explicit processing with nonconceptual content*; (3) *implicit processing with conceptual content*; and (4) *implicit processing with nonconceptual content*. Existing theories of emotion readily identify two types of emotional processing: explicit processing with conceptual content, and implicit processing with nonconceptual content. Strong cognitivists favour the former type of processing and noncognitive affect programme theorists the latter, whereas multi-level appraisal theories maintain that both forms of processing are possible in different emotions or even in the same emotion at different points of time. On the other hand, emotions with explicit processing and nonconceptual content are paradoxical because even if such emotions exist, the rules involved in their processing cannot be semantic (yet see Moors, 2010). In contrast, emotions with implicit processing and conceptual content abound among humans, as multi-level appraisal theories point out (e.g. Clore & Ortony, 2000; Smith

---

1.   Psychologists typically discuss mechanisms of information processing in emotion, and philosophers often frame the question in terms of representational content, while cognitive scientists analyse both content and processes. The two approaches can be seen as overlapping insofar as explicit, rule-based mechanisms operate on conceptual representations, whereas implicit, associative mechanisms employ nonconceptual representations. However, I suggest that this dichotomy is inadequate for implicit processing.

& Kirby, 2001; Moors, 2010; Moors et al., 2013). These theories emphasize re-peated practice and learning in the automatization of rule-based, explicit process-es. However, it is important to realize that differences in the nature of content remain in spite of change in the nature of processing.

Dual-process theorists widely agree that implicit, or more generally, "type 1" processing is an umbrella term for several processes that share some or many fea-tures of the property cluster (automatic, associative, implicit, fast, etc.) attached to this type of processing. The fact that implicit processing has been invoked in the explanation of so many different kinds of phenomena, such as biases in human reasoning and decision making, probabilistic judgment, stereotypic responses to members of socially stigmatized groups, and elicitation of emotional responses, indicates that these processes do not belong to a single system but only overlap in terms of their functional properties to a greater or lesser extent (e.g. Evans, 2008, 2009; Samuels, 2009; Stanovich, 2009). This is obvious: implicit processing in hu-man reasoning and social cognition for instance operates on garden-variety beliefs, stimulus distinctions, and decision-making principles whose rule-based process-ing has become implicit and automatic through repeated practice, whereas auto-matic processing in the context of perception, attention, and acquisition of motor skills operates right from the outset on strongly modular, evolutionarily pre-wired contents (see e.g. Evans, 2008; Stanovich, 2009). The difference between acquired and inherent automaticity undermines a central assumption of many dual process models that all implicit processes operate on similar contents. This can be seen in the context of human emotions.

Human emotions can be divided into those that emerge from implicit process-ing as if by default on the one hand and those whose activation has become im-plicit through their recurrent emergence through explicit processing on the other hand. Emotions of the first type are evolutionarily older than those of the latter type: they have been learned in the ancestral rather than the individual past. Ac-cordingly, the learning mechanism of these emotions is biased even if it also requires personal experience. Yet a single exposure to such evolutionarily prepro-grammed stimuli as coiling snakes, menacing wolves, and rotten food items is capable of associating these objects with persistent implicitly emerging emotional responses in later encounters. In empirical studies, both humans and monkeys developed strong fear that resisted extinction after conditioning to such fear-rele-vant stimuli as snakes, spiders, and angry faces, compared to when the condi-tioned stimuli were fear-irrelevant, such as flowers, toys, and happy faces (Öhman & Wiens, 1994). Likewise, humans like other animals have the tendency to develop persistent disgust and aversion to foods whose consumption has been followed by illness even if their causal association is understood to be contingent (e.g. Logue, Ophir & Strauss, 1986). No similar effect is forthcoming for suspicion towards an overeager real estate agent or pride in one's beautiful house – emotions about objects and events with socially learned meanings in general. Repeated emotional encounters of the same kind are required for producing an associative link between emotions and objects in these cases.

It is important to observe that the contents of these two kinds of emotions remain dissimilar even after their elicitation has become implicit. The emotions whose elicitation becomes implicit after a single exposure to their eliciting object have nonconceptual content. The perceptual features of coiling snakes, menacing wolves, or rotten food rather that conceptual information about the dangerous or disgusting qualities of these objects render them emotionally salient (Deigh, 2008). In contrast, perceptual cues merely *activate* personally learned semantic meanings in such emotions as suspicion about an overeager real estate agent or pride in one's beautiful house. The content of these emotions remains conceptual even after their elicitation has become implicit. A sight or thought of the estate agent immediately elicits suspicion but this does not mean that the perceptual features of the person would have become emotionally salient in the meanwhile. Instead, these features are immediately associated with the person's overeager behaviour and its underlying deceitful intentions that become the focus of wary suspicion. Evidence on highly automatic and implicit yet conceptually structured emotion-eliciting appraisals can also be found from various psychological disorders such as depression, social and generalized anxiety disorders, and panic disorder, as cognitive-behavioural psychotherapists have pointed out (e.g. Leahy, 2004). This indicates that emotional processing does not employ merely one but several types of representations, as Darlow and Sloman (2010) have argued, against some other dual-process theorists who have associated emotion categorically with type 1 processing (e.g. Epstein, 1994; Slovic, Finucane, Peters, & MacGregor, 2004).

Another important question concerns the relation of the two modes of processing. Alternatively, the two modes are parallel and mutually exclusive in determining emotional responses, or they are sequential, partially overlapping, and interactive in producing emotional responses. Evans (2009) has characterized these two versions of dual process theories as *parallel-competitive* and *default-interventionist* models.

> In the former, two parallel processes propose their own judgments or decisions which may or may not conflict. In this approach, one or the other kind of process ultimately takes control of the behaviour. In the default-interventionist approach, a fast type 1 process provides default intuitions which are always subject to at least minimal scrutiny by type 2 processes which may approve them or intervene with analytic reasoning (Evans 2009, p. 43).

Minimal scrutiny involves monitoring the quality of intuitively produced proposals which type 2 processing may endorse, correct, or override. When it endorses an intuitive response, the influence of type 2 processing on overt behaviour remains minimal. Nevertheless, counterfactual reasoning indicates that the role of such processing is significant even in those cases because analytic processing could have intervened if it had not endorsed the intuitive response.

Multi-level appraisal theorists of emotion are not very articulate about their position as parallel-competitive and default-interventionist dual processing models, in part because they often focus on the generation of emotion instead of looking at entire emotional responses from beginning to end. If the parallel-competitive model is correct about human emotions, then we should have blue-ribbon cases of both main types of emotion: emotions with implicitly processed nonconceptual content and emotions with explicitly processed conceptual content, and nothing in between. Indeed, Griffiths (1997, 2004), in his criticism of multi-level appraisal theories, represents this kind of view indirectly in claiming that human emotions divide sharply between complex, coordinated, and automated affect programs on the one hand and cognitively complex emotions that are associated with higher cognitive processing and social roles on the other hand. In a like manner, Clore and Ortony (2000), for instance, appear to suggest that emotional appraisals emerge either through rule-based, online "bottom-up" processing or through associative, reinstated "top-down" processing. Even so, they allow that rule-based processing can become associative, and suggest that bottom-up and top-down processes form a continuum from appraisals with more online computation at one end to appraisals with more reinstatement of previously learned significance at the other. The appraisal theories of Lazarus (1991) and Scherer (2001, 2009) exemplify default-interventionist views more explicitly since they understand emotional appraisal as a process that typically begins from noncognitive appraisals and proceeds to cognitive appraisals. Studies of emotion regulation offer more support to the default-interventionist view in suggesting that explicit, semantic processing is capable of influencing emotions from their onset until their extinction or transformation into other states (Gross & Thompson, 2007).

Instead of engaging in a direct discussion on the merits of the two kinds of dual processing models in the context of human emotions, I have chosen another, more indirect strategy. It focuses on analysing different types of emotional content, and asks whether any single type of content is capable of explaining the properties of all or even most human emotions. Implications of this survey to the dispute between parallel-competitive and default-interventionist views of dual processing in the context of emotional processing will be presented in the end of this and the following chapter. I shall analyse types of content rather than types of processing because implicit processing is capable of operating with many kinds of content, conceptual and nonconceptual, as I emphasized above, and because, unfortunately, the distinction between conceptual and nonconceptual content is also ambiguous.

Everyone agrees that conceptual representations are cognitive, and most theorists maintain that nonconceptual representations are noncognitive.[2] However, nonconceptual representations can be divided into several subtypes. My primary task is then to determine whether particular types of nonconceptual content are cognitive or noncognitive. Yet it is also important to determine whether any single type of representation is capable of accommodating the properties of all or most human emotions at the algorithmic level of analysis. This is my secondary task whose outcome is important for determining the overall strength of the cognitive claim. If only few human emotions qualify as cognitive at this level, then cognitivism is worse off than if many human emotions have cognitive content. Since the full answer to this question depends on how the different types of processes and representations interact in the dynamics of emotion, it can only be given only in the next chapter. Here it is sufficient to establish the strengths and limitations of different types of representation in accounting for human emotions. I begin with conceptual content because nonconceptual content is a contrastive term that is defined by its divergence from conceptual content.

Conceptual content

The notion of conceptual content can be characterized by means of mental states and linguistic utterances that possess content of this kind. A paradigm case for a state with conceptual content is a propositional attitude – an attitude towards a proposition or a thought whose content remains the same in spite of a change in the attitudinal mode.[3] Thus I can believe, desire, hope, fear etc. that the soccer

---

2.   There is no wide agreement on the term "cognitive", even less so that it refers exclusively to conceptual representations. However, there is considerable agreement that conceptual representations are cognitive, whether other representations are cognitive or not.

3.   This Fregean understanding of conceptual content is not the only game in town, however. In The Representational Theory of Mind, concepts are understood as mental representations that function as constituents of structured mental representations whose type is identified by the functional role of the representation in the subject's mind. Accordingly, the representational theory of conceptual content can be associated with the functional account of cognition discussed above. Moreover, some philosophers maintain that propositional structure is not limited to conceptual representations but applies to nonconceptual representations as well. Peacock (1992) for instance presents such a view about the content of perceptual experiences, and Döring (2004) applies it to affective perceptions (emotions). Therefore, propositional and conceptual content are not synonymous or even coextensive even if conceptual content typically has propositional.structure.

team of United States will win the 2014 FIFA World Cup in Brazil. York Gunther (2003) calls this property of conceptual content its *force independence*: the content of a propositional attitude can be individuated independently of its illocutionary force. The fact that conceptual content is constituted of concepts allows us to form and grasp an infinite number of thoughts and expressions by combining concepts in different ways. This *compositionality* of conceptual content explains how language can be both systematic and productive and why states with conceptual content can enter into inferential relations with each other. For instance, if I believe that "Tom is a pianist" while also believing that "if Tom is a pianist, then Alice was his teacher", I can infer from the content of these premises that "Alice was Tom's teacher". The content of a propositional attitude specifies its *determinate reference*, which can be either an actual, conditional, historical, or a fictitious state of affairs. Each type of attitude also has its own condition of success. Thus beliefs succeed when their content is true, whereas desires succeed when their content is satisfied or desirable (Green, 1992; de Sousa, 2002).[4]

Emotions can have conceptual content in many ways. First, some emotions qualify as propositional attitudes in an ordinary sense by having propositionally specified content. For instance, investors fear *that stock prices will plummet* or diplomats are relieved *that an international conflict was avoided*. Sometimes propositional content can be fully expressed without a that-clause. Such emotion is, for instance, pride in *graduating from a prestigious university*. Yet some emotions resist propositional specification of their content. "A description of someone as pitying, hating, resenting, or loving that *p* would be syntactically deviant", as O.H. Green (1992, p. 39) remarks. Instead, these emotions take direct objects, as when Mike pities refugees or Lisa despises a treacherous friend. Even so, a cognitive theorist may suggest that it is possible to specify the propositional content of such emotions in terms of a thought or belief that describes the respect in which the object is comprehended in the emotional state (ibid., p. 40). Thus Mike's pity for refugees involves a belief that the refugees have suffered a loss, or Lisa's despising of her friend involves a belief that the friend has betrayed her confidence. However, this response is not entirely satisfactory as the emotion is still felt towards the whole person rather than towards some aspect of him or her that figures as a reason or motive for the emotion. Therefore, it may not be possible to spell out *specific* propositions that define emotions with direct objects but only the *type* of thoughts or beliefs that essentially rather than contingently belong to these emotions (e.g. Goldie, 2000). Finally, Green (1992) suggests that evaluative judgments or thoughts

---

4.   Satisfaction and desirability are different kinds of success conditions for desires, as Green and de Sousa emphasize. My desire that p is satisfied if I get p, but the desire is not successful if the object of my desire is not desirable.

can be analyzed further into semantically interrelated beliefs and desires. In this approach, fear is a combination of an uncertain belief that p and the desire that *not-p*; sadness a compound of a certain belief that p and the desire that *not-p*; hope is a synthesis of an uncertain belief that p and the desire that p, whereas happiness comes out as a certain belief that p together with the desire that p. Other emotions differ from these basic emotions by involving more elaborate beliefs.

The main problem with conceptual accounts of emotional content is that we sometimes feel emotions even if we do not believe or judge or think that our goals are affected favourably or adversely by external events. Fear of flying, fear of spiders, and pathological fears such as a fear of crossing a bridge are examples of rationally recalcitrant emotions that we can feel in spite of our judgments of being safe. The conflict between emotion and judgment is a problem for theories that analyse the content of emotions in terms of propositional attitudes. If emotions are or involve ordinary beliefs or judgments, the subject of a recalcitrant emotion logically contradicts himself in the same way as a person who attempts to believe contradictory statements p and not-p. The fact that emotional recalcitrance is both logically and psychologically possible, whereas it is impossible in both respects to believe that p while consciously believing that *not-p*, indicates that the content of all human emotions cannot be fully analysed in terms of propositional attitudes (see e.g. Oeigh, 1994).

Cognitive theories have tried to adjudicate the problem of recalcitrant emotions in various ways. Strong cognitivists who analyse emotions in terms of evaluative judgments with propositional content are most vulnerable to this problem. They suggest that the extra-semantic, attitudinal qualities of emotional judgments such as their freshness, haste, self-involvement, and intensity allow these judgments to conflict with nonemotional evaluative judgments (e.g. Solomon, 1988; Armon-Jones, 1991; Nussbaum, 2001). However, these proposals are metaphorical at best and incapable of offering a satisfying response to the problem of recalcitrance. Other cognitivists, sometimes referred to as "quasi-judgmentalists" (D'Arms & Jacobson, 2003), have suggested that the propositional content of emotions should be analysed in terms of evaluative thoughts that – unlike beliefs and judgments – do not involve an epistemic commitment to the truth of the content (e.g. Neu, 1977; Greenspan, 1988). The appeal of this solution is reduced by its reliance on defining-propositions methodology that unites both traditional versions of cognitivism because it is not obvious that the contents of recalcitrant emotions are inferentially related to the contents of evaluative judgments (D'Arms & Jacobson, 2003; Döring, 2004). If the content of a recalcitrant emotion were analysable in terms of a propositional attitude short of belief, the emotion would still be in rational conflict with the subject's assented belief, which should dispel the emotional thought or construal in the long run. However, the persistence of recalcitrance of some, especially phylogenetically ancient, emotions shows that this need not happen, which in turn suggests that those recalcitrant emotions do not have conceptual content. Finally, perceptual cognitivists invoke the idea of *gestalt* perception in which feeling-infused thoughts or concern-based construals hold the mind in more or less temporary grip (Goldie, 2002; Roberts, 2003). The affect explains the salience and compellingness of an emotional thought or construal and its capacity to persist in spite of conflicting belief or evaluative judgment. Perceptual cognitivists offer the best solution to the problem of emotional recalcitrance. However, their main challenge is to explain how emotions come to have this kind of affective-cum-evaluative content. The claim that emotions are *sui generis* in this respect amounts to little more than giving up the challenge of explanation in favour of a dogmatic view that hybrid states of this kind exist.

In spite of these problems with rationally recalcitrant emotions, cognitive theories are capable of accommodating the lag it normally takes from disconfirming evidence to the propositional content of emotion to "sink in", so to speak. An emotion whose conceptual content has been disproved does not immediately go away because the other noncognitive components of an emotion such as strong physiological arousal, bodily sensations, and action tendencies are capable of keeping it going for a while. A lingering emotion may also skew the subject's epistemic perspective, urging him or her to come up with other reasons for the emotion, as Peter Goldie (2004) has pointed out. Yet this kind of lag is common to all cognitive phenomena and should not be mixed up with the kind of persistent rational recalcitrance that is characteristic to phylogenetically ancient affect programme emotions on the one hand and to ontogenetically specific pathological emotions on the other hand. The fact that emotions of the latter kind exist indicates that the content of all human emotions is not conceptual.

Nonconceptual content

Nonconceptual content is a contrastive term that can be explicated in relation to conceptual content whose properties it lacks in some or several respects. Accordingly, the notion of nonconceptual content has been invoked in explaining many types of mental states whose content cannot be circumscribed by the subject's conceptual capacities. These states include representational states at the subpersonal or subdoxastic level of information processing; sense perceptions by virtue of their phenomenological or logical properties or both; and representational states of non-human animals and human infants who do not seem to possess concepts in the first place (Bermudez, 2008). However, the third category is theoretically redundant because the representational states of non-human animals and human infants are nonconceptual in some other sense and do not constitute a kind of nonconceptual content of their own. Therefore, I focus on three types of nonconceptual content – subdoxastic, phenomenological, and inferential – and their role in emotions. I first introduce each version of nonconceptual content. Then I examine how each of these versions has been applied in the discussion on emotional content and whether any of these versions offers a valid account of the content of all or most human emotions at the algorithmic level of analysis.

A.   *Subpersonal and subdoxastic nonconceptual content*

Characterizations of nonconceptual content as *sub*personal, *sub*doxastic, *pre*-linguistic and *non*-propositional are negative as they focus on properties that nonconceptual content lacks in comparison with conceptual content. Dual-process models of information processing place subpersonal and subdoxastic representations within the implicit and associative type 1, but as I have argued above, this categorisation alone is not very informative because implicit processes can operate with either conceptual or nonconceptual content. Subpersonal and subdoxastic representations are evolutionarily old and shared by humans and animals alike, and their computational system is highly independent from rule-based explicit processing. A classic analysis of such a computational system is Jerry Fodor's (1983) distinction between central and modular processing that some advocates of affect programme theories have applied in their accounts of emotional processing.

Affect programme theorists argue that emotions are special kinds of information-processing devices that emerge rapidly in situations that are relevant to the organism's fundamental life tasks. The rapid onset of emotions suggests that they are independent from conceptual processes. Yet the fact that mutually similar emotions emerge in otherwise dissimilar situations indicates that there is an internal system that is capable of appraising the emotional relevance of situations very quickly on the basis of salient perceptual cues. Accordingly, Paul Ekman (1999; 2003) has posited, following the work of Charles Darwin (1965 [1872]) and Silvan Tomkins (1962), the existence of basic emotions with distinct affect programmes. On the one hand, Ekman describes affect programmes as the *operating mechanisms* of basic emotions whose characteristics are distinctive universal signals, distinctive physiology, automatic appraisal mechanism, distinctive universals in antecedent events, distinctive developmental appearance, presence in other primates, quick onset, brief duration, unbidden occurrence, distinctive thoughts, memories and images, and distinctive subjective experience. In this sense, "the affect programme of an emotion is situated in the central part of the somatic component and is put forward as the cause of several other components (motivational, peripheral somatic, motor) in the emotion", as Moors (2012, 259) points out. On the other hand, Ekman suggests that the different elements of response "enter into" affect programmes that come out as "complex, coordinated, and automated" emotional responses, as Griffiths (1997, p. 77) has summarized. However we interpret the concept of affect programme, these programmes involve automatic appraisal mechanisms that compare perceptually submitted information to stored information about classes of stimuli that have previously, in either the ancestral or the individual past, elicited similar emotional responses. Biologically determined stimuli can be amplified or dampened by social learning. The automatic appraisal mechanisms are implemented in developmentally ancient, subcortical brain structures such as the amygdala, basal ganglia, and lateral temporal cortex that we share with many other vertebrates, especially with other mammals, and they operate without the control of conscious thinking and semantic memory.[5] Instead, their functioning is modular in the sense suggested by Fodor (1983).

Affect programmes exhibit several characteristics of Fodor's modular systems, as Griffiths (1997) has pointed out. Their operation is opaque, informationally encapsulated, mandatory, domain specific, and neurally hard-wired in identifiable circuits and locations of the brain. Affect programmes are opaque as we can be aware of their inputs and outputs but not of the automatic appraisal processes themselves. Due to their informational encapsulation, automatic appraisals cannot access information that is stored in specific cognitive systems, and they can store information that contradicts consciously available or retrievable information. Informational encapsulation explains the mandatory and recalcitrant nature of many emotions: they cannot be chosen, prevented, or terminated at will, and they can persist even if we know that they are off the mark. This is possible because the appraisal system that evaluates the stimulus and determines a fixed response to it operates on infradoxastic representational items that are semantically less complex than propositional attitudes and conscious thoughts (see Charland, 1996). Finally, each affect programme operates in its own domain, defined by its characteristic "core relational theme", and there is evidence that basic emotions, such as fear, anger, and disgust, possess specific command circuits with distinct neurochemical coding systems in the mammalian brain (Panksepp, 1998).

Jaak Panksepp advocates the most sophisticated and ambitious version of contemporary affect programme theories in his view that there are seven fundamental emotional-motivational systems in subcortical regions of the mammalian brain: SEEKING, RAGE, FEAR, LUST, CARE, GRIEF/PANIC, and PLAY. Each emotional system consists of neural networks that coordinate specific patterns of arousal,

---

5.   Ekman emphasizes that an "appraisal is not always automatic. Sometimes the evaluation of what is happening is slow, deliberate, and conscious" (Ekman 1977, 59; quoted from Ekman 1999, 51). Ekman associates his view of emotional appraisal with multi-level appraisal theories and Lazarus (1991) in particular. However, extended appraisals are not part of basic emotions and their role in Ekman's theory remains open because he explicitly states that there are no "non-basic" emotions.

distinctive instinctual behaviours such as flight or freeze in fear and aggression in rage, as well as certain "raw" affective feelings that are closely enmeshed with the neural circuits that engender instinctual emotional behaviours. Phenomenally, emotional feelings are characterized by a certain valence, arousal, and power, but they do not relate to anything beyond the organism even if they are elicited by certain evolutionarily hard-wired environmental stimuli; hence their "raw" quality. Emotional affects are also "raw" in an evolutionary sense as their underlying neural networks reside in the subcortical areas of the brain that are among the most ancient in the brain. Coherent emotional behaviours and the adjacent raw feelings can be provoked by applying unpatterned electrical stimulation to the relevant subcortical area of the brain. The same responses remain intact also in animals that are decorticated at a young age. These observations provide Panksepp evidence for the independence of emotion from cognition, as no higher cognitive activity is required for the elicitation of emotions at the *primary-process* level that we share with non-human mammals. Panksepp's affect programme theory is based on his research of primary-process brain networks in the mammalian brain. However, he believes that the results of animal studies are relevant to human emotions as well by virtue of homologous subcortical networks in the mammalian brain.

Nevertheless, the main limitation of affect programme theories – including that of Panksepp – is their applicability to post-infantile human emotions. The problem is not that we do not have pure primary-process level emotions – hard-wired responses to unconditional stimuli – but that they constitute only a small minority of our emotional episodes, as Russell (2012a, 282) points out. Panksepp admits this point in his notion of *tertiary-level* emotions that emerge when our unconditional emotional-affective responses are blended with learning, conceptual thinking, and cultural norms. Indeed, Panksepp argues that the emotional system in humans extends beyond primary-process brain networks, involving interrelations between emotion and cognition in both directions: emotion controlling cognition and cognition instigating emotion. He even writes that "in the intact adult human brain, the relations between affect and cognition are enormous and almost impossible to disentangle" (Panksepp, 2012, 59). Yet he sees the primary-process level emotional circuits as underlying mechanisms that also control emotions at higher levels. However, psychological constructionists reject this assumption about the noncognitive core of all human emotions, maintaining that empirical evidence does not support the existence of emotion-specific subcortical neural networks any more than it supports the existence of emotion-specific facial expressions, autonomic nervous system responses, action tendencies, or subjective experiences (see Russell, 2012a, 281 for a summary, and Lindquist et al., 2012 for a meta-analysis of brain studies). Accordingly, constructionists argue that the human brain typically processes emotions holistically rather than in a bottom-up fashion as affect programme theorists suggest.

Considerations of modularity provide further arguments against the wide applicability of affect programme theories. Even if some human emotions are strongly modular in the Fodorian sense, the global validity of affect programme theories is undermined by the fact that many human emotions are weakly rather than strongly modular.[6] The pervasive regulation of emotional responses before, during, and after their generation shows that their malleability far exceeds that of sense perceptions, Fodor's paradigmatic modular states. The apparent similarity between sense perception and human emotion emerges from the fact that all human emotions are capable of persisting in the face of rational counterevidence when we are in their grip, so to speak, before contrary information is taken in, as I pointed out above. Yet this weak modularity of ordinary human emotions does not render them similar to strongly modular sense perceptions and evolutionarily primitive emotions. "Emotional lag is less like visual illusion than it is like the ordinary cognitive phenomenon of beliefs outlasting acceptance of the evidential base on which they were first formed" as Karen Jones (2007, p. 23) remarks. It appears to me that this claim applies, with reservations, even to those pathological emotions whose dysfunction lies in the context of emotion regulation rather than in the underlying organismic structures and pathways. Contrary to persistent perceptual illusions, such as the Müller-Lyer illusion, there is a real possibility of bringing pathological emotions of the former kind in line with our considered judgments in therapies that may involve several types of treatment; cognitive, behavioural, and pharmaceutical (e.g. Leahy, 2004; Young, Klosko, & Weishaar, 2003; Dobson, 2001). This is the main reason for regarding those emotions as weakly or moderately rather than strongly modular.

Griffiths' (2004) own example of an affect programme emotion, anger aroused by being unexpectedly poked in the small of the back in a nightclub queue, is a case in point. Griffiths suggests that the event launches an affect programme of anger that prepares the agent for an aggressive behavioural response. However, the interpretation of the situation is defused and the response aborted as soon as one turns around and finds out that the "hit" was actually caused by the stumbling of a feeble old man. If this is an example of a "pure" affect programme, as Griffiths maintains, then it testifies *against* strong modularity of subpersonal emotional processing instead of supporting this view, for "one of the basic principles of automaticity contends that genuinely automatic processes cannot be disrupted by controlled processes", as Lieberman (2003, p. 55) points out.

An affect programme theorist may object that instrumental behaviour is not part of emotion, unlike the "square-mouthed" facial expression of anger that the

---

6.   The argument that modularity in emotion is a matter of degree was first presented by de Sousa (1987). For more recent discussions on the topic, see Faucher & Tappolet (Eds.) (2007).

subject expresses while turning around with clenched fists. However, we can grant this concession to Griffiths without defusing the argument because it is important to notice that in addition to the abortion of instrumental behaviour, the entire response would not have arisen in the first place if full perceptual information about the situation had been available to the agent during emotion generation. Visual information about the feeble old man would have supplemented tactile information, overriding the unfitting automatic appraisal of an intentional offence as soon as such an appraisal had been made. Indeed, if the automatic affect programme appraisals can be overridden by slower and more careful semantic appraisals before these programmes run their course from elicitation to full-fledged emotional response, these emotions are weakly or moderately rather than strongly modular, and therefore significantly dissimilar from sense perceptions. Accordingly, subpersonal and subdoxastic content may accommodate the emotions of subjects whose personal-level semantic processing is hindered for developmental, psychopathological, or physiological reasons but it is hardly capable of accommodating all human emotions.

B.   *Noninferential nonconceptual content*

The logical version of nonconceptual content maintains that states with nonconceptual content are not inferentially related to each other or states with conceptual content. Perception is the paradigm mental state in exemplifying this aspect of nonconceptual content as well.

Tim Crane (1992) elucidates nonconceptual content in terms of those logical properties of conceptual content that content of this kind lacks. Crane distinguishes between three kinds of inferential relations: logical, semantic, and evidential. The logical and semantic relations come down to the idea that "if a thinker has a belief, then he or she must also have many others... [because] the content of any intentional state depends, to some extent, on the contents of the others" (Crane 1992, p. 145). Thus if I believe that p while also believing that q, then I also believe the obvious logical consequences of these beliefs, such as *p and q, not (p and not-p)*, and *not (q and not-q)*. Furthermore, I believe propositions that are semantically related to p. For instance, if the content of p is that cheese is nutritious, then by believing p I also believe that cheese is edible because anything that is nutritious is also edible. Finally, evidential relations refer to the sensitivity of beliefs to perceptual evidence as well as to other pieces of conceptual evidence. If I believe that it is raining outside then I believe that I will get wet if I go out without an umbrella or waterproof clothing. If my perception does not support this belief, I revise my belief accordingly.

Crane argues that beliefs are holistically related to one another by all three kinds of inferential relations – logical, semantic, and evidential – whereas perceptions lack all these relations. First of all, "there is no such thing as deductive inference *between* perceptions. If I perceive that *a is F*, and I perceive that *a is G*, there is no such thing as inferring the perception that *a is F and G*" (Crane 1992, p. 152). It is also possible to have perceptions with explicitly contradictory contents whereas this is impossible in the case of beliefs. The Waterfall Illusion in which water seems to be both moving and not moving is a case in point. No semantic inferences from perceptual content are possible either. For instance, if one believes that a table is brown, one can also infer from this belief that the table also has shape because anything that has colour also has some shape. In contrast, "the content of the perception that the table is brown *already contains* the perception of its [actual] shape" (ibid., p. 153). Therefore, unlike believing that *p* which entails that "there are other beliefs that you *ought to have* if that belief is to have the content *p*... to perceive that *p*, there are no other *perceptions* that you *ought to* have. ...You simply perceive what the world and your perceptual systems let you perceive" (ibid., p. 154, original italics). A visual perception of any object gives rise to a series of anticipations of how the object would look from different angles. Yet this does not entail that one ought to perceive the object from another angle in the anticipated way, nor does a failure to see the object in the anticipated way preclude the perception from having the content it has. The object we take to be a barn may turn out to be a barn façade when we see it from another angle.[7] Finally, perceptions are resilient to conclusive counterevidence, which shows that they are not evidentially related to other states. The Müller-Lyer visual illusion is a well-known example: conclusive evidence that the two lines are the same length does not adjust our perception accordingly. All these differences in the properties of belief and perception indicate that perceptual content is not inferentially related to the contents of conceptual representations and therefore not subject to the constitutive ideal of rationality.

Noninferential structure is Sabine Döring's main argument for the nonconceptual content of emotion and perception. She illustrates this claim with the phenomenon of "conflict without contradiction". Döring (2003, p. 223) claims that the emotional content "resembles the content of sense-perception in that both kinds of representational content need not be revised in the light of belief and better knowledge". She compares emotions to the Müller-Lyer visual illusion and remarks that emotions may persist in the face of belief or knowledge in the same way as our visual perception that the two lines differ in length survives our belief that the lines

---

7.   A person who detects a barn façade may think that the content of his previous perception of the same object from another angle cannot be a barn and should be modified accordingly. However, this thought does not create an ought to perceive the object differently but only a new expectation that the object's façade character may be detectable also from the other angle by taking a closer look. Yet this expectation cannot rationally influence the content of perception: the façade either is perceivable also from that angle, or it isn't.

are the same length. Döring argues that this kind of recalcitrance is not restricted to evolutionarily basic emotions and pathological emotions but applies to ordinary human emotions as well. Love for an unfit partner may linger on in spite of the partner's abusive behaviour, or one may feel guilty for an accident even if one knows that the accident could not have been prevented. These examples indicate that a subject can coherently have a sense perception or experience an emotion of the content that p, while consciously believing that $\sim p$, whereas this is impossible in the case of explicitly contradictory beliefs. In spite of a rational conflict in content, no logical contradiction is involved, because there are no inferential relations between the contents of emotion or perception and belief. Instead, perceptions and emotions noninferentially justify perceptual beliefs and evaluative judgments, respectively. Neither are there inferential relations between emotions and other states, including other emotions. There is no such thing as inferring an emotion or a sense perception with a conjunctive content from the contents of distinct emotions or sense perceptions.

The question whether emotional content is noninferential boils down to the question whether or not it is subject to the constitutive ideal of rationality. Donald Davidson (1980) famously argued that a person's individual beliefs, desires, intentions, and actions as well as many emotions are intelligible only insofar as they fit into a coherent and holistic pattern that also determines their rationality. Perception is not subject to the constitutive ideal of rationality due to its noninferential structure, and insofar as emotion and perception resemble each other in this respect, emotion should not be subject to this ideal either. However, Bennett Helm has presented an elaborate theory of the nature and rationality of emotions on the basis of an opposite view, arguing that emotion participates in the holistic ideal of the mental.

In his *Emotional Reason* (2001), Helm proposes that emotions are evaluative feelings of import that both constitute and display the value of their focus, a particular object. Moreover, emotions with a common focus impose rational constraints on each other and on the subject's other states, including desires and evaluative judgments. Thus, individual emotions are warranted by virtue of their being elements of a projectable pattern of rationality, formed by the subject's felt evaluations and evaluative judgments. This means that one is *prima facie* committed both actually and counterfactually to experiencing rationally required emotions if the focus of one's emotion is or would be affected favourably or adversely. For instance, if Sam fears that his prize Ming vase is about to be destroyed, he is committed to hoping that the vase will remain intact, feeling relieved if the vase escapes unscathed, and becoming sad or angry if the fear of its breaking is borne out. Helm admits that there may be occasional and isolated gaps or anomalies in the overall pattern of rationality. Sam may for instance be too exhausted or depressed to actively care about his Ming vase. But if Sam generally does not feel relieved when he sees the vase escape undamaged from dangers or shocked when he witnesses its breaking into pieces, and so on, we find it hard to believe that Sam was afraid of its breaking in the first place, because he *ought to* have felt one of those ways if the vase has import for him. Paraphrasing Crane, 'to feel that *p* there are other emotions that you ought to feel about *p*', where this ought is not reducible to mere anticipation of other emotions but represents a requirement of rationality.

Obviously, Sam's failure to feel relieved when he sees the vase escape undamaged does not rule out the possibility of his having felt afraid of the vase's breaking; the fact of experiencing an emotion is distinct from its rationality. Indeed, only a wider pattern of Sam's felt evaluations and evaluative judgements is capable of determining which of these responses are subjectively rational for him. To some extent, the situation is similar for perception. Other perceptions lead us to conclude that some perceptions are illusory. The perception of a bent stick in water counts as a visual illusion because the same stick is consistently seen as straight in other surroundings. However, an important disanalogy between emotion and perception emerges here. There can be no 'rational ought' to perceive the stick as straight, because we cannot bring the perception in line with our other perceptions and beliefs in any case. We renounce the belief that the stick is bent in the face of conclusive counterevidence, but the content of perception is not revisable on the basis of this evidence, which shows that perceptions are not evidentially related to other states.

Döring claims that ordinary emotions of ordinary people are similar to perception in the sense that they persist in spite of the subject's better knowledge. Indeed, evolutionarily primitive emotions, such as fear of snakes or heights, as well as pathological emotions are resilient to rational counterevidence. However, ordinary emotions of ordinary people are not like this. They are evidentially related to other states even if they do not immediately vanish in the face of better knowledge. Yet the fact that we regard many recalcitrant emotions as well as pathological emotions as irrational rather than *arational*, and try to get rid of them, implies that the problem with recalcitrant emotions is not so much whether they *need* to be revised in the light of better knowledge, but rather whether they *can* be so revised.

Since ordinary emotions of ordinary people are weakly or moderately rather than strongly modular, as I have argued above, the phenomenon of conflict without contradiction is an untypical case which does not exempt emotions categorically from the constitutive ideal of rationality. In fact, Döring admits this point in maintaining that emotion, perception, and belief are different cognitive systems that provide us with information about the world. More importantly, she argues that conflicts between perception and belief as well as emotion and belief are *rational conflicts* because they are "conflicts *in content* about how the world actually is" (Döring 2009, p. 240; original italics). However, the fact that the content of most human emotions, unlike perceptual content, is both semantically and evidentially related to other states suggests that only conflicts between emotion and belief are rational conflicts in a more robust, Davidsonian sense of being conflicts within a coherent and holistic pattern of mental states and attitudes. Conflicts between perception and belief are rational conflicts in a thinner sense, or rather psychological conflicts because perception unlike emotion is not subject to the constitutive ideal of rationality. These considerations show that typical human emotions do not have noninferential nonconceptual content.

C.   Fine-grained nonconceptual content

The final, phenomenological version of nonconceptual content highlights the fine-grained nature of such content. This property of nonconceptual content plays a significant role in the argument from noninferential structure, but it constitutes an independent argument leading to the same conclusion as well. This argument refers to the qualitative and informational richness of nonconceptual content in comparison to conceptual content. Dretske (1981) illustrates this point with his distinction between analogue and digital forms of representation. Their main difference is that when a representation carries the information that *s* is *F* in digital form, it only carries this piece of information, whereas an analogue representation of the same information always carries some additional information about *s*. The sentence, "There is a table in the room" is an example of a digital representation, while a photograph of the table in the room represents the same information in an analog form. The photograph contains much more information than the sentence because it also carries information about the shape, colour, and texture of the table, its location in the room, objects placed on the table, and so on. A picture is literally worth a thousand or even more words as these can never capture and reproduce the qualitative richness of the picture in a conceptual form. The same point applies to visual experience whose details and nuances evade an exhaustive propositional rendering. We can also perceptually discriminate scenarios with determinate shapes and shades without possessing concepts that characterize specific aspects of those scenarios (Crane, 1992; Peacocke, 1992).

Emotions typically strike us with an immediacy and vivacity comparable to sense perceptions. Vividness, in turn, is related to intensity, another phenomenological aspect of emotion. In contrast to beliefs and thoughts where intensity is a measure of their subjective probability, the intensity of an emotion refers to its motivational force and vividness, both of which are reflected in the urgency and compellingness of the emotional experience. Some emotions such as fear and anger or love and hate can also be distinguished from one another by their phenomenal *qualia* in the same way as perceptual qualities. Last but not least, the *what-is-it-likeness* and intentionality appear to be inseparable in the representational content of both emotion and sense perception even if they obviously do not have the same phenomenology. Emotional content is shot through with feeling which renders it verbally ineffable. This inseparability of phenomenology and intentionality, affect and attitude in the emotional content, is the core idea behind arguments for the fine-grained phenomenology of emotions. Nevertheless, most theorists who emphasize the fine-grained character of emotional content believe that this content is conceptually structured (see Roberts, 1988, 2003; Helm, 2001; Goldie, 2000, 2002, 2009). This leaves Döring (2004, 2007, 2009) as the sole protagonist of nonconceptual content on the basis of fine-grained phenomenology of emotion.

Döring (2004) argues that emotional content is structured by perceptual *gestalt* qualities such as fearsomeness and offensiveness that organize the various details of emotional content in the same way as the *gestalts* of duck and rabbit organize the content of the picture that can be seen either as a duck or rabbit, depending on the dominant gestalt. A *gestalt* cannot be inferred from a detailed description of its parts and their relations. Instead, it is the whole that organizes the parts and determines the terms in which the parts are perceived. Thus for instance the *gestalt* of fearsomeness organizes the sensory properties of an aggressive-looking pit bull terrier, such as its raised hackles, sharp bared teeth, low growl, and fixed glare, which together give rise to an affective perception of the dog as fearsome. We can respond to this affective perception with fear even before realising that the animal is a dog of notorious breed that has all the classic symptoms of canine aggression and therefore is fearsome. Nor do we need concepts of those perceptual properties that together constitute an affective perception of the dog as fearsome. Instead, we are capable of responding to this property emotionally even before our perceptual system has produced a conscious representation – let alone a conceptual classification– of the object. In a like manner, Deigh (2008) suggests that the content of some emotions resembles perceptual content in being constituted of sensory evaluative representations of objects as, for instance, scary (fear) or rotten (disgust). Unlike Döring, however, Deigh does not generalize this claim to all human emotions. Instead, he distinguishes between primitive and tutored instances of the same emotion type: primitive emotions with sensory, nonconceptual content, and tutored emotions with evaluative, propositional content.

Döring's phenomenological argument for the nonconceptual content of emotion runs together two claims that are actually separate. One is the feeling-laden content of emotions and the other is the capacity of emotions to emerge from simple perceptual cues before a conscious categorisation and evaluation of the situation. The first claim is true of all emotions whereas the second applies only to some emotions. The separation of these claims is important because only the latter requires explanation in terms of nonconceptual content.

Emotions always have phenomenologically fine-grained content as they are multimodal states whose constituents intertwine in emotional experiences, giving rise to intentional affective experiences (Salmela, 2002, 2005). However, emotions may come to possess content of this kind in many ways. Döring describes one instance in which the emotion emerges from a sense perception before the subject conceptually recognizes the object of his or her emotion. Yet affective perceptions can emerge in another ways as well, as Goldie (2000) has pointed out. He gives an example in which we look at a gorilla in a zoo and think of it as dangerous without fear because the gorilla seems to be in a cage behind bars. But then we notice that the cage door has been left open. This perception frightens us, giving our thought that the gorilla is dangerous a new affective flavour that Goldie describes as "thinking with feeling". Goldie claims that thinking with feeling involves a direct and original type of affective intentionality. This means that when we come to think of an object as dangerous with fear, "the dangerousness of the object, and the determinate features towards which the thought is directed, is grasped in a different way. That is to say, one's way of thinking of it is completely new. It is not just the old way of thinking of it, plus some new element" (Goldie 2002, p. 243). Yet as important as the new phenomenological features of thinking *with feeling* are, as a form of *thinking* this activity still has conceptual content, albeit shot through with feeling. This shows that emotions may have conceptual content in spite of their fine-grained affective phenomenology.

In contrast, emotion generation on the basis of perceptual *gestalt* qualities relates to the kind of affective or automatic information processing that Jenefer Robinson, Paul Griffiths, Paul Ekman, and other affect programme theorists have associated with basic emotions. Indeed, these two forms of nonconceptual content complement each other as perceptual *gestalt* qualities are good candidates for elicitors of emotions that operate on subdoxastic and subpersonal representations. Perception of such qualities does not require conceptual capacities from the subject; an ability to recognize perceptually similar objects in light of the subject's active goals and to respond to those objects with the same, specific emotion is sufficient. The emotions of nonhuman animals and human infants who do not possess concepts are likely to operate in this manner.[8] The same mechanism continues to operate in language users whose emotions may then emerge from either evaluative perceptions or evaluative judgments, as Deigh (2008) points out. His

---

8.   Thus McDowell (2009, p. 130) observes that "If an animal has in its repertoire behaviour appropriately conceived as fleeing, it must be able to discriminate (perhaps not very accurately) between situations that pose danger to it and situations that do not. But given my stipulation, *this ability to discriminate does not suffice for having the concept of danger*. The concept requires a subject who can respond to dangerousness as the reason it is. And that requires in turn the ability to take dangerousness into account in reasoning" (my italics).

distinction between primitive and tutored emotions with dissimilar content, sensory and evaluative, offers a viable hypothesis of this difference while being consistent with the distinction between conceptual and nonconceptual content. However, conceptual capacities bring an important new dimension to post-infantile human emotions as they allow further information processing during emotion generation, allowing us to modulate the emerging emotional response if perceptual impressions and conceptual appraisals of the emotion-eliciting situation differ from each other. Again, we must conclude that emotions with perceptually organized nonconceptual content are a minority among human emotions.

Nonconceptual content: Cognitive or noncognitive?

The previous discussion has shown that neither account on the nature of emotional content, conceptual or nonconceptual, is capable of accommodating all human emotions at the algorithmic level of analysis. Some emotions have conceptual content whereas others have nonconceptual content, but the divide is not sharp because most actual emotions incorporate representations of more than one type. This result brings us back to the first question on whether particular types of nonconceptual content are cognitive or noncognitive. Everyone agrees that subdoxastic and subpersonal nonconceptual content is noncognitive. Therefore, the question is relevant only for the inferential and phenomenological types of nonconceptual content. Advocates of these types of content usually regard noninferentially structured or phenomenologically fine-grained content as noncognitive (see e.g. Griffiths, 2004; Gunther, 2003; Deigh, 2008). An exception is Döring (2004), who suggests that affective perceptions qualify as cognitive by virtue of having the hallmarks of cognitive content: propositional structure, the mind-to-world direction of fit, and a correctness condition. This proposal calls for more elaborate examination.

Döring's argument for the cognitive character of nonconceptual content is founded on the idea that emotional content is structured by nonconceptual *gestalt* qualities such as fearsome (fear) or outrageous (anger). She invokes a distinction between two kinds of propositional content: propositional in the Fregean sense, or 'propositional$_F$' in short, and 'propositional$_S$' in which the subscripted 'S' stands for sentential or conceptual content. For the former kind of propositional content, a mental state must only ascribe a property to the particular object that it represents. Both perceptions and emotions qualify as propositional$_F$ as they ascribe certain sensory properties such as colours, shapes, and affective *gestalt* qualities to their particular objects. The content of perceptions and emotions need not be conceptually available to the subject unlike the content of beliefs and evaluative judgments that is propositional in both senses of the term. In essence, propositional content in the Fregean sense boils down to a predicative structure that Döring associates with the mind-to-world direction of fit and a correctness condition. However, these epistemic notions are problematic in the context of perceptions of affective *gestalt* qualities.

It is true that emotions ascribe such properties as fearsome, disgusting, and outrageous to their particular objects. Yet in order to have the mind-to-world direction of fit, these ascriptions should not be fitting in every token emotion. Unfortunately, this seems to be the case because there is a difference between affective *gestalt* properties and ordinary perceptual properties as the former properties are projective rather than merely response-dependent. Typical perceptual properties such as colours and sounds are secondary properties that can be defined through their appearance to normal subjects in normal conditions of perception. To be, for instance, green is to appear green to normal subjects in normal conditions, where normality refers to capacities of visual perception, health, freedom from the influence of substances, and so on, while normal conditions include bright daylight, short distance, and so on. In contrast, affective properties are "tertiary" as their perception depends on the perception of primary and secondary properties such as a pitbull terrier's fearsome-making properties. More importantly, affective properties are response-dependent in a deeper sense than secondary properties because any object that gives rise to an emotional response receives the relevant tertiary property in emotional experience. Thus, everything that appears fearsome is fearsome, whereas everything that appears green is not green, because green is not an entirely phenomenal property but depends both on the subject and her conditions of perception. However, without a meaningful *is/seems* distinction there is no correctness condition either because this condition *is* such a distinction.

Emotion theorists have recognized this problem in discussing the formal objects of emotion. In order to qualify as a standard of fittingness, a formal object cannot be a property that every token emotion of the same type ascribes to its particular object (McDowell, 1997b, p. 207; Prinz, 2004, pp. 60–64; de Sousa, 2011, p. 64). Fear, for instance, is fitting only if its object *merits* fear by being dangerous; not merely frightening or fearsome or scary. Therefore, the formal object of fear is the property of being dangerous rather than the property of being frightening. Unfortunately, language does not allow us to make the same kind of distinction between evaluative and phenomenal properties in the context of all emotions. The concepts of being enviable and being shameful, for instance, can be used in both an evaluative and a phenomenal sense. Thus, we describe as shameful both acts that we actually feel ashamed of and acts that we or other people should feel ashamed of, whether or not we do so. Yet these properties qualify as formal objects of envy and shame only if they are interpreted in the evaluative sense that refers to fitting envy and shame, respectively. Döring's affective *gestalt* properties, in contrast, are those phenomenal properties that figure in all emotional experiences of the same type – otherwise they could not phenomenally structure those experiences.[9] Yet the phenomenal role of affective *gestalt* properties undermines their role as formal objects because no plausible *is/seems* distinction can be grounded on such properties that trivially fit their particular objects.

Therefore, I conclude that nonconceptual content is noncognitive. Attempts to expand cognition to cover both conceptual and nonconceptual representations blur important distinctions between different kinds of representations involved in emotion. Delicate distinctions such as Deigh's divide between primitive and tutored emotions rather than sweeping generalizations are needed in order to understand how the emotions of pre-lingual infants differ from those of adult humans. Even so, a structural approach to emotional content can only lay out the elements of which human emotions are composed. It is another thing how these elements enmesh and interact in actual human emotions. Therefore, a structural approach must be complemented with a dynamic approach to the content of emotions.

Conclusion

In this chapter I have discussed the role of cognition in the content of human emotions from a structural point of view. I have argued that cognition is always involved in emotional content at the functional level of analysis, whereas emotional content can be divided schematically into two kinds, cognitive and noncognitive, at the algorithmic level of processes and types of representation. My discussion focused on the analysis of cognitive and noncognitive content in terms of conceptual and nonconceptual content; on subdoxastic, logical, and phenomenological subtypes of the latter; and on the possibility of analysing the content of all or most human emotions in terms of any single type of representation. Unsurprisingly, no single type of content was found to fit the bill: some human emotions involve representations with conceptual content whatever other components they involve; while others involve representations with nonconceptual content in the subdoxastic, noninferential, or phenomenological sense, or several of them. Nevertheless, instances of pure types were found to be rare as most human emotions have contents that mix properties of conceptual and nonconceptual content, being more or

---

9.   Actually this is not the case because the content of an emotional experience depends on the subject's focus of attention during the experience. An intentional affective perception emerges only if the subject's attention is focused on the particular object of emotion. Focus on the unfolding bodily response gives rise to a different kind of emotional experience. See e.g. Lambie & Marcel, 2002; Salmela, 2002, 2005; Deonna & Teroni, 2012, Ch. 7.

less conceptual or nonconceptual on a continuum from strongly conceptual to nonconceptual.

This result shows first of all that a quest for a single type of emotional content is misdirected. Human emotions are neither cognitive nor noncognitive, categorically, but typically have aspects of both to varying degrees. This conclusion also speaks against a sharp dichotomy between radically dissimilar types of emotion such as "pure" affect programme emotions and cognitively complex emotions. These types are idealisations that actual human emotions resemble to a greater and lesser extent. Secondly, the blended or mixed character of emotional content speaks against parallel-competitive views of dual processing in the emotional domain. Emotional processing is parallel but the two types of processing, implicit and explicit, typically do not compete with each other – rationally recalcitrant emotions are an exception – leaving the determination of response to just one type of processing. Instead, emotional processing is sequential, especially when the emerging emotion is about a present state of affairs whose unfolding the subject perceives with all her senses. Implicit nonconceptual processing launches the initial stages of responding on the basis of immediate perceptual impressions, but explicit conceptual processing immediately joins in to refine the appraisal of the situation and to monitor the adaptiveness or fittingness of the emerging response. The question is whether such a role of explicit processing renders even implicitly elicited human emotions cognitive in a robust sense at the algorithmic level of analysis. The following chapter about the role of cognition in dynamics of emotion is organized around this question.

CHAPTER 3

Cognition in the dynamics of emotion

The previous chapter ended in the conclusion that the discussion on the cognitive or noncognitive nature of human emotions must be brought from the level of representations and processes to their interaction and integration in real emotions. This approach focuses on the *dynamic* character of emotions as processes that have a temporal structure. Emotions are elicited, they unfold as multimodal responses that are regulated in various ways, and they attenuate towards an affective baseline or transform into other emotions. Yet it is not obvious on which part of the emotional response we should focus in defining emotions because an emotion can last from fractions of seconds to several minutes or even days, depending on one's theoretical approach.

Noncognitivists typically understand emotions as short-lived responses that are triggered more or less automatically by perceptually salient cues even if remote cognitive causes sometimes elicit emotions as well. However, cognitive causes are never constituents of emotion for noncognitivists. Instead, emotions involve stereotypic patterns of changes in central and autonomic nervous system activation, action readiness, facial and vocal expressions, and subjective feelings but not for instance instrumental behaviours or regulatory processes. In contrast, cognitivists prefer to analyze emotions in terms of longer time frames. In their view, appraisal processes evolve and interact with other components of emotion during the generation of emotional responses whose regulation is also often seen as an integral part of emotion. The challenge is to determine where an emotion begins and ends on the continuum of emotional processing and what if any role do cognitions have within this temporal frame.

Both cognitive and noncognitive theorists have traditionally assumed that the cognitive or noncognitive status of emotions depends on the nature of the mental states that are involved in the elicitation of emotions. If emotions emerge from either sub- or supraliminal perceptions with nonconceptual content, they are noncognitive, whereas they are cognitive if the constitutive causes of emotions are evaluative judgments or thoughts. Accordingly, the dispute on the nature of emotions has focused on the character of emotion-eliciting mental representations, and the disagreement between cognitivists and noncognitivists has moved one step further and now centres on the correct level of analysis for these representations. Cognitivists advocate functional accounts in which all mental representations that give rise to emotions of the same vernacular type qualify as cognitive, whereas noncognitivists favour algorithmic accounts that highlight differences between eliciting representations and processes. This dispute is familiar from the classic Zajonc-Lazarus debate whose repercussions in contemporary emotion theories were analysed in the previous chapter.

Yet the plausibility of the traditional approach depends on the extent to which initial perceptions or appraisals determine the identity of the emerging emotions as well as their duration, intensity, and expression. Insofar as the "late cognition" that emerges after the initial eliciting representations participates in the shaping of emotional responses and their type, it should perhaps be included in the constitution of emotion. The status of emotion as either cognitive or noncognitive could not then be judged on the basis of its eliciting representations but by an overall contribution of cognition to the phenotype of emotion. This approach is particularly relevant in the context of human emotions that become thoroughly integrated with conceptual information processing in normal ontogenetic development.

The first hurdle to any cognitive account of human emotions concerns the question of whether or not mental causes of emotion, either cognitive or noncognitive, are also constituents of emotion. Emotions come out as noncognitive if their mental causes do not belong to emotion, or if their type-identifying appraisals are noncognitive, whatever cognitive representations are sometimes or even always involved in the regulation of emotions. Jesse Prinz (2004) and Jenefer Robinson (2005) advance these two arguments for noncognitivism. Prinz distinguishes elicitors of emotion from emotional responses and defines emotions in terms of the latter, whereas Robinson suggests that emotions are always elicited by automatic affective appraisals that determine their status as noncognitive states even if these appraisals are invariably followed by cognitive monitoring. I shall first argue against Prinz that elicitors of emotions must be included in the definition of emotion. Then I shall turn this conclusion against Robinson's view about noncognitive elicitors of all human emotions. Robinson turns out to be more ambiguous about the nature of emotions than she proclaims. Her process model associates closely with cognitive process models of emotion that explicate the essential role of cognitive representations in the generation and regulation of emotional responses. I discuss two such models, process-oriented appraisal theories and psychological constructivism, at some length. Finally, I turn the overlap and integration of emotion generative and regulative processes into one more argument for a robust role of cognition in human emotions. However, the journey towards this conclusion begins from the role of mental causes in the constitution of human emotions.

Mental causes in the constitution of emotion

Noncognitive theories typically employ two strategies in keeping cognition out of emotional content. They either treat cognitions as contingent elicitors of emotion that do not belong to emotion proper, or they maintain that the eliciting appraisals of emotion that determine the quality of emotional content are always rather than contingently nonconceptual – subpersonal and subdoxastic – representations. Prinz (2004) employs the first argumentative strategy, whereas Robinson (2005) and affect programme theorists (e.g. Ekman, 1992, 1999; Levenson, 2003) advance the second, the latter especially for basic emotions. I shall argue against Prinz that elicitors of emotion belong to emotion proper and that they often, though not always, qualify as cognitive states. This conclusion can be turned against Robinson's view about noncognitive elicitors of all emotions. In conclusion, the elicitors of human emotions divide into cognitive and noncognitive appraisals. This means that the cognitive status of human emotions depends on whether or not cognitive processes are essentially involved in all emotions after their elicitation, a question which will be discussed in the next section.

Prinz argues that evaluative judgments contingently elicit emotions that qualify as embodied appraisals with a representational content by virtue of their evaluative function, without involving appraisals as their components. This claim is founded on a sharp distinction that Prinz makes between the *initiation* and *response* pathways of emotion. Initiation pathway contains the elicitation and calibration files of distinct emotions, whereas the response pathway is constituted of changes in the bodily state and their somatosensory perception. A noncognitive view of emotions as perceptions of bodily changes results from defining emotion exclusively in terms of the response pathway.

Two crucial distinctions for Prinz's argument are those between (1) *elicitors of emotion* and *emotions proper* on the one hand and between (2) *direct* and *indirect causes* of emotion on the other hand. The first distinction purports to establish the noncognitive view of emotions proper as perceptions of bodily changes that nevertheless, on account of the second distinction, represent their indirect causes, that is, core relational themes, rather than those bodily changes that directly cause the emotion. This idea can also be expressed by distinguishing between the *real* and *nominal contents* of emotion: "Core relational themes are the *real contents* of emotions, and bodily changes are their *nominal contents*" (ibid., p. 68). Even if emotions are reliably caused by both bodily changes and core relational themes in the organism's environment, they represent only the latter because they have the *function* of detecting core relational themes, which they do by registering changes in the body.

Elicitors of a particular emotion type constitute its *elicitation file*. These are mental states that internally trigger individual emotions of a particular type when the relevant core relational theme is instantiated in the subject's environment. Yet elicitors need not have anything else in common. For instance, the elicitation file of fear may contain perceptions of a snake or a pointing gun, as well as judgments like "That's poison!" or "I'm in danger!" Elicitation files of basic emotions have been fostered by natural selection, but response patterns of basic emotions can be retuned to respond to other properties that they were not genetically set up to detect. For instance, the response pattern of anger may come to represent infidelity (jealousy) and moral transgression (moral indignation) as well. One response type can then function as a *calibrated* detector of several core relational themes. Items of a particular elicitation file contain all those states that elicit an emotional response of a certain kind. However, emotions are constituted of perceptions of bodily changes alone because elicitation and calibration files are only causes, not constituents of emotion.

A major problem with Prinz's theory is its incapability to accommodate particular objects as intentional objects of emotion. Emotions as embodied appraisals have been set up to be set off by core relational themes, not particular objects that figure in the theory as mere triggers of emotion. Thus for instance "Sadness represents the loss of something valued. If I am sad about the death of a child, I have one mental representation that corresponds to the child's death *and* another, my sadness that corresponds to there having been a loss" (Prinz, 2004, p. 62). Since representations of particular objects are not components of emotion, individuals must scan their environment for particular objects or situations that instantiate the relevant core relational theme. The actual elicitors of emotions obviously give clues here, but the process still involves more or less interpretation because emotions do not include representations of particular objects. Worse still, psychological construction of this kind extends to the type of emotion as well since Prinz allows the same bodily response patterns to represent several core relational themes.

Prinz argues that anger, fear, happiness, sadness, and disgust are embodied appraisals that are identifiable in terms of their bodily response patterns, whereas all other emotions are blends of basic emotions or cognitive elaborations of basic emotions. The key to nonbasic emotions is calibration, a mental mechanism "that establishes a link between judgments of a particular kind and embodied appraisals" (ibid., p. 100). Thus, "for instance, guilt may be sadness brought on by the belief that one has committed a harmful transgression. [Or] pride may be happiness brought on by the belief that one has achieved a difficult task" (ibid., p. 93). But since nonbasic emotions can be elicited by both evaluative judgments and perceptual stimuli that are not part of emotion, the subject may have to rely on her emotional experience in identifying her emotion. Indeed, some theorists suggest that bodily feelings distinguish between different emotion types (e.g. Deonna & Teroni, 2012). However, Prinz does not invoke this argument. Instead, he maintains that the same bodily response patterns serve several emotion types. Consequently, the subject of emotion may have to engage in an interpretation of the environment in order to figure out which emotion – guilt or sadness; pride or happiness, jealousy or anger – she is experiencing, in addition to finding a suitable particular object for the emotion. Even if constructive processes of this kind are in some cases necessary to identify our emotions and the objects that "make us feel the way we do... there is no reason to think that this subset of cases captures the typical epistemological situation we are in when we feel emotions", as Deonna and Teroni (2012, p. 74) point out.

Another problem for a sharp distinction between initiation and response pathways emerges from the twofold nature of emotional dysfunctions. Prinz argues that dysfunctions of emotion parallel those of perception that result from accidents, diseases, lesions, substance abuse, and other organismic damages or failures. Indeed, some dysfunctions of emotion involve or emerge from failures in the emotional 'hardware', so to speak. Alexithymia, which Prinz discusses in passing, may be such a failure. Antonio Damasio presents several dysfunctions of this type in *Descartes' Error* (1994) and his other books. However, there are also disorders whose pathology resides in the misconnected emotional 'software', such as phobias, panic disorders, OCD, PTSD, as well as other mood and anxiety disorders. These affective disorders can be conceptualized as normal emotional responses to misplaced or inappropriate objects.[1] Prinz mentions those phenomena as well; not as dysfunctions in the emotion system, which he identifies with the response pathway, but in another context, in discussing the initiation pathway that houses calibration files for emotional responses.

Prinz's refusal to characterize anxiety and mood disorders as dysfunctions of emotion is idiosyncratic considering that they are widely, for instance, in the DSM-V manual of psychopathology, classified as such.[2] However, this terminological choice is in line with Prinz's definition of emotions as perceptions of bodily changes. Even so, the choice is not entirely warranted if Prinz thinks, as he does, that the function of emotions is to detect core relational themes rather than bodily changes.

---

1. In neurophysiological terms, the amygdala of a clinically anxious or phobic person, for instance, may operate normally. The dysfunction lies in the context in which the emotion is experienced rather than in the response itself. Accordingly, Davidson, Fox and Kalin (2007, p. 56) suggest that mood and anxiety disorders may be best conceptualized as disorders of the context regulation of affect, involving the expression of normal emotion in inappropriate contexts (see also Beer & Lombardo, 2007; Healy, 1990).

2. Obviously, anxiety disorders both in DSM-V and here are understood as involving several episodes of anxiety within several weeks rather than a single, prolonged anxiety episode.

This means that an inappropriate emotional response, such as fear of an innocuous object, quite literally is a dysfunctional emotion; an emotion that does not serve its function, which is to detect dangers in the subject's environment. In order to serve their function of delivering information about how we are faring, the calibration files of emotions must be "well-tuned", as Prinz (2004, p. 240) puts it. But then calibration files become part of the emotion system that cannot be limited to pathways and neural representations responsible for somatosensory perception. Prinz observes this difference between emotion and sense perception in pointing out that "vision does not require an initiation pathway. It is not mediated, under ordinary conditions, by mental states outside the visual system" (ibid., p. 239). However, he does not realise that this mediation of emotions, which is necessary for the emergence of emotions and crucial for their proper functioning, undermines the theoretical divide between initiation and response pathways. An emotional system encompasses both pathways, which allows us to see the essential role of mental causes in emotion.

The more inclusive definition of emotion in terms of both initiation and response pathways refutes Prinz's argument for the noncognitive character of all emotions. Instead, emotions appear to divide into cognitive and noncognitive, depending on the nature of their mental causes that divide into nonconceptual perceptions and conceptual judgments at the algorithmic level of analysis. Nevertheless, this conclusion can be rejected by suggesting that the *immediate elicitors* of emotions are always fast, automatic and noncognitive appraisals, whatever conceptual thoughts or judgments precede or follow these affective appraisals. This Robinson's strategy, who emphasizes the nature of emotions as processes but limits the role of cognition to emotion regulation.

Nonconceptual appraisals as constitutive causes of emotion

Robinson's argument for noncognitivism is founded on distinguishing the noncognitive elicitation of emotions from their cognitive monitoring and treating the former as decisive in determining the identity of emotion. Robinson admits that conceptually complex thoughts and beliefs sometimes participate in the evaluation of emotion-eliciting stimuli at early stages of appraisal. Yet the affective appraisals that ultimately elicit emotions and function as their components are nonconceptual and noncognitive. "Emotions are processes in which a rough-and-ready affective appraisal causes physiological responses, motor changes, action tendencies, changes in facial and vocal expression, and so on, succeeded by cognitive monitoring" (Robinson, 2005, p. 97). If this argument is correct, then all elicitors of emotions qualify as noncognitive at the algorithmic level of analysis whereas the role of cognition is limited to emotion regulation that begins only after emotion elicitation.

Robinson illustrates her view by analysing the fright caused by a significant economic loss. She admits that sophisticated conceptual appraisals may be necessary to realise that the evaporation of 10 000 USD from one's stock portfolio during a recent economic crisis constitutes a significant loss. Yet she suggests that this appraisal only paves the way for a causally efficient, fast and automatic affective appraisal about the loss. "It is only after lengthy cognitive evaluations that I realise how badly I am doing, but once I make this discovery, then all of a sudden I make an affective appraisal that rivets my attention on this discovery and its implications for my well-being," (Robinson, 2005, p. 62). Robinson argues that this subdoxastic and subpersonal affective appraisal is decisive as it gives rise to the other noncognitive components of emotion: physiological changes, changes in facial and vocal expression, action tendencies, and subjective feelings. In contrast, the preceding conceptual appraisal has only a contingent role in emotion elicitation because all affective appraisals do not have conceptual appraisals as their antecedents. More importantly, conceptual appraisals that either precede emotions or participate in their regulation after their elicitation do not influence the identity of emotions but only their duration, intensity, and expression. Therefore, all human emotions have nonconceptual content.

Robinson characterizes affective appraisals of the contents of conceptual thoughts or judgments as "meta-responses" that appraise the cognitively evaluated situation as **bad for me** (in bold to emphasize the qualitative difference to cognitive appraisals) or **good for me** in a "rough and ready" manner (ibid., p. 62). The problem with this proposal is that appraisals of this kind are hardly sufficient for determining the type of the emerging emotion as fear, anger, sadness, grief, joy, pride, and so on. Goodness and badness for the self only imply the valence of an emotion as either positive or negative, not its distinct type. Nor does a general appraisal of goodness or badness for the self represent the particular situation that figures as the particular object of emotion. Instead, an affective meta-appraisal appears to *implement* the higher-level cognitive appraisal whose content – an unexpected economic loss – determines both the identity of the emerging emotion as fright and its particular intentional object. The insistence on the necessary role of affective appraisal in emotion elicitation seems to refer to the activation of amygdala that is found in both bottom-up and top-down processes of emotion generation as neuroscientists have pointed out (e.g. Ochsner, Ray, Hughes, McRae, Cooper, Weber, Gabrieli, & Gross, 2009; Ochsner & Gross, 2007).

Robinson appears to recognize the problem with the content of affective appraisals as she suggests that the components of these appraisals may be the same as those identified by cognitive appraisal theorists. Her examples include This threatens me (or mine)! (fear) and This is an enemy! (hate), or, more concisely, Threat! (fear) or Offence! (anger). The argument is that affective appraisals of this kind always elicit emotions "regardless of how little or how much cognitive work it takes to detect the threat in question" (ibid., p. 94). If this proposal works, then an affective appraisal could specify the identity of the emerging emotion and represent its particular object after all.

Unfortunately, an elaborate affective appraisal appears superfluous in both respects in situations where such an appraisal has been preceded by a cognitive appraisal of threat or offence or some other core relational theme. Robinson correctly argues that cognitive thoughts and evaluations "are never the whole story" (ibid., 91), but her insistence that an affective appraisal that belongs to the emotion must nevertheless reiterate the entire evaluation in noncognitive terms strikes one as an unnecessary overlap that evolution would have eliminated if it had belonged to our emotional repertoire, given that the function of emotions is to facilitate fast responding to situations that bear on the subject's life or well-being. Alternatively, if there is no overlap between cognitive and affective appraisals, then affective appraisals are "meta-responses" that rely on cognitive appraisals in implementing emotions whose type and particular object are determined by cognitive appraisal. In this way, cognitive appraisals figure essentially in the elicitation and constitution of emotions after all.

The crux of Robinson's theory is her view that "affective appraisals can be automatically evoked not only by simple perceptions such as a sudden loud sound but also by complex thoughts and beliefs" (ibid., p. 97). If affective appraisals are capable of taking conceptual appraisals on the personal significance of events as their input, then affective appraisals are not so modular – opaque, cognitively impenetrable, informationally encapsulated, mandatory, domain specific and neurally hard-wired – as Robinson and affect programme theorists who support similar views about the nature of emotional appraisals suggest. Instead, affective appraisals are flexible as they are capable of mediating emotional responses to both perceptual stimuli and semantic information (Roberts, 2003). In functional terms, affective appraisals qualify as garden-variety cognitions by virtue of their causal role in emotion elicitation. However, these appraisals also qualify as cognitive at the algorithmic level of analysis insofar as they are capable of relying on the outcome of conceptual appraisals in their functioning. This conclusion seriously undermines Robinson's noncognitive interpretation of affective appraisals and her entire theory.

Prinz is then right in arguing that emotions can be elicited by both cognitive appraisals and noncognitive perceptions. However, this upshot does not determine the cognitive or noncognitive status of human emotions because we must look beyond the first fractions of seconds in emotion generation to see whether or not cognition has an essential role in emotion. Noncognitive theorists admit that cognitive appraisals and reappraisals may influence the duration, intensity, and expression of emotions but not their identity. Therefore, these theorists exclude late cognition from emotion proper and associate it with emotion regulation instead. Robinson is an exception as she emphasizes the nature of emotions as processes that involve cognitive monitoring by default rather than contingently. In fact, Robinson admits that cognition may amount to more than merely monitoring as these "secondary appraisals" have the capacity of influencing the identity of emotions. Her example is the distinction between fear and anger. Robinson notes that "both fear and anger may occur when someone has done something to us which we regard as a wrong or a threat. Fear is associated with an appraisal that one is unable to deal with the situation... [whereas] anger is associated with an appraisal that I can deal with the situation" (Robinson, 2005, p. 202).

This is a striking – indeed a theoretically fatal – concession from a noncognitive theorist whose main argument for noncognitivism is that cognitive appraisals have only a monitoring function in regulating noncognitively elicited emotions. If cognitive secondary appraisals are sometimes needed to distinguish between such basic emotions as fear and anger, they do not merely monitor the unfolding of emotional responses but take an active role in shaping those responses as empirical emotion regulation researchers have pointed out (e.g. Shaver, Schwartz, Kirson, & O'Connor, 1987; John & Gross, 2007). Such influences on the duration, intensity, and expression of emotions as well as on their identity allow us to treat cognitive appraisals as necessary components of emotion after all. Indeed, Robinson seeks to present her account as a plausible synthesis of noncognitive and cognitive theories of emotion while remaining subtly on the noncognitive side. Nevertheless, my previous discussion has shown that Robinson is actually a subtle cognitivist as her insistence on the pervasive role of cognitive monitoring in all human emotions associates her view with cognitive process models of emotion.

Cognitive process models of emotion

Cognitive process models argue that it is not possible to restrict the role of appraisal to two separate stages, elicitation and regulation, in emotional processing. Instead, appraisal continues during the entire process of emotion generation and regulation, shaping the emotion in light of constant feedback from other response domains and perceived changes in the emotion-eliciting situation. "The interpretation develops over time, and so does the feeling in a continuously interactive sequence, often a very rapid one. Neither interpretation, nor bodily feedback, nor subjective experience comes first; at the very most, one can talk about which of these complex temporal processes *starts* first", as Phoebe Ellsworth (1994, p. 227) points out. The continuity of emotional processing makes it difficult to draw a sharp distinction between emotion generation and regulation and to maintain – *pace* Robinson – that affective and cognitive appraisals map neatly onto these two facets of continuous emotion processing. By virtue of this processing, human emotions may have a strong cognitive imprint even when they are triggered by affective appraisals.

The basic idea of cognitive process models of emotion is that thematically coherent appraisal themes such as "an irrevocable loss" (sadness) or "a demeaning offence against me or mine" (anger) do not cause emotions but are constituted in the process of emotion generation together with other elements of emotional response. All process models emphasize the dynamic, parallel, nonlinear, and recursive character of emotional processing. Appraisal theories of this variant maintain that initial phases of stimulus appraisal trigger initial changes in the various response modalities such as autonomic physiology, action tendencies, motor, vocal and facial expression, and feeling state, whose feedback then influences both subsequent stages of appraisal and reappraisals of previous appraisals. In this way, appraisal and response modalities modify and update each other through parallel distributed processing and recursive feedback, proceeding through amplification to a stabilization phase in which parallel appraisal and response activities begin to constrain each other in a self-organizing manner. Along with increasing stability emerges a coherent appraisal in which different appraisal dimensions consolidate into a superordinate appraisal, which in turn holds the subordinate appraisals in place. "Emergent appraisals (or appraisal-emotion amalgams) are construed as globally coherent states arising and stabilizing through nonlinear causal transactions among appraisal and emotion constituents", as Marc Lewis (2005, p. 174) states. This kind of dependence between wholes and their constituent parts has been characterized as *circular* or *bidirectional* causality, and it has been argued to constitute the other main form of nonlinear causation along with feedback in emotional processing (Lewis, 2005; Scherer, 2009).

Cognitive process models maintain that the initiating appraisals in emotion generation process are often implicit, subpersonal, perceptual, and stimulus-driven, and if a satisfactory match to an existing appraisal schema is detected, an emotion ensues effortlessly. However, if further processing is required for determining the meaning of the stimulus to the subject, the level of processing tends to rise in tandem with the progress of the appraisal process. The continuous, parallel, and recursive nature of emotional processing ensures that the outcome of 'slow and careful' semantic appraisals becomes integrated with the result of 'quick and dirty' automatic appraisals that have initiated the emotion. After all, perceptual information reaches the subcortical domains of emotional processing in the centromedial nuclei of the amygdala and its subcortical circuit that includes the striatum, the brainstem, the hypothalamus, and the basal forebrain only a few milliseconds before arriving, through the basolateral nuclei of the amygdala whose function is to integrate sensory information, at the cortical areas of orbitofrontal, anterior cingulate, and ventromedial prefrontal cortex (e.g. Pessoa, 2010; Rolls, 2013; Bzdok et al., 2013). The minor lag in the cortical processing allows the subcortical processing to trigger endocrine, autonomic, and somatomotor responses as well as rudimentary behaviours such as attentional reallocation, orienting, avoidance, and approach before conceptual appraisals begin to influence and control the various response modalities. Indeed, recent neuroscientific evidence suggests that the divide between a subcortical 'low road' and a cortical 'high road' with their distinct types of appraisal, advocated by LeDoux (1995), is misleading (Pessoa & Adolphs, 2010; Rolls, 2013; see also Furtak, 2010). Instead of functioning automatically without top-down influences, the amygdala's responses are strongly dependent on task context and attention, a paradigmatic cognitive process. This suggests that instead of being a hub of the 'low road', the amygdala is a convergence zone for highly processed sensory information from both the subcortical and cortical structures with which it is connected (Pessoa, 2008; Pessoa & Adolphs, 2010; Bzdok et al., 2013). Therefore, its contribution to stimulus evaluation is not unambiguously subcortical. Moreover, the orbitofrontal cortex together with the anterior cingulate cortex engages in more complex processing of stimulus value and its rapid changes than the amygdala especially in primates such as humans, allowing greater flexibility in their emotional behaviour (Rolls, 2013). Thus the different pathways of emotional processing become strongly connected in the normal development of the human prefrontal cortex, allowing us significant control over even those emotions that are elicited through the subcortical circuit of the centromedial amygdala (Bluhm, 2007; Thompson, 2011; Rolls, 2013).

The main theoretical approaches that support the dynamic, parallel, nonlinear and holistic character of emotional processing are *process-oriented appraisal theories* (e.g. Smith & Lazarus, 1990; Ellsworth, 1991; Lazarus, 1991; Frijda, 1993; Frijda & Zeelenberg, 2001; Smith & Kirby, 2001; Scherer, 2001, 2009) and *psychological constructionism*, whose main advocates have been James Russell (e.g. 2003, 2009, 2012a,b) and Lisa Feldman Barrett (e.g. 2006a,b, 2009). Both approaches emphasise parallel distributed processing of appraisal and other response components that together constitute emotions. They also share a default-interventionist view about the relation of noncognitive and cognitive processes in emotion generation in maintaining that nonconceptual processes trigger affective responses but conceptual appraisals are required to shape these responses into emotions. Nevertheless, contrary to appraisal theorists, psychological constructionists claim that an actual appraisal process is only typically but not necessarily needed for determining the type and object of emotion. Instead, they suggest that emotions are constructed by categorising states of core affect on the basis of salient conceptual knowledge about emotions and their objects. Appraisals are conceptually constitutive of emotions, but they do not cause emotions in all cases, as appraisal theorists maintain.

These theoretical disputes are serious to appraisal theorists and psychological constructionists who frame each other as their main theoretical opponents. Even so, I suggest that those disputes are nevertheless relatively minor in comparison to their equally important consensus on the nonlinear and parallel character of emotional processing, which ensures the constitutive role of cognitive processes in human emotions. In what follows, I first discuss the merits and flaws of these two approaches in more detail. Then I outline a novel argument for the constitutive role of cognition in the dynamics of emotion. This argument suggests that the dynamic character of emotional processing blurs the distinction between emotion generation and regulation.

Process-oriented appraisal theories

Process-oriented appraisal theories maintain that dynamic, parallel, non-linear and holistic emotional processing is both elicited and driven by appraisals. Appraisal "is a process that detects and assesses the significance of the environment for well-being," as leading contemporary appraisal theorists Agnes Moors, Phoebe Ellsworth, Klaus Scherer, and Nico Frijda (2013, 120) summarise. Different appraisal theories have somewhat dissimilar conceptions about the components of the appraisal process but commonly suggested dimensions include novelty, intrinsic pleasantness, certainty or predictability, goal significance, agency, coping potential, and compatibility with social or personal standards (Ellsworth & Scherer, 2003). Some appraisal theories argue that the appraisal process follows a certain fixed logical order so that, for instance, the relevance and implications of a stimulus must be evaluated before proceeding to the dimensions of coping ability and normative significance. The sequential view of emotional appraisal can be reconciled with parallel and nonlinear processing by assuming that each "stimulus evaluation check" (Scherer's term for appraisal dimension) has a particular point in time at which it achieves a preliminary closure. The closure yields a result that warrants efferent commands to various response modalities – ANS physiology, action tendencies, motor expression, and feeling state – and allows the evaluation to proceed to the next phase even if the previous stages remain open to revision according to the results of subsequent appraisals. Other appraisal theories deny the sequential assumption as overly restrictive, suggesting that subordinate appraisals need not unfold in any particular order, especially in recurring appraisal cycles (e.g. Lazarus, 1991; Smith & Kirby, 2001). However, both versions of appraisal theories emphasise that emotional appraisal may occur at different levels of processing; fast, automatic, implicit, and schematic on the one hand, and slow, controlled, explicit, and conceptual on the other hand. "Appraisal may be a single process at the functional level of analysis, but it covers multiple processes (i.e., mechanisms) at the algorithmic level of analysis," as Moors (2012, 266) points out. A cognitive view about the nature of ordinary adult human emotions at the algorithmic level of analysis can be maintained if all emotions involve the latter kind of conceptual processing at some stage of the appraisal process even if the process may have been triggered by appraisals of the former, nonconceptual type.

What reasons are there to believe that cognitive, conceptual appraisals regularly rather than just contingently participate in the formation of human emotional responses in situations where the computation of personal meaning occurs online rather than by association to an existing appraisal pattern? The first reason focuses on the nature of certain appraisal dimensions. Appraisal theorists maintain that the early appraisals in the emotion generation process on such themes as novelty and intrinsic pleasantness may operate on a sensory basis without cognitive processing. Accordingly, those appraisals are also present in most animals, including newborn humans. These appraisals launch the initial physiological, behavioural and affective consequences whose feedback influences later stages of appraisal at which the level of processing is expected to move upwards. This is particularly the case with appraisals on the self and the normative significance of the emotion-eliciting event. These appraisals focus on such issues as coping ability, credit or blame, and the compatibility of the response with social and personal norms (Scherer, 2001, 2009, 2013). Scherer argues that "the normative significance of the event... is expected to be appraised last, as it requires comprehensive information about the event and comparison with high-level propositional representation" (Scherer, 2009, p. 1318). In this way, noncognitively elicited emotions turn into cognitive through the noncontingent involvement of cognitive processing at later stages of evaluation that bring the evaluation process into a closure.[3]

The second reason for the involvement of cognitive appraisals in emotional processing emerges from the recursive character of emotional appraisal. Appraisal

---

3.   Brian Parkinson and Antony Manstead (1992) argue that it is possible to detect normative significance effortlessly on the basis of implicit interaction and feeling rules that associate with interpersonal roles and status differences. Accordingly, these authors contrast "contextual meaning apprehension" with cognitive appraisal. However, the dichotomy is exaggerated since adequate responsiveness to social interaction and feeling rules is nevertheless mediated by the processing of meaning, which qualifies as cognitive activity. I shall return to the argument on the contrast between implicit emotion regulation and cognitive appraisals below in the section on emotion regulation.

is not a one-shot affair that gives way to other aspects of emotional response after having initiated them but a process that evolves during the entire emotional response, updating and modifying the various response elements on the basis of both internal and external feedback. This means that initiating appraisals on the various stimulus evaluation themes give way to reappraisals of the same themes during the dynamically unfolding emotion process. Scherer maintains that the recursive "checking process repeats the sequence continuously, constantly updating the appraisal results that change rapidly with changing events and evaluation... until the monitoring subsystem signals termination of or adjustment to the stimulation that originally elicited the appraisal episode" (Scherer, 2009, p. 1317). Thus if the level of processing has not risen from schematic to conceptual towards the end of the first round of appraisals, it will do so during the recursive appraisal cycles. In this way, conceptual appraisals join the appraisal process during recursive reappraisals in determining the type and shape of the evolving emotional response, including its experienced evaluative content.

Appraisal theories have often been contested on methodological grounds. Even if there is conclusive evidence that people associate distinct emotions with certain appraisal themes in self-report studies, this evidence alone does not support an empirical connection between emotions and appraisals but only a conceptual one (e.g. Parkinson, 1997, 2001; Barrett, 2006a,b). In order to support the empirical claim, process-oriented appraisal theories have sought to find correlates of various dimensional appraisals in diverse domains of emotional responding, such as vocal and facial expression, ANS response, and action tendencies. Scherer (2001; 2009) has presented detailed predictions for specific effects of appraisal outcomes in all response modalities, some of which have been supported in empirical research. Thus, Aue and Scherer (2008, 2011) found out that the appraisals of intrinsic pleasantness and goal conduciveness had somewhat similar but still not identical somatovisceral response patterns, with similarities in facial activity and differences in mean skin conductance, forehead temperature, and finger temperature. Lanctôt and Hess (2007) obtained similar results about the difference and sequential order of intrinsic pleasantness and goal conduciveness in facial EMG. Likewise, Kaiser and Wehrle (2001) detected stages of appraisal from filmed sequences of dynamically unfolding facial expressions. Finally, facial muscle activity over the brow and cheek regions marking the process of stimulus relevance appraisal occurred significantly earlier than that of goal conduciveness appraisal in the study of Aue et al. (2007). Some correlations between physiological responses and appraisals have also been established. Differences in appraised task difficulty and coping potential have been associated with dissimilar cardiovascular reactivity and electrodermal activity (Pecchinenda, 2001). However, these are only a small fraction of the hypothesized correlations between distinct appraisals and the various central nervous system, neuro-endocrine system, autonomic nervous system, and somatic nervous system changes, which means that the empirical validation of the theory is still at an early stage. Nevertheless, some work has been done on finding the neurophysiological correlates of distinct appraisals as this issue bears heavily on the default-interventionist claims of the theory.

Tobias Brosch and David Sander (2013) propose a model of neural mechanisms that underlie the processing of distinct appraisal criteria on the basis of existing research in affective neuroscience. They suggest that the novelty of stimuli is detected subcortically and automatically in the perirhinal cortex, the hippocampus, and the amygdala. The amygdala also detects concern relevance, but whether or not automatically is a debated issue. Goal congruence is processed in a "conflict-control loop consisting of anterior cingulate cortex (ACC) and dorsolateral prefrontal cortex (DLPFC). This circuit subserves the monitoring of performance toward a goal, the detection of goal conflicts, and the adjustment of top-down cognitive control to resolve potential conflicts" (165). Here emotional processing enters the cortical sphere in being related to individual differences in higher-order belief systems. Even so, the detection of goal congruence may occur automatically. Different neural regions underlie attributions of internal and external agency "with temporo-parietal junction (TPJ), precuneus, dorsomedial prefrontal cortex (DMPFC), presupplementary motor area involved in attributing external agency, and insulate and motor-specific regions are involved in attributing self-agency" (ibid.). Finally, an appraisal of norm or value compatibility is related to activation in the superior anterior temporal lobe for norms and in the medial prefrontal cortex and the dorsal striatum for values. With the last two appraisal themes, both automatic and controlled processes are possible. Brosch and Sander argue, with reference to Pessoa and Adolphs (2008), that emotional processing proceeds in the form of "multiple sweeps of activation with numerous feedforward and feedback loops that refine neural processing patterns and underlying computations with each iteration" (166). When cortical refinement of the amygdala-induced response reaches a stable state, the ventromedial prefrontal cortex (VMPFC) represents a conceptualization of the appraisal outcome. From the perspective of different levels of analysis, this evidence shows that "appraisal may or may not be a single process at the functional level, but it does not correspond to a single process at the algorithmic level, nor to a single process at the implementational level" (Moors, 2012, 267).

Psychological constructionism

Psychological constructionism has emerged to deal with the problems of other emotion theories, particularly the problem of establishing discrete emotions with distinct causal mechanisms and response patterns. Instead of continuing to search for evidence for discrete emotions, constructionists suggest that the problems of finding such evidence are chronic and diagnostic of the constructed character of emotions. Construction requires ingredients such as facial and vocal expressions, ANS changes, feelings, behaviours, appraisals, attributions, and regulation, but these occur both inside as well as outside of emotional episodes and do not require the category of "emotion" for their explanation. Insofar as correlations among components exist, these patterns are loose and do not require separate emotion-producing mechanisms for their explanation. Instead, experiences of emotions emerge from interpretations of existing multimodal psychological states in terms of contextually and socially viable emotion categories that impose meaning and structure on the components of ongoing psychological processes *as* components of emotion.

Even so, psychological constructionism retains the basic idea of multi-level processing, but with a twist. The twist is its reinterpretation of the two levels of emotional processing, nonconceptual and conceptual, as different domains and types of processing that associate only contingently. At the lower, nonconceptual level is *core affect*, feelings with a certain hedonic valence and intensity of arousal. Changes in core affect emerge from continuous and automatic appraisal of situations and objects for their relevance to the subject's well-being at developmentally early stages of information processing. However, the variety of core affect both underdetermines and outnumbers discrete emotions. Therefore, the theory posits a higher, conceptual level of processing at which emotions are constructed by categorising particular highs and lows of core affect in terms of contextually salient conceptual knowledge about distinct emotions. This knowledge is established via context-specific memories captured across instances when core affect has been categorised as this or that emotion, such as anger or guilt or fear. Yet "the key here is that membership in the emotion category does not require a set of necessary and sufficient features. Resemblance is a matter of degree", as Russell (2009, p. 1275) emphasises. Some instances of emotion may involve further appraisal of the situation in terms of such cognitively complex themes as coping potential, normative significance, accountability, future expectancy, and so on. However, psychological constructionists disagree with process-oriented appraisal theorists in claiming that such appraisals are not necessary for the categorisation of core affect even if appraisals are typical ingredients of emotion because the appraisal dimensions of different emotions are built into our conceptual understanding of discrete emotions.

Yet the difference between appraisal theories and psychological constructionism may be only in their dissimilar focus, as Moors (2012) and Russell (2012a) have recently suggested. Moors points out that both process-oriented appraisal theories and psychological constructionists deny the existence of a single process that is the common cause of the other components. In the former theories, each appraisal variable exerts its influence on the remaining components of emotion via a separate mechanism, whereas the latter propose component-specific processes that are not characteristic to emotions alone. In a like manner, Russell has (2012a, 297) contended that "Appraisal theorists emphasise appraisals and have offered detailed hypotheses and supporting data, [whereas] I emphasise components, one of which is an appraisal, and I have not offered details."

Psychological constructionism emphasizes the non-linear, parallel, and holistic nature of affective processing. The experience of core affect emerges from the simultaneous activation of several output systems, some of which such as autonomic and endocrine changes, voluntary behaviour, and facial movements typically associate with emotional responding, whereas others such as selection of attention and memory are influenced by nonaffective processes as well. Some patterns of core affect become labelled as discrete emotions and integrated into situated conceptualisations of those emotions. As instances of the same emotion accrue, information about the specific emotion type develops into a conceptual system which "is a distributed collection of modality-specific memories captured across all instances of a category" (Barrett, 2006b, p. 34). A specific emotion can then be triggered by priming any aspect of the category: sensory, motor, or conceptual. Whatever route this priming takes, "conceptual and affective processing proceed in parallel, with the processing in each limiting, shaping, and constraining the way in which the brain achieves a single coherent interpretation and action plan that suits the particular goals of the individual and constraints of the context" (ibid., p. 35). Along with categorising core affect as this or that emotion, we imbue it with intentional directedness to an object that the subject believes to have caused the affect. This ascription is made on the basis of situational cues together with knowledge about typical causes of distinct emotions. Intentionality becomes then a property of emotion only at the stage of emotional meta-experience. However, the same applies to discrete emotions that do not have an ontological status separate from our categorisation of their ingredients in terms of mental prototypes of emotion.

Evaluation of the two process models

Psychological constructionism emphasises the dynamic interplay of affective and conceptual processing that operate in parallel in producing emotional states and experiences. Even so, the theory is also default-interventionist about the relation of noncognitive and cognitive processing in the context of emotions as these are built upon states of core affect. The distinction between core affects of babies and beasts and post-infantile human emotions that depend on concepts offers a nice solution to the traditional problem of cognitive theories concerning animal and infant emotions. Moreover, the theory explains how conceptually elaborate emotions like anger, shame, and guilt can emerge from appraisals that are minimal in complexity. These cases are anomalous to traditional process-oriented appraisal theories that invoke complex patterns of appraisal as both causes and constituents of emotion. In contrast, those cases are paradigmatic to psychological constructionists who maintain that the core-affect aspect of emotions is always elicited by primitive appraisals; the complex evaluative content is imposed on core affect when the affect is categorised in terms of this or that emotion category. Indeed, appraisal theorists have moved towards the constructionist view by admitting that "appraisals can be outcomes of the emotion process as much as its antecedent conditions. They involve cognitive elaborations motivated by affect and action readiness", as Nico Frijda and Marcel Zeelenberg (2001, p. 151) have pointed out.

In spite of increasing convergence, appraisal theories and psychological constructionism do not coincide. Appraisal theorists maintain that the complex appraisals that figure in emotional experiences have been constructed during actual processes of emotion generation rather than ascribed to states of core affect. Complex appraisals can also be stored in the associative memory and reinstated on the basis of perceptual cues when similar situations are encountered. Appraisal reinstatement does not contradict the fact that knowledge about emotion types and their characteristic appraisal patterns is also learned from others in socialisation. Yet the question about the psychological origin of coherent appraisal patterns remains. Do these patterns emerge from actual appraisal processes, initially shaped by the evolutionary process, as Scherer and other appraisal theorists propose, or are they cultural scripts that pass on through social learning as constructionists suggest?

On the one hand, constructionists admit that appraisal processes sometimes continue from noncognitive appraisals of relevance and implications for subjective well-being that underlie fluctuations of core affect to such complex themes as coping potential and normative significance in determining the meaning of the emotion-eliciting situation. Appraisal theorists, on the other hand, are capable of explaining the cases in which emotions emerge from minimal processing by appraisal reinstatement. But then it seems that conceptual knowledge about emotions cannot replace actual appraisal processes as the *sole* source of coherent appraisal patterns. Instead, both theories appear to be partially right: conceptual knowledge about emotions influences actual appraisal processes in emotion generation, and these processes vary between minimal and elaborate depending on the particular case and its similarity to previous emotion-eliciting situations whose appraisal schemas are available for immediate reinstatement upon recognition of their match to the present situation.

Unfortunately, psychological constructionism has some other problems that reduce its appeal. Deonna and Scherer (2010) argue that the theory performs a disappearance act on the intentional object of emotion by elevating exceptional cases into paradigmatic ones. The point is that we sometimes find ourselves in situations where an ambiguous core affect must be interpreted and labeled as this or that emotion. However, these cases cannot provide the basis for a general theory of emotions. Too much room is given to categorization as one and the same core affect can be interpreted in terms of several emotions and ascribed to many different objects, depending on situational cues. Psychological constructionists assume that core affect typically emerges from primitive appraisals of external objects or events to which the affect is attributed when it is categorized as this or that emotion. Yet the concept of "appraisal" implies that something is already being appraised here, and even if this something may not rise to awareness together with the affect, it is curious to maintain that core affect has "*no* object until the subject has conceptually investigated and decided what, if at all, the experiences could be about" as Deonna and Scherer (2010, p. 47) remark. "Conceptual investigation" and "decision" are overly intellectual terms for effortless conceptual acts in the constructionist sense but the main point of this criticism holds: the divide between non-intentional core affect and intentional emotion is unwarranted in the context of typical emotions in which the subject is acutely aware of the object of emotion at the time the emotion emerges.

The attached, non-original intentionality of emotions also makes it difficult for psychological constructionism to accommodate emotions whose affective quality is experienced without an awareness of what the feeling is about. Since affective quality underdetermines emotions, it is often difficult to identify whether or not a particular feeling is part of an emotion – feelings of chill, for instance, may be associated with fear as well as with fever, as Goldie (2002) points out. Instead of digging deeper into the context of feelings, however, constructionism seems happy to accept any emotional categorisation of a core affect as long as it somehow fits the situation. Thus a person may come home from work and snap at his or her spouse without realizing that the true cause of the irritated feeling is a rough encounter with one's boss earlier in the day. Smith and Neumann (2005) use this example to point out that emotions can be misattributed to their true cause and misidentified in terms of their type. Unfortunately, psychological constructionism has meager theoretical resources to criticise people for such behaviour as it maintains that emotions come to exist only when a core affect is labeled in terms of some emotion category and attributed to some object. Even if it were possible to misattribute the true cause of one's core affect, the same is not possible for an emotion because according to this theory it has *no* cause or intentional object before a causal attribution to some salient situation.

Russell (2012b) has responded to some of these claims about the lacking intentionality of core affects and emotions. He points out that core affects can come to have intentional directness in the same sense as localised bodily sensations.

When a core affect is interpreted in terms of its source, such as the pleasure of tasting caviar, it becomes an Attributed Affect; and when a core affect is projected to an external object, we perceive it as an Affective Quality. Yet neither Attributed Affects nor Affective Qualities are emotions because they lack other components such as appraisal of the eliciting event, attribution, beliefs, desires, plans, impulses, and behaviours that typically associate with core affect in constituting emotional episodes whose criteria rely on folk concepts of emotion. Russell maintains that individuals may have emotional episodes without categorising them as this or that emotion – indeed, many of our most intense emotions seem to occur without an emotional meta-experience. Moreover, he argues that it is possible to err in the categorisation of one's emotional episode as a particular emotion.

On what grounds can a psychological constructionist maintain that there is an emotional episode without categorisation if emotions come to exist only through a categorisation of core affects? Russell replies that this occurs simply because ingredients of a specific emotion without an emotional meta-experience are present in the subject's psychophysical state. However, this response is more problematic than meets the eye. The problem is that even if criteria of discrete emotions rely on folk concepts that are communal rather than private, the theory rejects external perspectives on the same criteria in emphasising the *psychological* rather than the *social* construction of emotions. "Whether a pattern of ingredients constitutes an emotional episode is the question of whether the pattern crosses a *subjective* threshold of resemblance to a mental prototype" (Russell, 2012b, p. 92–3, my italics). This suggests that a pattern of ingredients may cross a subjective threshold without the subject realizing that it does, and here we may have an emotional episode without a categorizing meta-experience. This is the distinction between *being* in the state of emotion and the *feeling* of being in the state of emotion that the philosopher Robert Roberts (1988; 2003) has emphasized.

An emotional episode need not then involve a meta-experience of being in the state of emotion. However, it seems that some kind of *recognition* of resemblance to a mental prototype is nevertheless needed for an emotional episode in the constructionist account. And since the identity of an emotional episode depends on this subjective recognition, there is no room for error about the identity of an emotion at the time of recognition. Others may categorise the subject's emotion differently on the basis of its visible ingredients, and the subject may change his or her identification accordingly. Yet from the subject's point of view, which is decisive for psychological constructionism, this is not a detection of an erroneous categorisation – an insight that "this is how I have felt all along" – but instead a new interpretation of the same ingredients in terms of another mental prototype. This suggests that psychological constructionism has problems with accommodating the phenomenon of mistaking emotions and their intentional objects.

Together, these considerations suggest that psychological constructionism has some serious problems in spite of its sound claim that the appraisal process need not always go all the way to produce an emotion, nor to proceed in a fixed order, which are the main problems of Scherer's sequential appraisal theory. The appraisal process typically begins from the implicit processing of nonconceptual representations and proceeds to explicit processing of conceptual representations before reaching a closure on the type of emotion unless a match to an existing appraisal schema is found. Yet there is little evidence beyond Scherer's and his associates' studies that the process must proceed in a fixed order and go through all or even most stimulus evaluation checks in order to produce an emotion. In spite of these problems, process-oriented appraisal theories and psychological constructionism are promising approaches to accommodate the interplay and integration of nonconceptual and conceptual representations and their implicit and explicit processing in human emotions.

The argument for cognitivism from emotion regulation

Emotion theories have traditionally regarded emotion regulation as a temporally and ontologically separate process that either precedes or follows emotion generation. In the former case, regulation is about controlling the occurrence of emotions by deliberately seeking out or avoiding potentially emotion-evoking situations, whereas the latter type of regulation focuses on modulating the duration, intensity, and expression of already generated emotions by suppression, savouring or other means of response modification. An envy-prone individual who morally disapproves of this emotion for instance may avoid situations involving social comparison in order to ward off experiences of envy and purport to suppress its displays whenever he feels this emotion. In both cases, regulation is *extrinsic* to the process of emotion generation that determines the identity and constituents of the emerging emotion. Extrinsic regulation that precedes or follows emotion generation involves conscious planning and control but insofar as regulation is not capable of being an *intrinsic* part of emotion generation, the two processes appear to be distinct and only contingently associated with each other in some emotional responses of adult humans. Indeed, most theorists of emotion, cognitive and noncognitive alike, with the exception of Frijda (1986) and Parrott (2007), have until recently shared this assumption about the contingent, limited, and extrinsic role of regulation in human emotions.

In contrast, the theories I have discussed above, both process-oriented appraisal theories and psychological constructionism, emphasise the constitutive role of regulation in human emotions. Appraisal theories incorporate reappraisals into the process of emotional evaluation, whereas constructionists see regulation as an ongoing process that accompanies and influences the other ingredients of emotion. Both theories regard regulation as an intrinsic aspect of emotions and their generation. The connection between emotion generation and regulation emerges through a process of meaning-making that continues from the beginning of an emotion to its end. "The same processes may be considered to be generative when they occur at the beginning of a new emotional episode... but considered to be regulatory when they occur later in the episode", as James Gross and Lisa Feldman Barrett (2011, p. 14) remark in their useful review on the relation of emotion generative and regulative processes in different types of emotion theories:

> In appraisal views, the emphasis is on making sense of one's external surroundings, and internal changes are assumed to result from this meaning analysis in a way that reflects it. In psychological construction views, the emphasis is on making meaning of internal body sensations, and this meaning then makes it possible to construct a unified awareness of both body and the world. This similarity in emphasis on meaning-making (albeit with a different focus) means that one key target of emotion regulation for both perspectives will be the meaning-making process (ibid.)

However, it is important to note that an essential involvement of regulation in emotions does not support a robust role of cognition in emotion without a few further conditions. The intrinsic regulation of emotions must be cognitive itself and it must be always present in ordinary post-infantile human emotions in one form or another. The process of meaning-making that continues during the entire emotion is obviously cognitive at the functional level of analysis, but we are here interested in its status at the algorithmic level of analysis. Emotion regulation comes in many forms some of which are implicit, instinctive, nonconscious, and effortless rather than explicit, learned, conscious, and deliberate, and the former kind of regulation does not seem to involve cognitive representations or processes. If this is the case, then cognition is only contingently involved in emotion regulation, quite similarly to its role in emotion elicitation. The challenge is then to determine whether or not intrinsic yet implicit, nonconscious, and effortless emotion regulation may qualify as cognitive. The first task, however, is to clarify the distinction between intrinsic and extrinsic emotion regulation.

The efficiency of intrinsic emotion regulation

In his widely accepted theoretical model of emotion regulation, Gross argues that emotion regulation is a process with several possible entry points and strategies (see e.g. Gross, 1998; Gross & Thompson, 2007). Gross distinguishes five distinct emotion regulation families, which he divides into two broad categories:

antecedent-focused and response focused. The former type of regulation occurs before emotion-eliciting appraisals give rise to full-blown emotional responses, whereas the latter type of regulation follows only after the response has been generated. Two forms of antecedent-focused regulation, attentional deployment and cognitive change, in particular, allow extensive modification of emerging emotional responses, including their type. These two strategies also constitute the main forms of intrinsic emotion regulation.

Attentional deployment and cognitive change operate at early stages in the emotion-generative process. The main attentional strategies are distraction and concentration. Distraction focuses attention on different aspects of the situation with the purpose of avoiding an emerging emotion, whereas concentration draws attention to the emotional features of a situation, thus amplifying the process of emotion generation. Looking away from aversive events and focusing on pleasant ones are ways of attentional deployment. Cognitive change occurs one step further in this process as a way of altering the meaning of an emotion-eliciting situation or its implications to the individual by means of a reappraisal or reappraisals that change the emotional impact of the situation. An emotional construal of the situation can be modified by such means as a reappraisal of one's coping potential that may transform a nascent humiliation into anger, for instance, or downward social comparison that counters or decreases the impact of negative social emotions by revising one's emotional construal of the situation into a more positive one.

Several empirical studies have compared the efficiency of reappraisal and suppression – the only response-focused regulation strategy – in the modification of emotional responses. These studies have established that reappraisal is an effective means of modifying all aspects of emotion – autonomic physiology, action tendencies, motor expression, and feeling state; even the type of emotion – whereas suppression is merely capable of dampening emotional expression (see e.g. John & Gross, 2004, 2007):

> Reappraisal – which occurs early in the emotion-generative process before emotion-response tendencies have been fully generated– permits the modification of the entire emotional sequence, including the experience of more positive and less negative emotion, without notable physiological, cognitive, or interpersonal costs. By contrast, suppression – which comes relatively late in the emotion-generative process– primarily modifies the behavioural aspect of the emotion-response tendencies, without reducing the experience of negative emotion. (John & Gross, 2007, p. 352–3)

Consequently, researchers of emotion regulation promote reappraisal as an adaptive and "healthy" form of emotion regulation in comparison to suppression that consumes cognitive resources "that could otherwise be used for optimal performance in the social contexts in which the emotions arise" (ibid. p. 353). Together, attentional deployment and reappraisal manifest the capacity of cognition to shape even noncognitively elicited emotions during their generation as these emotion regulation strategies draw on similar cognitive processes and mechanisms as other forms of cognitive control (Ochsner & Gross, 2005, 2007).

The efficiency of attentional deployment and reappraisal in moulding emotional responses is based on the integration of bottom-up and top-down appraisal processes in emotion generation and regulation. Ochsner and Gross (2007, p. 89) argue that "emotion generation and regulation involve the interaction of appraisal systems, such as the amygdala, that encode the affective properties of stimuli in a bottom-up fashion, with control systems implemented in prefrontal and cingulate cortex that support controlled top-down stimulus appraisals". Emotions can be generated and modulated by either bottom-up or top-down processes. Therefore, "once bottom-up generation has begun (and sometimes even before, if one anticipates a negative event), top-down processes can regulate, redirect, and alter the way in which triggering stimuli are being (or will be) appraised" (ibid., p. 90). Reappraisal functions in this manner, reinterpreting the meaning of an emotionally evocative stimulus and leading the appraisal system to respond to the new description. Yet it is no exception to the general pattern of emotional processing since both emotion generation and regulation follow from interactions between top-down cognitive appraisal processes which control bottom-up affective appraisal processes. The brain areas that are active in both emotion generation and regulation overlap to such an extent that "there may not be brain centers uniquely dedicated to emotion generation or emotion regulation per se", as Oschner, Ray, Hughes, McRae, Cooper, Weber, Gabrieli and Gross (2009, p. 1330) point out. Accordingly, individual human emotions fall somewhere in the automatic – controlled continuum, always manifesting some degree of both types of processing.

> The generation of an emotion episode results from a heterogeneous network of bottom-up (stimulus-driven) and top-down (goal or organism-driven) processes that are organised into a coherent interpretation and action plan. All this occurs in parallel, and in real time probably happens in the blink of an eye. The result is an emotional episode that people experience more or less as a gestalt. (Barrett, Ochsner, & Gross, 2007, p. 194)

Together, these considerations show that emotion generation is not an impervious black box between eliciting appraisals and programme-like response tendencies but a process that can be penetrated and influenced by cognitive regulation at several points. Even so, the seeming automaticity of many instances of intrinsic emotion regulation demands an explanation before we can justifiably turn the pervasive role of regulation in human emotions into an argument for the essential involvement of cognition in ordinary human emotions. How can nonintentional, effortless, implicit, and nonconscious regulation that appears as a direct opposite of cognitive activity nevertheless qualify as such?

Implicit, effortless, and nonconscious regulation

Dual-process models of information processing, discussed in the previous chapter, provide a possible answer to this question. These models emphasise that even complex cognitive processes may become implicit, automatic, and effortless through their recurrent employment. With the exception of those emotion regulation strategies such as thumb sucking or gaze turning that are present already at birth, all other forms of regulation are learned from their repeated use in the individual rather than the ancestral past. Therefore, Bargh and Williams (2007, p. 436) suggest that emotion regulation strategies "should be capable of nonconscious activation and operation to the extent the individual has employed them routinely, in a frequent and consistent manner, whenever he or she is in the given situation". The cognitive regulation strategies of attentional deployment and reappraisal are similar to more behavioural strategies, such as situation selection, in this respect. All regulatory strategies are capable of becoming automatic and nonconscious through their repeated and consistent use in similar emotional situations. Therefore, insofar as emotions are regulated by ideational factors such as feeling and display rules, emotion scripts, and ethnotheories about emotions, or more by general societal values, norms, rules, scripts, schemas, and mental models that have been internalized over the course of socialisation, cognitive representations of these factors are capable of influencing both emotion generation and regulation effortlessly and nonconsciously.

Nevertheless, the argument from acquired automaticity may not establish the cognitive character of all instances of intrinsic emotion regulation if Parkinson, Fischer, and Manstead (2005) are right. They point out that "long before any of us is able to decode the meanings of cultural messages explicitly, we accumulate a vast store of practical expertise in the local workings of emotion at an implicit level" (ibid., p. 226). Values, rules, and other cultural representations with emotional implications are not acquired "as a result of deliberate inculcation, but simply as a function of participation in everyday social practices" (ibid.). Moreover, representations embodied in social practices and cultural artefacts continue to exert direct and implicit influence on our emotional experiences and behaviour even after we have internalised those prescriptive and descriptive representations that explicitly influence our emotions. Thus, participation in social practices and interaction with others have real-time effects on emotional appraisal and regulation that often operate in a socially distributed manner. Guilt, for instance, can be elicited by another person's blame rather than by an appraisal of one's own blameworthiness, although some kind of minimal endorsement of communal norms is probably necessary for understanding blame *as* blame. Yet the function of guilt is to maintain a relationship with the blaming subject, whose response to an appropriate display of guilt is capable of directly influencing the blamed person's regulation of his guilt, without a prior appraisal of the situation's changed personal meaning, as appraisal theorists would suggest. In this way, implicit emotion generation and regulation respond to the changing dynamics of social forces and interpersonal relations, whose aligning and realigning human emotions serve in the first place.

Together, Parkinson, Fischer, and Manstead's arguments purport to establish that emotion regulation does not require internal mental representations because it is capable of functioning directly through participation in social practices and interpersonal encounters that have their own constitutive rules that we learn in socialization into those practices and forms of interaction. At the same time, the emphasis on the inherent relationality of emotions offers an additional argument for the noncontingent regulation of human emotions. If emotions are more or less strategic moves that adjust social interaction as the late Robert Solomon (1980) suggested, their smooth and efficient regulation in relation to other people's reactions is vital to their successful functioning. Indeed, social feedback from significant others is perhaps even more important than internal feedback from the various response dimensions in influencing emotion regulation. The observation that both emotion generation and emotion regulation typically take place in a developing dialogue with other people rather than in isolated individual processing is an important amendment to other process models – both appraisal theories and psychological constructionism – that focus too much on intraindividual processes. Most importantly, the dialogical character of implicit emotion regulation need not be in conflict with a cognitive claim about this kind of regulation, contrary to Parkinson, Fischer, and Manstead's own interpretation.

Parkinson, Fischer, and Manstead think that cognitive regulation requires representations of meaning that influence emotion regulation explicitly in the form of internalised rules, norms, scripts, and schemas. However, if we understand cognition in terms of recognition of *meaning* and appropriate responsiveness to it, adjusting one's emotion on the basis of other people's responses qualifies as cognitive regulation because it depends on understanding the meaning of others' responses as praise or blame, for instance. Others' blame conveys incompatibility of one's action with social norms directly, without recourse to an appraisal about the blameworthiness of one's action. Yet identifying others' verbal or nonverbal response *as* blame *for* one's particular course of action and responding to it by guilt is still a cognitive mental operation as it involves an interpretation of others' response in relation to one's own action as authoritative within the context of established social interaction. Parkinson, Fischer and Manstead characterize interpretations of this kind in passing as "habitual appraisals" (ibid., p. 227) without elaborating to what extent these appraisals resemble or differ from the more sophisticated appraisals of appraisal theories. My suggestion is that "habitual appraisals" or something alike are appraisals that register meanings directly in habitualised social interaction, thereby serving implicit and effortless yet cognitive emotion generation and regulation. Internal representations that guide explicit emotion generation and regulation are acquired from participation in social interaction, but adequate responsiveness to embodied representations in social practices qualifies as cognitive activity as well because it is mediated by the processing of meaning.

Causally efficacious cognitive monitoring

Finally, there remains the question of the role of intrinsic cognitive regulation in situations where its impact on the trajectory of emotional responses seems to remain minimal. If we exclude cases in which the subject's abnormal physiological or psychological condition undermines her capacity of emotion regulation, such as intoxication, diseases, phobias, PTSD, OCD, or pathological fear of flying, the remaining cases include rationally recalcitrant emotions of ordinary people, such as survivor guilt, and evolutionarily pre-wired emotional responses, such as fear of snakes or heights. Regulation may be ineffective in altering the identity of these emotions, but it is surely capable of influencing their intensity, duration, expression, and action tendencies. Regulation can prevent fleeing from a sightseeing balcony or from the vicinity of a snake, for instance. Yet it is possible to maintain that instrumental behaviours of this kind do not belong to emotion and therefore their regulation does not count as emotion regulation. Emotions involve spontaneous expressive behaviours and action tendencies that may remain active even if their motivational impulses are overruled in instrumental behaviour. A fearful person displays expressions of fear and has an urge to flee even if she sticks to her rational judgment about the situation and decides to stay. Where is the influence of cognitive regulation in emotions of this kind, and is it significant enough to support the claim that cognitive processing plays a robust role in ordinary post-infantile human emotions?

The Stoic philosophers famously argued that emotions are evaluative judgments or opinions, not mere impressions or appearances of the goodness or badness of things from a subjective point of view. As judgments, emotions are impressions to which reason has given its assent. The Stoics admit that evaluative impressions spontaneously induce physiological changes, feelings and sensations, such as flushings, agitations, and palpitations, or involuntary behavioural responses such as facial expressions that can sometimes be so intense that an observer cannot distinguish these responses from impulses to act that belong to emotions proper. The Stoics, however, see this difference as significant. They emphasise that insofar as we do not assent to evaluative appearances, the involuntarily emerging mental and bodily perturbations amount to mere "first movements" or "pre-passions" that are less intensive and less consuming than the affections and behavioural responses that follow from assented appearances (Knuuttila, 2004; Sorabji, 2000; Nussbaum, 1993). This Stoic view indicates that cognitive regulation is capable of influencing not merely instrumental behaviour but *all* aspects of noncognitively elicited emotions through reappraisals that either *withhold* or *give assent* to the emotion-eliciting noncognitive evaluative appearances as these appraisals either attenuate or intensify the relevant emotional responses.

Anecdotal evidence in favour of this Stoic view is available from everyday social interaction where most people are adept at avoiding blowing up at their superiors and other people with higher power status, whereas they easily snap at those with inferior power status or those whose attachment they take for granted. Bosses sometimes behave irritatingly but we usually manage to shrug off their behaviour during the encounter and express our resentment only when alone or in the company of reliable co-workers or significant others. The usual interpretation is that intense anger is felt in the situation but the emotion is supressed by keeping a stiff upper lip. However, an alternative interpretation suggests that the experience is moderated by reappraising an angry response as maladaptive and socially inappropriate in the situation. There is evidence that facial expressions covary with subjective experience, and even if this linkage is strongest when there is no reason to manage or modify the expression because of social circumstances, the connection implies that successful expression management influences subjective experience and other components of emotion such as distinct appraisals and physiological responses that covary with expression (Matsumoto, Keltner, Shiota, O'Sullivan, & Frank, 2008). Reappraisals on the situational warrant of emotions are guided by feeling and display rules. The more internalised the rule, the more capable it is of influencing the emerging emotion, as can be seen in my discussion on the authenticity of professional emotions in Chapter 5.

Empirical evidence for the influence of reappraisals on unfolding emotional experience can be found also from studies in which people's emotional responses to films with aversive content have been manipulated by the conditions in which they have watched the film. A classic study of this kind is Lazarus and Alfert (1964) in which students watched a film on a circumcision ritual with and without a soundtrack. The soundtrack was manipulated to distance the viewer from the negative impact of the film by denying the pain involved in the ritual and emphasising the joyful aspects of the procedure instead. When the viewers' heart rate, skin conductance, and mood were measured, and it was found that those with a manipulated soundtrack had a slower heart rate, a lower skin conductance levels, and a more positive moods in comparison to those who watched the film without a soundtrack. These findings indicate that reappraisals, by withholding assent from noncognitive affective appraisals, significantly alter evaluations of threat and reduce the stressfulness of otherwise distressing experiences. The same cognitive mechanism underlies all instances of emotion-focused coping that Lazarus and Folkman (1984; Folkman & Lazasus, 1990) have studied in depth. Similar findings are available from more recent studies where the pleasantness of an odour was influenced by its labelling as either "Cheddar cheese" or "body odour". The different pleasantness ratings were correlated with dissimilar activations in the orbitofrontal cortex and the amygdala (De Araujo et al., 2005), highlighting the influence of cognition on sensory processing and experience. Together, these findings show how far linguistic representations can modulate emotional states, emotional behaviour, and emotional experience through altering emotional representations in the orbitofrontal cortex, as Rolls (2013, 129–32) has pointed out. Accordingly, cognition is capable of influencing all constitutive aspects of emotions instead of mere instrumental behaviour that is contingently associated with emotions.

Finally, when considering the role of cognition of human emotions, we should not forget that cognitive assent can be short-sighted and founded on situationally salient prescriptive and descriptive representations rather than on thoughtful reflection. Indeed cognitive assent is often of the former kind. For instance, to modify Griffith's example from above, a racist may lash out against a coloured person who has accidentally poked him in the back in a nightclub queue. Yet this does not mean that the emotion is a "raw" affect programme response because the racist's cognitive regulation could have toned down the anger and aborted the aggressive response if the subject had attempted to do so. Instead, his racist beliefs and values warranted the emotional response, leading the subject to assent to the appearance of culpable harming and the aggressive response to it.

I believe that this account generalizes to other less idiosyncratic cases in which cognitive regulation does not appear to take hold of emotional responses. Cognitive regulation has a robust role in ordinary post-infantile human emotions by virtue of its monitoring function that allows regulatory processes to modulate emotional responses on the basis of their appraised situational adaptiveness or fittingness. Therefore, if such regulation remains minimal in an ordinary human emotion, we should not conclude that the emotion is a "pure" noncognitive affect programme response. Instead, we should infer – in accordance with default-interventionist theories of dual processing – that the seemingly noncognitive response bears a cognitive imprint through its approval by cognitive monitoring that could have influenced the response more thoroughly if it had not endorsed the response.

Conclusion

In this chapter I have discussed and defended cognitive process models of emotion after first arguing that mental representations that cause emotions are also their constituents and that these representations are not categorically noncognitive. Cognitive process models emphasise that emotion generation is a process that cognitive, semantic representations join sooner or later. The overlap and integration of emotion generative and regulative processes also supports a strong influence of cognition in even noncognitively elicited human emotions. This influence manifests as cognitive monitoring also in those cases where the influence of regulation on the trajectory of emotional responses remains minimal because a cognitive assent to a noncognitive appraisal allows the emotional response to unfold without interference. In contrast, a cognitive dissent from a noncognitive appraisal amounts to moderating the emotional response, showing the influence of cognitive regulation on the duration, intensity, and expression of emotion even in those cases where cognitive regulation is incapable of altering the identity of emotions.

I agree then with Robinson (2005, p. 76) that "emotion is a *process* that unfolds, as the situation is appraised and reappraised, and as continuous feedback occurs". However, my conclusion is contrary to hers. Cognitive appraisals paradigmatically influence the identity of emotions by participating in the appraisal process, in addition to monitoring the situational warrant of emotions and thereby modulating the experience, intensity and duration of human emotions. These findings show that the proper dual process model of emotional processing is default-interventionist rather than parallel-competitive: explicit processing of conceptual representations intervenes in the implicit processing of nonconceptual representations by default rather than contingently. Therefore ordinary post-infantile human emotions are cognitive at both the functional and the algorithmic levels of analysis. This conclusion wraps up my discussion on the role of cognition in the structure and dynamics of human emotions.

CHAPTER 4

Emotional authenticity

The antinomy of emotional authenticity

Authenticity is an important ideal of emotional life. Yet it is not obvious what we mean by an authentic emotion. Ronald de Sousa illustrates this problem in *The Rationality of Emotion* (1987) with an example of a homosexual who comes out to his best friend. The friend's spontaneous reaction is violent and hostile: she expresses disgust, disappointment, and anger, and walks away without wanting to discuss the matter. But the next evening she calls him and apologizes for her unreasonable, unkind, and prejudiced reaction, assuring him that she wholeheartedly accepts his sexual orientation, which need not affect their friendship in any way. Comments de Sousa:

> In favour of spontaneity, one can say that the first reaction was unreflective, uncensored, and therefore presumably genuine. – On the other hand, might her prejudiced reaction not be a mere reflex, unrelated to her character? It stemmed perhaps from effects of a narrow-minded education that she has not yet had time to mend (de Sousa, 1987, p. 12).

The problem of deciding which reaction is more authentic is complicated by the fact that "both spontaneous emotion and deliberate attitudes are intimately bound up with our conception of people's character and moral worth" (ibid., p. 13). De Sousa believes that this antinomy remains unsolved even if by relating authenticity to appropriateness and emphasising that "going with one's feelings is not the royal road to authenticity" (ibid., p. 264) he, no doubt, takes a stance on the reflective side.

 This chapter investigates the notion of emotional authenticity with the purpose of resolving de Sousa's antinomy. This is a significant task for even if authenticity is an important notion in the contemporary research of emotion, it lacks a proper theoretical foundation. True enough, philosophers, such as Martin Heidegger (1962), Jean-Paul Sartre (1956), and more recently, Charles Taylor (1991), have produced extensive and sophisticated accounts on authenticity and or related notions ("Eigentlichkeit", "mauvaise foi"). However, their influence on contemporary discussion on emotions and authenticity has remained scarce. In part, it may have been difficult to apply philosophical accounts of authenticity to emotions, especially as their originators have not generally provided guidelines for that purpose.[1] Yet a more fundamental reason lies in the normativity of the philosophical concept of authenticity, which scientists find difficult to accommodate. For the normative sense of authenticity raises the question of whether one should feel in a particular way, quite independently of what one actually feels "deep inside" as the cliched expression for a descriptive understanding of authenticity goes. Accordingly, a descriptively inauthentic emotion is somehow less genuine as an emotion, whereas a normatively inauthentic emotion lacks justification of certain kind, whether or not it is genuine or authentic in the descriptive sense (Mulligan, 2009).[2] This fundamental difference between the normative and descriptive perspective on authenticity appears to set the two discourses wide apart.

However, I shall argue for a reconciliation between normative and descriptive views on emotional authenticity. In particular, I shall argue that certain anomalies of the descriptive analysis of emotional authenticity in terms of sincerity and spontaneity suggest that we must distinguish between sincerity and authenticity. Sincerity is a psychological concept, whereas authenticity is a normative notion. In addition, I shall put forward an integrity view of emotional authenticity that takes its lead from normative accounts of authenticity. In this view, authenticity is analyzed in terms of coherence between an emotion and one's internally justified values and beliefs. However, an authentic emotion must also be sincere in the sense of being psychologically real. Moreover, authenticity is a regulative and open-ended ideal as our spontaneous emotions frequently challenge the coherence of our present emotions, values, and beliefs, thereby urging change, learning, and growth on a way towards a new, more enlightened coherence. But since all authentic emotions need not emerge spontaneously, spontaneity, unlike sincerity, is not a necessary condition of emotional authenticity.

---

1.   Sartre is an exception with his *Sketch for a Theory of the Emotions* (1939). In this little essay, Sartre suggests that the function of emotion is to change the world in an indirect way by changing its meanings when all ways to direct change by purposeful action seem to be barred. In these self-manipulative acts of "magic" that Sartre compares to sleep, dream, and hysteria, consciousness degrades both itself and the world by captivating itself to a distorted world of affective meanings that deny or freeze the fundamental capacity of consciousness to transcend itself, whatever the situation. Therefore, emotions constitute an example of "bad faith" and qualify as categorically inauthentic for Sartre.

2.   Mulligan focuses on the descriptive meaning of authenticity in arguing that inauthentic emotions are not real emotions, whereas authentic emotions are merely emotions. Even so, he recognizes the normative meaning of inauthenticity in remarking that "we sometimes speak about inauthentic emotions or beliefs that are in fact beliefs or emotions. In those cases the inauthenticity of a belief or an emotion is constituted by its *relation* to other beliefs and emotions" (my translation). Mulligan does not discuss this meaning of authenticity besides remarking that it relates to "the difficult phenomenon of personal integrity".

Emotional authenticity as sincerity

Most contemporary researchers of emotion, both philosophical and empirical, associate emotional authenticity with sincerity and spontaneity (see e.g. Mulligan, 2009; Bolton, 2005; Steinberg & Figart, 1999; Pugmire, 1998; Erickson & Wharton, 1997; Ashforth & Humphrey, 1993; Wentworth & Ryan, 1992; Hamlyn, 1989; Dilman, 1989; Hochschild, 1983). An authentic or genuine emotion, according to this view, is a sincere and spontaneous response to the eliciting situation. The emotion is founded on the subject's spontaneous apprehension of the object that reliably manifests his or her concern for it. David Pugmire contends: "My emotions must be allowed to take the form they seek to take; and they must be acknowledged as authoritative expressions of part of my actual valuational attitude, as bearing witness to my real beliefs" (Pugmire, 1998, p. 129).[3] I shall focus on Pugmire's version of the sincerity view because it is the most detailed and theoretically elaborate one.

Since most emotions are not entirely transparent to their subject, it is quite easy to misidentify one's emotion or its true object and cause. For example, lust can be mistaken for love, anger at one's bullying boss can be misinterpreted as anger at one's spouse, and drunken confidence can be misconstrued as good self-esteem. Yet none of these difficulties qualifies as a flaw of authenticity as such. Pugmire suggests that an emotion turns inauthentic only when the subject purposefully sticks to his or her misidentification and thereby distorts or masks the underlying real emotion or the lack of it. But how can we distinguish such "counterfeit" emotions from real articles?

Pugmire is a cognitivist who argues that emotions essentially involve thoughts, either in the form of affirmed beliefs or judgements, or in the form of ideas, construals, or imaginings that are merely entertained maintains. However, some emotions demand actual belief instead of a mere construal in order to qualify as genuine. A person may construe a situation as dangerous without believing this to be true, whereas beliefs and affirmed appraisals aim to be true, whether they succeed in this or not. Yet construals are verisimilar in the sense of having an appearance of truth for the construer, as Robert Roberts (1988) points out. Since construing is capable of evoking experientially identical or similar feelings as an appropriate belief, it is easy to mistake these feelings for the manifestation of a genuine emotion. But now a problem emerges: "If I am unaware that what I am doing is construing rather than considering or affirming, I am not in a position to distinguish my construal from a belief" (Pugmire, 1998, p. 116).

---

3.   In his *Sound Sentiments* (2005) Pugmire defends *profundity* as a normative ideal for emotions. I shall discuss this rival notion of authenticity later in this chapter.

Pugmire claims that emotions become artificial "by being sustained by construals rather than beliefs where beliefs are what is really required" (ibid., p. 117). Emotions of this kind are misbegotten because a desire to experience an emotion is not directly concerned with the ostensible object of emotion. Pugmire suggests that there are two general external motives for having an emotion. The Experiential motive is central, for instance, in sentimentality. Sentimental people desire emotions for their intrinsic affective qualities and savour them in the same way as people who use drugs for the sensations and feelings they induce. The superficiality of such emotions is indicated by their subjects' failure to follow the emotion into action (ibid., 119; Hamlyn, 1989). The relational motive figures in an emotion that places its subject in an advantageous position in some way. Pugmire surmises that "choice will centre on emotions that provide advantage of power (e.g. pity), moral advantage (e.g. forgiveness, and above all, righteous anger) or that reassuringly affirm personal qualities (e.g. compassion, remorse)" (ibid., p. 120). Such emotions are often adopted for the purpose of masking another, existing emotion that the subject does not like to experience. Thus, spite can be mistaken for righteous indignation and disdain for pity.

Pugmire argues that his account provides several reasons for the vitality of emotional authenticity. Firstly, a factitious emotion "misrepresents the agent both as to his true emotion and as to his true values" (ibid., p. 124). Secondly, a misrepresentation of the self creates a falsified and potentially dangerous point of departure for social interaction. By interpreting a factitious emotion as a genuine article, other people both support the original self-deception and become deceived themselves. Thirdly, Pugmire claims that "factitious emotions – lack the function that is frequently the warrant for emotion as distinct from dispassionate rational appraisal, namely, creating an immediate urge to act in accordance with the appraisal" (ibid.). And finally, inauthentic emotions are self-defeating as they cannot achieve what they want. It is not a facsimile but a real article that we are after.

The sincerity view offers several important insights into emotional authenticity. The undistorted perception of one's immediate psychological reality is certainly an essential foundation for authenticity. One should therefore recognize one's spontaneous emotions for what they are – with "warts and all" as Pugmire demands. I also agree with Pugmire that emotions are "authoritative expressions of part of my actual valuational attitude". But I do not believe that emotions always bear witness to my "real beliefs", nor that my "actual valuational attitudes" are equivalent to my values. I believe that the following analysis of two significant emotional phenomena, recalcitrant emotions and managed emotions, supports this view.

Recalcitrant and managed emotions

Recalcitrant emotions

Emotions that we experience in spite of our contrary beliefs or appraisals of the eliciting situation are familiar in our everyday lives. Some of these recalcitrant emotions are quite unavoidable and harmless. For instance, most people feel a little nervous or afraid while standing on the edge of a steep cliff even if they know that they are quite safe behind a bar. These feelings are echoes from our evolutionary past when avoidance of heights was an adaptive strategy for the survival of our species.

However, more pervasive and pernicious emotional recalcitrance is common among persons with phobias, obsessive-compulsive disorders, panic reactions, and other affective disorders. These people invariably report that they can see how unfounded their responses are but they still cannot help experiencing them. The same applies to people with extremely sensitive and repressive moral senses that censor their thoughts, desires, and actions, contrary to their considered opinions. At times we may even get carried away within emotions that we disapprove of before and after the emotional experience. This phenomenon of emotion contagion is common in family life, social rituals, political rallies, and mass meetings (Hatfield, Cacioppo, & Rapson, 1994). All these cases appear as counterexamples to the claim of the correlation between a person's spontaneous emotions and his or her personal values or concerns that many philosophers have characterised as a semi-analytic truth about emotions (e.g. Roberts, 2003; Stocker, 1996; Oakley, 1992).[4]

Robin S. Dillon discusses anomalous recalcitrant emotions in her article "Self-Respect: Moral, Emotional, Political" (1997). Dillon distinguishes between three forms of self-respect: recognition, and evaluative and basal self-respect. The first one centres on the issue of status worth, whereas the second one is oriented around merit. Emotions enact both these forms of self-respect as we resent people who do not respect our status as persons with equal moral worth or feel ashamed if we fail to live according to our normative self-conceptions. Basal self-respect is no exception to this involvement with emotions. In fact, basal self-respect manifests itself primarily through emotions because it does not involve explicit beliefs, judgments, or evaluations. Yet it has a cognitive function of providing us with an experiential, nonpropositional understanding of our worth.

---

4.   Anatomically, these pervasively and perniciously recalcitrant emotions seem to depend on very strong amygdala links between conditional stimuli and unconditional stimuli, learned in the ontogenetic development of the individual. Longer term values of the subject that are processed in the prefrontal areas do not have direct control over those amygdala links. My thanks are due to an anonymous reviewer of the manuscript for this point.

The fundamental role of basal self-respect is displayed in the distortions of recognition and evaluative self-respect. These manifest themselves as recalcitrant emotions that conflict with the subject's explicit beliefs and judgments of his or her worth and with his or her reflexive or "second-order" emotions. The latter are emotions about emotions, such as shame at feeling afraid in a situation that according to one's considered judgment does not merit fear. Dillon illustrates the psychology of anomalous recalcitrant emotions by providing a real-life example of "Anne", a respected and successful professor who

> cannot feel proud of herself or take pleasure in her accomplishments or feel satisfied with her life. Instead, she feels wholly inadequate and undeserving: each success feels like a fluke, those who praise her are only being nice. Anne is harshly critical of herself, dwells incessantly on her failures, feels that her screw-ups give a better picture of her than her so-called successes, and fears the inevitable unmasking of her mediocrity. Anne's emotional experience of herself testifies to a lack of evaluative self-respect. At the same time, however, she knows that she deserves to take pride in her accomplishments and that she lives self-acceptably. She believes she is respect-worthy and regards her lack of self-acceptance as ungrounded and disrespectful of herself. She is ashamed of her emotional incongruity; yet try as she might, she cannot bring her emotions into line with her beliefs, so she is ashamed of what she regards as weakness of will (Dillon, 1997, pp. 232–233).

Anne is torn between her avowed beliefs and second-order emotions that affirm her worth and her first-order emotions that persistently deny it. The latter are inappropriate and anomalous because they do not enact Anne's self-respect in a proper way. For "her second-order self-evaluations and emotions, and her struggles to correct the first-order emotions provide strong evidence that her real beliefs about her worth are what she says they are" (ibid., p. 237). Dillon argues that Anne's self-reproaching emotions make sense as manifestations of her damaged basal self-respect. Such profound damage may originate from one's experiential history of interactions with other people, especially with one's earliest caretakers. Many basal frameworks arise from institutionally structured and enacted social, cultural, and political contexts as well. Still, whatever the cause, Dillon argues that the subject of a damaged basal self-respect is a victim of mistreatment or oppression.

I believe that Dillon's account of damaged basal self-respect provides us with a poignant case against identifying sincere and authentic emotions. As such, Anne's recalcitrant emotions constitute a vital source of self-knowledge which, in turn, may contribute to her emancipation from the oppressive basal frameworks. Sincerity is, thus, an important virtue of self-knowledge. Nevertheless, it is not obvious that anomalous recalcitrant emotions should count as evidence of Anne's authoritative evaluative attitudes. Moreover, Anne is not a helpless victim of her anomalous emotions. On the contrary, she may attempt to transform her emotional dispositions through improved self-understanding, through her present relationships, by deliberately changing her way of being in the world, or through political engagement with the aim of removing the oppressive basal frameworks (ibid., pp. 247–249).

Managed emotions

The subject of emotional change brings us to emotion management, which is part of our pervasive capacity to regulate emotions. Even if passivity of emotion, the fact that emotions happen to us rather than our choosing them, has been one of their defining characteristics both in common sense and academic psychology, it has become equally evident that regulatory processes are present in almost all human emotions and that these processes can occur at all levels and phases of an emotional episode, as I pointed out in the previous chapter. Regulation can be conscious and unconscious, voluntary and involuntary, anticipatory and reactive, intrapersonal and interpersonal (see e.g. George, 2002; Gross, 1998; Walden & Smith, 1997). The general function of regulation is to attune emotions to everyday events, and we seldom need articulate considerations for this. The same goes with emotion management for social purposes.

Emotion management is so commonplace that we hardly even recognize it. In everyday life, we engage in situations and interpersonal relations that demand observation of delicate feeling rules. These largely unarticulated rules set criteria for the appropriateness or fittingness of emotion in a particular situation. These rules determine the proper duration, strength, time and placement of an occurrent emotion and guide emotion management by establishing the sense of entitlement or obligation that governs emotional exchanges between best friends, parents and children, wives and husbands, subordinates and superiors, customers and salespersonnel, and so on (Hochschild, 2003). Thus, we take on a joyful mood when we invite friends to a dinner party or a mourning feeling when we pay our last respects to a deceased relative. If everything goes well, the emotion appears to emerge quite spontaneously from our construal of the situation. We do not merely put on a happy or sad face but actually live through the appropriate emotion. Herein lies the difference between *surface acting* and *deep acting*: in surface acting, we merely imitate a feeling through its manifestations without experiencing it, while in deep acting, we induce a real feeling in ourselves.[5] In fact, emotion management is usually detected only on those occasions when automatic emotion work fails to achieve the goal and we have to finish the task by conscious means.

---

5.   John Sabini and Maury Silver (1998, pp. 56–57) suggest that even a feigned emotion can be authentic (or "sincere" as they put it) if the self-presentation is motivated by a sincere commitment to a person or role or value. I agree that a feigned emotion can be an expression of one's authentic self but it is nevertheless defective, and therefore, inauthentic as an emotion because it relies on mere "surface acting" and does not reach psychological genuineness through "deep acting".

The pervasive phenomenon of emotion management blurs the distinction between authentic and factitious emotions. If all adult human emotions in social situations are managed according to social and cultural feeling rules, it becomes impossible to maintain that an authentic emotion should be unmanaged, because we have no access to "pure emotions" – if there are any – before they are influenced by feeling rules. Neither can we distinguish between coaxed and sincere emotions, for it is plausible to assume that coaxing and regulation merely remain unconscious in the latter case. The appropriate evaluation and emotion – not just facsimiles – are there, even if we may have had to do a considerable amount of subterranean emotional work to evoke them.

But if emotion management cannot distinguish between authentic and inauthentic emotions, where should we draw the line? As an empirical researcher, Hochschild wavers in terminology. On the one hand, she contrasts authentic – genuine and spontaneous – feelings with all managed emotions. On the other hand, she admits that we do and must engage in deep acting in our private lives for the purposes of our "real selves", in contrast to deep acting in a corporate setting for the employer's goals. Since the former purposes are obviously more congenial to ourselves than the latter, some managed emotions should qualify as authentic for Hochschild as well. In fact, she may need to admit that even some occupational emotions can qualify as authentic for she writes that "When the feelings are successfully commercialised, the worker does not feel phony or alien; she feels somehow satisfied in how personal her service was. Deep acting is a help in doing this, not a source of estrangement." (Hochschild, 2003, p. 136). Later research in work psychology and sociology supports this conclusion as I shall show in detail in Chapter 6.

Both recalcitrant and managed emotions thus present problems for the sincerity view of authenticity. Even if many recalcitrant emotions are authentic and some managed emotions obviously qualify as inauthentic, my counterexamples indicate that the divide between authenticity and inauthenticity does not fall in line with the divide between spontaneous and nonspontaneous or the divide between managed and nonmanaged emotions. In the remaining part of this article, I attempt to outline a plausible account of this divide and of the puzzling notion of emotional authenticity itself. I will start by analysing the elusive notion of authenticity and its relation to sincerity.

Authenticity and sincerity

Both authenticity and sincerity refer to genuineness according to the Oxford English Dictionary. Sincerity, however, lacks the aspect of authorisation that is involved in the meaning of authenticity. In fact, I believe that there are both semantic and philosophical reasons for distinguishing between the two notions.

In his classical essay *Sincerity and Authenticity*, Lionel Trilling remarks that sincerity is "the state or quality of the self which refers primarily to a congruence between avowal and actual feeling" (Trilling, 1972, p. 2). Sincerity is a virtue of introspective self-knowledge and/or expressive behaviour. We are sincere if we admit to our conscious selves what we actually experience, and present ourselves to others accordingly. Hence the ideal of sincerity amounts to transparency both within mental life, and between mental states and conduct. Sincerity is then a matter of presenting an existing emotion to ourselves frankly, without dissimulation or duplicity.

Yet sincerity is not sufficient for authenticity. The problem is that sincerity is consistent with a wide and restless variation or vacillation in one's beliefs, desires, and emotions as far as the person is undeceived and forthcoming about his or her actual states of mind. The character *Him* in Denis Diderot's classic novel *Rameau's Nephew* illustrates this problem poignantly. *Him* is an unabashed egoist and opportunist whose only concern is his own pleasure and happiness. However, he is also "an exceptionally clear example of sincerity in its basic form of uninhibited expression and enactment" as Williams (2002, p. 189) points out, for he does not pretend to be anything else than he is: "a lazy man, fool, and scoundrel". This total lack of hypocrisy elevates *Him* above ordinary people who think and act in the same way as he but disown those vices as soon as they are pointed out to them. Yet we hesitate to characterise *Him* as an authentic person, for he appears to be too whimsical and fluctuating in his principles, opinions, and emotions in order to qualify as a person with integrity, as his interlocutor, *Me*, remarks. Indeed, *Him's* mastery in imitation and impersonation together with his breathtaking vocal and mimic performances metaphorically represent the epistemic and attitudinal volatility of his mind.

The case of *Him* suggests that we must distinguish sincerity and authenticity from each other for it is just authenticity that *Him* seems to be missing in spite of his sincerity. If the notion of authenticity refers to "a more strenuous moral experience than 'sincerity', a more exigent conception of the self and of what being true to it consists in", as Trilling (1972, p. 11) suggests, then *Him* is the very opposite of authenticity (see also Golomb, 1995). For he openly confesses that "my mind is as round as a ball and a character as open as a wicker chair – . I've never thought about my life before speaking or while I'm talking, or after I've finished talking". This may sound like a commitment to unabashed spontaneity that could, after all, redeem *Him's* authenticity. But this is an illusion for he is merely describing his mind without any commitment, which is necessary for authenticity – or even having a self. For the self exists only in a moral space of questions about the good, as Charles Taylor (1989) has argued. Likewise, authenticity in the moral sphere requires creation and originality but also discovery and commitment to some conception of the good whose value does not rest on mere commitment. After all, we cannot confer value to a goal or activity by merely choosing it, quite independently of the reasons for choosing it (Taylor, 1991).

If we apply these insights about authenticity and the self to emotions, it seems that we cannot confer authenticity to an emotion by merely having it. Authenticity is a matter of striving towards a more steady, coherent, and committed self from the multifaceted resources of uninhibited spontaneity (Williams, 2002). Accordingly, authentic emotions are congruent with, or integral to one's self, not just passing episodes that occur in one's body and mind (see also Roberts, 2003). To call an emotion "authentic" is then to evaluate it in a wider context of the person's identity, which is inextricably interwoven with his or her conceptions of the good (see also Erickson, 1995; Gecas, 2000). These conceptions may in some conditions be quite idiosyncratic from the social point of view but this does not cancel authenticity in so far as those values are nevertheless internally justified. A sincere emotion, in turn, is a veridical expression of one's actual affective state, whether or not it coheres with one's values. Adequate self-knowledge is, of course, an important precondition of authenticity, but the latter aims higher as it "depends on conquering emotional blocks and tensions that prevent us from understanding ourselves as we really are", as Anthony Giddens (1989, pp. 78–79) points out, with an allusion to the Nietzschean idea of "becoming what one is". Indeed, the normative and emancipatory aspect of authenticity has been important for existentialists and feminists.

Many feminists urge us to purge our personalities from the various oppressive or heteronomous influences that we have internalized. Alison Jaggar (1997) has argued that sincere "outlaw" and recalcitrant emotions that emerge spontaneously and resist rational reconceptualisation are epistemologically indispensable as symptoms of oppression. Women's recalcitrant feelings of anger, resentment, or fear, for instance, often betray the fact that they have been subjected to coercion, cruelty, injustice, or danger in a sexist society. Accordingly, outlaw emotions may give rise to a conscious insight into the sexist, racist, and other oppressive frameworks and thus pave way to emancipation from those frameworks. Yet in spite of their epistemological value, some recalcitrant emotions, such as fear, resentment, or self-contempt, may eventually become rejected in this process, as Dillon's example of Anne suggests. Therefore, the feminist project needs a positive goal as well, for the idea of emancipation remains unintelligible without some conception of its aim. Here the notion of authenticity comes in, as Morwenna Griffiths proposes:

> Without some grasp on authenticity, there is a mystery surrounding the identity of the liberated selves who are acting, feeling, being, changing. Therefore, an understanding of authenticity is essential. It is the key to understanding what is being called for in a liberation movement (M Griffiths, 1997, p. 175).

Moreover, the quest for authenticity remains an open-ended project for there is no objective human nature that would consummate it. Hence, Griffiths emphasises that "authenticity has to be achieved and re-achieved" over and over again (ibid.). This flexibility is also a core idea in the existentialist views, especially of Nietzsche and Sartre, that associate authenticity with an incessant movement of becoming, self-transcendence, and self-creation. There is no essence or determined self that would precede one's existence, as Sartre's ontological argument for authenticity maintains. Yet in spite of their pathos of continuous change, the existentialists also embrace coherence as a regulative ideal. For they seek "a whole, congruent, and harmonious personality –, [an] individuum, which rejects any symptom of divid-uum within one's authentic self", as Jacob Golomb (1995, p. 12) remarks. Obvi-ously, the existentialists knew only too well how distant such ideal is bound to remain for the fragmented and finite beings like us. But it did not prevent them from holding authenticity as "a kind of regulative and corrective ideal rather than a manifestly viable norm" (ibid., p. 81).

Thus, if sincerity is not the sufficient condition of authenticity, I conclude that we must distinguish between the two notions. Sincerity is a descriptive, psychologi-cal concept, whereas authenticity is a normative notion. True enough, sincere emo-tions may reveal important biographical truths about one's self, as feminists readily emphasise. However, the overall project of emancipation, whether sexual, racial, or political, requires a regulative ideal for the emotions of emancipated selves as well. This rendering still leaves open the possibility that sincerity nevertheless is a neces-sary condition of authenticity. Therefore, we must ask, whence do authentic emo-tions derive their authorisation as our true responses? In short, what does it mean to say that an emotion is congruent with or integral to one's self? Before sketching my own response to this question, I discuss de Sousa's response to the antinomy of emotional authenticity which is outlined in his article "Truth, Authenticity, and Ra-tionality" (2007) and reprinted later in the book *Emotional Truth* (2011).[6]

---

6.   David Pugmire presents an ideal of emotional profundity or depth in his *Sound Sentiments* (2005). This notion combines the ideals of authenticity and truth in requiring that profound emotions to be both *true to me* and *true to the world*. As an ideal of emotional authenticity, the main problem of Pugmire's account is that he denies the possibility of authentic emotional am-bivalence in claiming that "one does not really have an emotion unless one is subject to it with the whole of one's mind" (Pugmire, 2005, p. 189). By contrast, I believe that it is possible to have au-thentically ambivalent emotions if one belongs to two communities of sensibility whose feeling rules are opposed and resist reconciliation; for a more elaborate discussion on such cases see pp. 115–116 below. Moreover, it seems overly demanding to *conceptually* tie an ideal for an individ-ual person's emotions to the existence of objective facts and values in the manner of Pugmire.

De Sousa on emotional authenticity

De Sousa's account of emotional authenticity highlights the unique emotional repertoire that everyone of us has, thanks to dispositions and experiences that "derive from a multiplicity of social and environmental factors, which are unlikely ever to be identical for any two of us" (de Sousa, 2007, p. 329). These emotional patterns constitute "individual natures", personalised ways of emotionally apprehending the world and its values. However, authenticity understood in terms of "individual natures" must be supplemented with a suitable notion of coherence. The problem is what coherence means in the context of emotions.

First of all, we must distinguish between synchronic and diachronic coherence, depending on whether we assess the coherence of co-existing states or look at transitions between states. Moreover, coherence itself can mean either compatibility or consistency. Compatibility relates to the possibility of feeling two emotions simultaneously, whereas consistency focuses on the rational justification of contrary emotions about the same object.

Two states are compatible with each other if they can both exist together. For instance, one can feel both hungry and cold, or hungry and warm, but one cannot feel both hot and cold at the same time. In contrast, two states are consistent if the states of affairs represented in the intentional contents of those states are able to coexist. Admiration and contempt or love and loathing appear to be inconsistent, for it is hard to see how something could be both admirable and contemptible or lovable and loathsome in the same respect and at the same time. However, de Sousa argues that logical relations between emotional evaluations are insufficient as standards of inconsistency for emotions because many of our emotions do not heed principles of logical consistency. They persist despite clear knowledge of their falsehood as evaluations (e.g. fear of flying), and they are not responsive to rational evidence as motivating reasons (e.g. our lacking fear of driving cars). This fact connects to the relative independence of emotion and rational judgment as functionally and neurophysiologically distinct faculties.

Therefore, de Sousa surmises that standards of emotional consistency must be connected to laws of compatibility, which, in turn, are grounded in competition for physiological and behavioural resources between different emotions. Anger and fear, for instance, are practically incompatible, because one cannot both approach an object and withdraw from it. De Sousa suggests that practical incompatibility may suffice for a *weak* sense of inconsistency as incompatible emotions often also *felt* as inconsistent, "that is, as a problem requiring some sort of resolution" (ibid., p. 336). Even so, de Sousa claims that inconsistency is not entirely reducible to incompatibility because the latter cannot be clearly split off from inconsistency. Incompatible emotions can frame the same situation from different perceptual and behavioural perspectives that are irrational with respect to each other, and in this sense, inconsistent.

Compatibility and consistency are standards of synchronic coherence. However, this standard must be supplemented with diachronic coherence: constancy and flexibility of our attitudes through time. De Sousa discusses the book *The Hidden Genius of Emotion* (2002) by Carol Magai and Jeannette Haviland-Jones on three therapists, Carl Rogers, Albert Ellis, and Fritz Perls at some length. Magai and Haviland-Jones argue that each of these therapists had a unique ideoaffective structure, largely set up in childhood and characterised by the dominant role of certain emotions as well as the inhibition or rejection of others.

> Rogers, for example is found to be a life-long avoider of anger, whose main attractors are joy and shame. For Perls and Ellis, anger and contempt are the major attractors. Perls' dynamic is based on oscillation between contempt and shame. Ellis's pattern is much more rigidly fixed on avoidance of strong negative emotions. These differences account for the different potential for long-term transformation over the three subjects' lives. (de Sousa, 2007, p. 340)

Magai and Haviland-Jones maintain that these "emotional signatures" have a "fractal structure" as they can be detected at different levels of observation: in the therapists' life decisions, in the main tenets of their theoretical work, as well as in the specific gestures, attitudes, physical postures, and facial expressions revealed in the frame-by-frame analysis of their filmed therapeutic sessions. Magai and Haviland-Jones claim that fractal structures endure throughout our lives and are largely unavailable to consciousness.

De Sousa reads the study of Magai and Haviland-Jones as an argument for a specific conception of authenticity as "a certain fit between the basic emotional configuration that defines an individual nature and that individual's choices and habits" (ibid., p. 341). The opacity of authentic patterns of emotion is somewhat disturbing because it maintains that these patterns are beyond the subject's awareness and rational influence. Magai and Haviland-Jones do not see this as a problem, but de Sousa speculates about confronting Ellis (who was alive and active when the Magai and Haviland-Jones book came out) with the researchers' account of his fractal structure and observing his response. Irrespective of the consequences of such confrontation, its long-term effects on the fractal pattern of Ellis would have become discernible only when the new pattern had already passed out of awareness. Concludes de Sousa: "It follows that the relation of consistency or inconsistency that matters most at this level cannot be exhausted by the phenomenology of emotion, for the most important patterns will not show up as such in conscious experience at all" (ibid., p. 342).

Nevertheless, de Sousa emphasises the importance of taking at least an aesthetic interest in authenticity, regardless of whether such interest changes one's behaviour. A problem is that practical criteria of emotional consistency "do not get a grip on the aesthetic, both because the aesthetic by definition restrains all action-tendencies, and because resource-based physiological criteria of compatibility are not guaranteed to surface into awareness" (ibid., p. 343). However, an aesthetic approach allows an ascent to a meta-level of irony that is capable of reconciling *any* apparent inconsistencies with a second-order recognition of one's incoherence.

My qualms about de Sousa's discussion on emotional authenticity and coherence focus on his conclusion that ends up with aesthetic criteria for emotional coherence. The problem is that an aesthetic approach to one's emotions seems to involve a disengaged attitude towards them and irony certainly does. The disengaged attitude naturally associates with aesthetic emotions that do not manifest in action, and therefore do not compete for limited physiological and behavioural resources. Indeed, de Sousa's examples of apparently inconsistent but aesthetically reconcilable contraries are musical preferences such as Palestrina and Acid Rock rather than emotions. In this disengaged, aesthetic context, ambivalence is at home, as Pugmire (2005) points out. However, let us suppose that the subject is not an observer but deeply involved in the emotion-eliciting situation. Is it plausible or even possible to apply the idea of aesthetic coherence to cases of ambivalence in which we, for instance, both admire and despise a person for the same reason, or feel both proud and ashamed of the same act of ours?

If such cases are possible, they seem rare and inherently instable, not merely psychologically but also normatively because the balance of reasons may not provide equal warrant to both emotions. Think about a homosexual who is both proud and ashamed of his sexual identity but whose shame is merely a voice from his narrow-minded upbringing. Even if an aesthetic reconciliation may be possible, such strategy may be seriously irrational if it implies that the question about the relative warrant of normatively inconsistent emotions is supplemented or replaced with a question about factual compatibility in terms of physiological and behavioural resources. When it is possible to rationally adjudicate between normatively inconsistent emotions, reconciling them by taking an aesthetic refuge may not come without a price for emotional authenticity.

By adopting an aesthetic approach to her inconsistent emotions, the subject steps back from the underlying concerns of those emotions, as well as from their conflict, that may demand both rational and practical solution. Emotional ambivalence is a way of becoming aware of such conflict, which, by the means of an aesthetic reconciliation, is brought into *dissolution* rather than *resolution*. De Sousa seems to recommend *both*, depending on whether we understand reconciliation in terms of aesthetic criteria or practical compatibility – indeed, the mutual relation of these two standards of emotional consistency remains obscure in his discussion. Yet there seems to be an important difference between these two forms of solving emotional conflicts, which renders the former strategy suspicious in cases where the subject's vital concerns are directly involved. It seems that an ascent to a meta-level of irony is a way of robbing the full importance of these emotions and avoiding one's responsibility to face the question about the relative warrant of inconsistent emotions. An aesthetic reconciliation may amount to what Sartre (1939) mistakenly ascribed to all emotions: taking refuge from the situation in order to avoid one's responsibility for it. Indeed, we can ask, is it authentic to apply aesthetic standards of coherence to non-aesthetic emotions in the first place?

Nevertheless, I agree with de Sousa qualms about accepting a person's lifelong pattern of emotions as authentic without qualifications. Even if these emotional configurations are largely unconscious and resistant to change, I agree with de Sousa that it makes sense to speculate about a person's response if he or she were confronted with an adequate account of his or her fractal structure. We do not know in advance if such confrontation would have any effect on the person's emotional configuration and behaviour but such confrontation, even as a hypothetical condition, may have independent justificatory value for the authenticity of emotions.

Emotional authenticity as integrity

These considerations bring me to my account of emotional authenticity, first formulated in an article "What is Emotional Authenticity?" (2005) My account concurs with the later proposal of de Sousa in explicating emotional authenticity in terms of coherence and integrity within the cognitive and evaluative perspective of a particular person. Integrity, like authenticity, is a normative notion that is often applied both in the context of emotions and self-concepts. Central to both concepts is the ideal of being true to oneself, the ability to resist alien and corrupt influences. Inherent in the meaning of integrity is also the idea of undividedness or wholeness as a regulative ideal that must accommodate cases of ambivalence as well. Therefore, an interpretation of authenticity in terms of integrity is not tautological but informative.[7]

---

7.   Integrity is an ideal with several interrelated and partially overriding aspects. Calhoun (1995) distinguishes between three views of integrity: the integrated-self, the identity-view, and the clean-hands view. Calhoun argues that none of these views is adequate without the others, which rings true if we discuss integrity as such. However, my purpose is more limited as I wish to put forward an integrity account of emotional authenticity. Therefore, I will center on the view of integrity that can best accommodate my counterexamples against the sincerity view. This is the integrated-self view.

The integrity account is founded on Sousa's observation that our "emotions are linked to each other and to our other mental states" (de Sousa, 1987, p. 324). Accordingly, when discussing authenticity, we should not focus merely on the coherence between emotions but on the coherence of more comprehensive patterns of the subject's cognitive and evaluative attitudes, including her emotions. Even if recalcitrant emotions defy this rational linkage, the fact that many of these emotions are anomalous from the subject's point of view indicates that coherence between a person's emotions, values, beliefs, and action is the default mode.

A viable starting point for a coherentist account of emotional authenticity is Bennett Helm's theory of emotional rationality. In *Emotional Reason* (2001), Helm proposes that emotions are evaluative feelings of import that both constitute and display our commitment to the focus of emotion. Moreover, emotions with a common focus impose rational commitments on each other. Thus, individual emotions are warranted by virtue of their being elements of a projectable pattern of rationality, formed by the subject's felt evaluations – emotions, desires, and bodily sensations – together with his evaluative judgments. Helm admits that there may be occasional and isolated gaps or anomalies in the overall pattern. A person can, for instance, fail to regret his inability to give up smoking even if he would sincerely like to quit. But if he never regrets his recurrent failures to give up smoking, we may infer that he does not value that goal much or at all, because the projectable pattern of evaluative attitudes rationally demands such a response.

I propose that Helm's coherence theory of emotional rationality provides a good starting point for accommodating my counterexamples against the sincerity view. Anomalous recalcitrant emotions qualify as inauthentic because they do not cohere with the person's second-order emotions and evaluative judgments about the emotion-eliciting situation. This is the case with Dillon's example of Anne, who is ashamed of her emotional incongruity as she cannot help feeling insecure and inadequate even if she judges those emotions as unwarranted in her situation. Due to this internal conflict, Anne does not have a single and unified evaluative perspective that would establish her genuine commitments.

By Helm's account, we may give priority to the coherent pattern of Anne's evaluative judgments and second-order emotions as the latter are especially significant for determining her values. For Helm distinguishes between two evaluative attitudes, caring and valuing. First-order emotions and desires manifest care for objects, whereas valuing is a form of reflexive caring about one's objects of care and, thus, about the kind of person one is. Deliberate judgments about one's concerns obviously play a role here, but Helm argues that rational patterns of second-order emotions constitute value without explicit deliberation as well. This requires that one responds with a coherent and projectable pattern of such reflexive emotions as shame, remorse, pride, or self-approbation to one's first-order emotions or other motives in terms of their worthiness or baseness. This is the reason why Anne's feelings of self-contempt, inadequacy, insecurity, and fear do not qualify as authentic: they do not cohere with the projectable pattern of her second-order emotions and evaluative judgments.

Some managed emotions, on the other hand, qualify as authentic for the same reason. The subject of a managed emotion may not spontaneously experience the relevant first-order emotion. Yet his or her second-order emotions and evaluative judgments indicate that the subject has committed him- or herself to a feeling rule that prescribes him or her to feel in a particular way in the situation. Thus, I may feel ashamed and accuse myself of heartlessness if I do not feel sad upon receiving the news of my dear aunt's death. Accordingly, I induce the relevant first-order emotion of sorrow in myself by construing the situation as a loss for me and the persons I care about. Now my first- and second-order emotions are in synch with each other and with my evaluative judgments. This internal coherence qualifies the managed emotion as authentic even if it does not emerge spontaneously but only as a rational requirement of my values and beliefs.

Helm's theory of emotional rationality provides then a promising starting point for an integrity account of emotional authenticity by highlighting the rational interconnections between emotions and other evaluative attitudes. However, it is only a starting point for several important questions still remain unanswered. The first problem concerns the evaluative judgments that according to Helm constitute a coherent pattern of rationality together with one's felt evaluations. It seems that in order to contribute to such pattern, those evaluative judgments must themselves qualify as rational in the first place for mere coherence with one's felt evaluations does not render them rational. The challenge is then to pin down relevant criteria of rationality for evaluative judgments that together with emotions constitute a coherent pattern characteristic of emotional authenticity. I shall refer to this task as *the problem of rationality*.

The second problem concerns the origin of our evaluative attitudes, both emotional and judgmental. For it is obvious that mere internal coherence may not amount to authenticity because one's emotional dispositions or evaluative judgments or both may have been adopted in an improper manner, such as through guilt-provoking upbringing, manipulation or indoctrination, distortion of evidence, brainwashing, or through a restricted interaction with the outer world. This is *the problem of autonomy*.

The third problem focuses on the dynamic and open-ended nature of authenticity. For we would be astonished if someone would tell us that he or she has after years of torment reached a conclusive state of authenticity in his or her emotions. Such conviction would strike us as delusive or downright self-deceptive because authenticity is hardly compatible with any fixed sentiments. On the contrary, it is an ongoing process in which we come to evaluate and re-educate our emotional responses and dispositions on the basis of new information, both factual and evaluative. The challenge is then to provide a flexible account of emotional authenticity that gives sincerity its proper due. I shall call this challenge *the problem of flexibility*.

The problem of rationality

Helm argues that evaluative judgments that together with felt evaluations constitute a person's rational pattern of import must themselves be sincere and practical. Sincerity is here simply a technical matter of occupying a transitive role in the subject's chain of reasoning. Practicality, in turn, requires that an evaluative judgment must consistently motivate the subject to act in accordance with itself. No doubt, sincerity and practicality are important criteria for the rationality of evaluative judgments. Yet they are clearly insufficient as they stand as a simple thought experiment shows.

Consider an already slender anorexic who makes an evaluative judgment that she is fat and must therefore put herself to a strict diet. The anorexic may embrace Helm's requirement of sincerity for she is both able to justify this particular judgment in light of her broader evaluative framework, her skewed evaluative beliefs about herself and excessive concern for her weight, willing to use this judgment to justify further evaluative judgments. Furthermore, the subject is consistently motivated to follow her evaluative judgment to action as she is anxious to engage in dieting. If, moreover, the anorexic person's felt evaluations about the necessity of dieting cohere with her evaluative judgments on the same topic, we should on Helm's account conclude that dieting is a matter of positive import for the subject. However, this is an absurd conclusion because fierce dieting cannot rationally be a focus of positive import for a slender and anorexic person.

The previous example indicates that we must find some other criteria besides sincerity and practicality for the rationality of evaluative judgments. To begin with, we can divide evaluative judgments into their constituent parts, that is, beliefs and values. An evaluative judgment, for instance, that the bear I come across in the forest is dangerous can be rewritten as a belief or thought that the bear is capable of inflicting severe or fatal damage to my physical constitution, thus affecting my health and capacity to survive. Now we have two items for evaluation in terms of rationality instead of one. Firstly, I can appraise whether in fact the bear is capable of inflicting severe or fatal damage to my physical constitution. This may depend, for instance, on its distance from me, on my available weaponry, or on my estimated possibilities to escape the scene which, in turn, depend on my physical condition, fitness, and so on. Secondly, I can also evaluate the status of health and survival in my set of values, which is obviously quite high. In sum, an evaluative judgment is rational if its constitutive beliefs and values are rational. But what does this mean?

I suggest that both values and beliefs are warranted by internal criteria of rationality. Here we can follow the guidelines of de Sousa who distinguishes between the compatibility and consistency of mental states as standards of coherence. To rephrase, two states are compatible with each other if they can both exist together whereas they are consistent if the states of affairs represented in the intentional contents of those states are able to coexist. As evaluative attitudes with the world-to-mind direction of fit, two or more values can be held irrespective of their content. We can value all sorts of things as long as we do not have to worry about their joint realisation or coexistence. Even so, we can increase the compatibility of values by Helm's criteria of coherence. Here valuing is a form of reflexive caring about one's objects of care and it manifests as a coherent and projectable pattern of such reflexive emotions as shame, remorse, pride, or self-approbation about one's first-order evaluations, both felt and cool, whose projectable patterns constitute objects of care. If an agent's evaluative perspective is divided into several coherent subpatterns of first-order evaluations, projectable patterns of reflexive emotions may separate his values from mere cares. Thus for instance a former drug addict may crave for a fix, feel satisfied when he gets it, and angry at those who try to interfere with this drug use, but if the same agent at other times sincerely judges that he should quit, feels ashamed of his relapses, and proud of his periods of abstinence, then abstinence rather than drug use has value for the agent.

For beliefs with the mind-to-world direction of fit, the situation is somewhat different. It is psychologically possible to have inconsistent beliefs such as p and q that cannot be true to together as long as their incompatibility goes undetected. This may happen easily as people rarely think through all logical consequences of their beliefs some of which may be incompatible. Explicit logical contradictions such as p and *not-p* are dissimilar since it is psychologically impossible to believe p and *not-p* in a single act of assent. Nor does it seem possible to understand believing logical contradictions in terms of failing to confront those beliefs with one another, as de Sousa (2007, p. 327) observes. The psychological question is still different from that about rationality: having inconsistent beliefs is subjectively irrational whether or not it is psychologically possible to have such beliefs. Furthermore, subjectively rational beliefs must be warranted on the basis of all relevant evidence conceivably available to the subject at the time. By the condition of conceivable availability we can rule out evidence that is beyond the subject's reach due to historical, cultural, social, or other limitations. Rational beliefs need not be warranted in an externalist sense either. The subject must have reasonable grounds to presume that his or her beliefs have been produced by reliable causal processes. But whether this in fact is the case, is of secondary importance for subjective rationality.

The main problem for subjective rationality is then the consistency of values. Evaluative attitudes are consistent if the states of affairs represented in their contents are able to coexist. If I for instance value both health and wealth but must work like crazy for the latter, these values are not consistent if the means of getting rich inevitably involve such workload that damages my health permanently. The example indicates how two or more evaluative attitudes can be consistent with each other: on the condition that realizing the state of affairs represented in the content of one attitude does not defeat the possibility of realising states of affairs represented in the contents other evaluative attitudes either simultaneously or at some later point of time. Georg Henrik von Wright (1989) called this kind of justification of subjective values "value rationality". The point is to qualify an agent's choices of intrinsically valued ends with knowledge of the causal consequences and prerequisites that are connected with attaining those ends. A practical problem for a rational agent is how to anticipate the causal prerequisites and consequences of realising different states of affairs as our knowledge of such causal connections is necessarily limited. Even so, such knowledge may be all we have if there is no other way of evaluating the consistency of valued ends before pursuing them.

The suggested criteria of subjective rationality for beliefs and values are capable of denying the rationality of the anorexic person's favourable evaluative judgment about dieting. The judgment fails to qualify as rational because the subject has disconfirming evidence to her belief about her fatness available any time she steps on a scale or sees her slender image in a mirror even though she does not want to consider this evidence. Accordingly, the rational pattern of evaluative judgments and felt evaluations that warrants the person's reckless dieting is founded on and maintained by a systematic restriction and distortion of the subject's available evidence. For the same reason, the subject's positive valuation of fierce dieting fails to qualify as justified as it does not rest on her well-founded and consistent beliefs.

The problem of autonomy

The anorexic person's anxiety about her fatness does not then qualify as authentic even if it coheres with her beliefs and values because these fail to be justified on the criteria of subjective rationality. However, it seems that some emotions can meet these criteria without still qualifying as authentic. The problem is that one's beliefs and values may have been adopted in an inappropriate manner. This problem emerges poignantly in Helm's example of Betty, a traditional housewife. Betty is a woman who internalised conservative family values in her upbringing in the 1950s. Accordingly, she naturally came to adopt a subservient role in the family, catering to others and, just as naturally, came to find self-esteem in anticipating and fulfilling their desires and supporting their aspirations. To say that she finds self-esteem here is to say in part that she takes pride on her fulfilment of this role and, conversely, becomes disappointed in herself for more selfish pursuits instead of catering to the needs and aspirations of others (Helm, 2001, p. 102).

Betty exhibits a coherent and projectable pattern of first- and second-order emotions and evaluative judgments even if her values do not result from a self-conscious deliberation and choice. Nevertheless, a feminist might point out that Betty's subservient emotions originate from a sexist upbringing that she was not able to resist. Moreover, those emotions do not contain the seeds of authenticity that are involved in "outlaw" emotions. Therefore, Betty should rephrase her evaluative judgments in accordance with an adequate understanding of her upbringing and struggle to alter her emotions accordingly. After all, the normativity of authenticity entails that we may have to strive for it if our spontaneous emotions persistently conflict with our internally justified evaluative judgments. Indeed, Helm admits that if Betty's new understanding of herself is accompanied by relevant first- and second-order emotions, this coherent and projectable pattern provides her with a new set of import. However, the feminist might argue counter-factually that Betty's subservient emotions may qualify as inauthentic even if she were not able to effect the relevant emotional change in herself.

Counterfactual considerations about the origin of our emotional dispositions bring us to the notion of personal autonomy that often is associated with authenticity even if their mutual relation is far from clear. The example of Betty indicates that mere coherence between a person's emotions, values, and beliefs does not establish authenticity for some or all constituents of this coherent pattern may have been produced by, for instance, an oppressive or guilt-provoking upbringing, manipulation or indoctrination, distortion of evidence, brainwashing, or by a restricted interaction with the outer world. The subject whose personal autonomy has been violated in this way may find that his or her beliefs and values cohere with his or her emotion, but we hesitate to qualify the emotion as authentic because the values and beliefs that both set the stage for the emergence of particular emotions and settle their authenticity have been adopted in an improper way.

In order to highlight this point, let us consider a more extreme example than Betty, a person who loathes himself for seemingly rational reasons. This person has not succeeded in life, he has no proper education, no job, no family, no friends, no property, and so on. In all likelihood, a person who has ended up in such a predicament was abused, abandoned, oppressed, neglected, rejected, or otherwise mistreated in childhood and/or adolescence. Such person may find that his present emotion coheres with the available evidence that the subject regards as rational. Yet the main problem is the emotional disposition of self-loathing that has distorted and keeps distorting the person's evaluations of himself, the world, and the future. This maladaptive emotion schema that constitutes a coherent pattern of thematically interrelated memories, emotions, bodily sensations, perceptions, and cognitions continues to plague the person in his present life.

In order to exclude such cases from the scope of authenticity, I propose that coherence between an emotion and the subject's rational beliefs and values should survive critical acknowledgment of the manner in which those beliefs and values and/or the emotional disposition were adopted. This condition of personal autonomy associates with de Sousa's dimension of diachronic coherence, highlighting critical transparency about one's own mental constitution; not merely emotions but also cognitive and other evaluative attitudes. Thus John Christman (1991) argues that a person is autonomous if he or she is capable of critically attending to and approving the formation of his or her desires and values or if he or she would not have resisted their formation had he or she been able to critically attend to it. The latter, counterfactual criterion is especially relevant for emotions because many of our fundamental beliefs and evaluations about ourselves, other people, and the world live on in emotional appraisals that go back to our formative years when we were incapable of attending to their acquisition due to our lack of reflective abilities. A major problem with emotions of course is the fact that it is practically impossible to critically attend to and approve the formation of most emotional dispositions. True enough, a recruit to a racist group, for instance, may be capable of attending to the formation of his hatred of other ethnic groups through peer pressure and propaganda. In general, however, this is not the case because most emotional paradigm scenarios go so far back in our personal history that the idea of critically attending to and approving their acquisition may be implausible even as a theoretical fiction. Indeed, it is not obvious who would be the subject of such fiction: the present self with its more or less articulate beliefs and values, or past selves with their inchoate epistemic and evaluative attitudes? Further still, the idea of approving of an emotional disposition is seriously ambiguous until we specify criteria for the evaluation of emotions. Should we evaluate an emotional disposition in terms of its fittingness to the emotion-eliciting situations, or in terms of those behaviours that it motivates, or both?

Fortunately, we need not stumble to these seemingly insurmountable hurdles. First of all, the problem with autonomy can emerge only for emotional dispositions that have been adopted during ontogenetic development, not for phylogenetically ancient emotions such as fear of heights. Moreover, the counterfactual condition of attendance and approval does not force us to engage in laborious self-scrutiny provided that we remain open to new evidence that is capable of challenging the evaluative perspective of our emotions. Goldie (2004) has pointed out that emotions are capable of skewing the subject's epistemic and evaluative perspective in weighing evidence independently of her awareness of this mechanism. Such mechanism operates for instance in the case of a self-loathing outcast that was highlighted above. While it may be psychologically impossible to penetrate into the sources of many emotional dispositions, it is slightly easier to become cognisant of the ways in which those dispositions influence information processing in the present life. If this influence turns out to be distortive, the skewed epistemic and evaluative attitudes must be rejected and emotions must be brought in line with the more rational and autonomous beliefs and values in order to maintain coherence.

Therefore, we can settle with a counterfactual condition of autonomy which states that an emotion is authentic if its coherence with one's subjectively rational values and beliefs would survive critical acknowledgement of the manner in which those values and beliefs were adopted. The condition of autonomy does not guarantee that an oppressed or manipulated person will renounce her emotion as inauthentic after having discovered the origin of its authenticity-conferring values and beliefs. After all, it is not the content of those beliefs and values that is challenged but the procedure of their adoption. Thus my love of classical music may survive an acknowledgement of the fact that it originates in part from piano playing to which I engaged reluctantly as a child to please my demanding father. However, considerations of this kind force the person to reconsider the issue by breaking the previous, ignorant coherence. If the person is able to reach a new, enlightened coherence by critically re-evaluating and endorsing her beliefs and values, we must accept such coherence as authentic.

The problem of flexibility

The case of Betty shows that authenticity is a regulative and open-ended ideal that requires us to stay open to new information and evidence, both factual and evaluative. We strive to build a congruous whole from the diverse aspects of our selves. Yet, on the other hand, we do not want to commit ourselves to any particular self once and for all, however coherent that self may be. Instead, we want to remain open to new experiences that can trigger change, learning, and growth (even if it is dubious whether authenticity may require us to continuously seek for such growth). In fact, psychological studies on the notion of "true feeling" indicate a strong connection between authentic emotions and personal change (Morgan & Averill, 1992).[8]

---

8.   When asked to compare episodes of "true feelings" with ordinary emotional episodes of similar length and intensity, 92% of the subjects in Morgan and Averill's study endorsed the phrase "the true feelings taught me more about myself", while 73% subscribed to the phrase "the true feelings helped more in clarifying my values". Morgan and Averill summed up these results by concluding that 'true feelings' can reflect a renewed commitment to previously held beliefs and values, or they can signal a change in beliefs and values, a new self-in-the-making" (Morgan & Averill, 1992, p. 117).

This suggests that there is after all an intimate connection between sincerity and authenticity. Sincere and spontaneous emotions constantly provide us with new information that has the capacity to challenge our present understanding of the world and ourselves, including the emotions we conceive of as authentic in virtue of their coherence with our other mental states. For instance, I can feel happy that my friend got a tenured job that both she and I applied for and disappointed at the fact that she, rather than I, got the job. Here I have two conflicting emotions about the same event, my friend's success, evaluated differently by my two emotions. The emotions are ambivalent but I have equally good reasons for both of them.[9] Happiness for my friend's success is warranted by moral reasons that emerge from our friendship, while disappointment at the same outcome from my perspective is warranted by eudaemonistic reasons that focus on my personal well-being. Accordingly, both emotions in the example qualify as authentic even if one of them may come to dominate the other in my mental life because ambivalence is difficult to endure in the long run. Yet this kind of undistorted openness to our mental states is essential to self-knowledge and our personal development. Therefore, sincerity is a necessary condition of emotional authenticity after all (see also Averill, 2005).

In the first place, an authentic emotion must be sincere in the sense of being psychologically real, whether it emerges spontaneously or only through conscious emotion management. This means that sincerity must be distinguished from spontaneity in the context of authenticity even if our spontaneous emotions typically respond to perceived changes in the condition of our values and concerns quite reliably. For the same reason, mere display without a proper physiological-cum-experiential state does not qualify as an authentic emotion even if the display were coherent with one's internally justified beliefs and values.[10] In another sense, sincerity is necessary for authenticity because latter is not primarily a state but a

---

9.   I return to this example in the next chapter, where I will argue that this kind of ambivalence is not *strict* because the opposite emotions do not have the same object even if they are about the same event. Greenspan (1988, pp. 109–136) provides an example of strict emotional ambivalence: the simultaneous love and hate of a nonchalant person. Here love is warranted by the energising spur that it gives towards the socially valuable end of bonding, whether or not this end is achievable in the particular case. Yet the subject may also hate the person for his nonchalance because that trait hurts her feelings. I don't think that the impersonal, utilitarian reason warrants love in this case. Therefore, hate would come out as a more authentic emotion in my view. However, Greenspan does not discuss this case of strict ambivalence in terms of emotional authenticity but instead as an example of rationally appropriate emotional ambivalence.

10.   Of course, bodily expression of an emotion is one way of inducing a corresponding real if only faint emotional feeling in oneself, as a large body of psychological research attests (see e.g. Laird, 2007). However, if this causal link for some reason fails, there is no emotion to be appraised in terms of authenticity.

regulative ideal of a process. For it is essential to authenticity that one's coherent pattern of emotions, beliefs, and values remains open to revision and change. Indeed, authenticity is a regulative ideal just because all such coherent patterns are intermediary stops in a continuum that does not have a final end state. This flexibility is so vital to authenticity that the entire ideal becomes unattainable and incomprehensible if a person ceases to be responsive to new factual and evaluative evidence (see also Pugmire, 1998, p. 131).[11]

The flexible nature of authenticity is consistent with Morgan and Averill's research on "true feelings". Their finding that "true feelings" often relate to a resolution of a personal crisis or internal turmoil indicates that these experiences involve a transition towards a more coherent and integrated self. In fact, authentic emotions are often both constitutive and expressive of a restored or renewed integrity in one's self. The integrity account of authenticity is thus capable of combining both the normative and the innovative aspects of authenticity. Therefore, I agree with Averill and Nunley who argue that "an authentic response is one that stems from the self that reflects the true ideals and values of the person" (Averill & Nunley, 1992, p. 184).

Authenticity in cultural context

A final, more general, problem for emotional authenticity emerges from the fact that our understanding of rationality, autonomy, and flexibility is always mediated through cultural norms, quite the same way as feeling and display rules of particular emotions. There is an extensive debate among philosophers and social scientists on whether norms of rationality are the same for all people or whether they remain ineliminably different across cultures (e.g. Hollis & Lukes, 1982). Even coherence is a substantial, albeit minimal condition of rationality. Likewise, the value of autonomy appears to vary between Western and Eastern cultures – or even between Western men and women – and their respective construals of the self, independent and interdependent (Markus & Kitayama, 1991; Griffiths, 1997). The problem is then whether authenticity relates to some privileged conception of rationality and autonomy rather than to the best available accounts of those

---

11. I am aware that this conclusion goes against an influential folk understanding of authenticity as being resistant to change, come what may. I admit that authenticity may in some exceptional cases be manifested as steadfastness and robust commitment to values which together with equally firm beliefs result in resistance to change. More often, however, inflexibility and stubbornness are symptoms of a personality disorder. In any case, resistance to change is a contingent rather than a necessary feature of authenticity.

standards. This is an important question because an objective view of authenticity would declare the emotions of entire cultures and historical eras inauthentic.

True enough, many cultures have hampered innumerable people's emotions by denying their personal autonomy and rationality on grounds, such as gender or race, that we now regard as untenable. In those societies, the oppressed must have claimed authenticity through their recalcitrant "outlaw" emotions. However, an objective view of authenticity would suggest that even the privileged in oppressive cultures cannot reach authenticity if the warrant of their beliefs and values derives from a deficient conception of rationality or autonomy. This would entail, for instance, that the Medieval sailors' fear of falling from the edge of the world was inauthentic because it was founded on their locally warranted but actually false belief that Earth is flat. But surely a conclusion this awkward constitutes a *reductio ad absurdum* of the associated view of authenticity. Authenticity is a norm of internal justification and it can remain as such only if it we restrict the warrant for authentic emotions to the best available standards of rationality and autonomy. After all, we can still maintain that an emotion is inappropriate or unfitting from a more global perspective even if it is authentic for the subject.

It is important to realise that the relativity of emotional authenticity need not nevertheless leave it at the mercy of parochial folkways, science, and moralities. This conclusion looms large when we recollect that, for example, both the cognitive and moral grounds for sexual and racial discrimination were once widely accepted within the Western culture. Yet our intuitions suggests that, for instance, Huckleberry Finn, in Mark Twain's famous novel, acted on his authentic emotion when he helped Jim to escape from slavery even if Huck's sympathy for Jim violated against his explicit moral norms.

Alison McIntyre (1990) provides a justification for this intuition by arguing that even if Huck's action manifested akrasia, that is, weakness of the will, it was nevertheless rational because Huck was mistaken about his best reasons. In fact, Huck acted on his actual best reasons, and his action was inconsistent only what he falsely believed to be his best reasons. This can be seen by considering the fact that if an agent like Huck "had had more time, more information, more insight, or greater powers of self-observation, the agent would have been able to justify performing the action that was done akratically" (ibid., p. 390). And since the reasons for an akratic action can be derived, through reflection, from the agent's own basic motivations, they count as internal. Huck's case indicates then that even conservative and quite homogeneous communities can provide enough resources for critical reflection that allow an individual who puts those resources into full use to authentically transcend the prevailing social norms and feeling rules.

Although every culture has some conception of rationality, personal autonomy is more problematic because it appears to be so clearly a modern Western value. Yet it would be rash to assume that people with more interdependent selves are incapable of experiencing authentic emotions because autonomy is not an overarching value for them. No doubt, the phenotype of authentic emotions may differ between East and West as the former cultures favour indirect expression and communication of emotions, especially in close relationships. However, authenticity as self–realization is an important value in the traditional Asian cultures as well (Sundararajan, 2002; Averill et al., 2001). The purpose of indirect communication is not to stiffen the self but to contribute to its autonomy by creating a private space that a person can share with the like-minded. Louise Sundararajan concludes that this view of harmony as affinity-based resonance instead of conflict-based conformity "renders superfluous the conventional dichotomies in the IND[ividualism] – COL[lectivism] literature – such as the self versus the group, and independence versus interdependence of the self" (ibid., p. 256).

Nonetheless, the somewhat different understanding of autonomy and other values between Western and Eastern cultures makes the question of authenticity poignant for especially the second generation immigrants, such as Asian Europeans and Americans as well as for members of other minorities, either cultural, ethnic or sexual, who must learn to live with dissimilar, sometimes even conflicting, feeling rules (see Calhoun, 1995; Erickson, 1995). Their situation constitutes a challenge, both psychologically and theoretically, as an integration of their emotions, beliefs and values into a coherent pattern may not be readily available. The integrity view of authenticity enjoins us to dissolve ambivalence whenever that is possible. However, some people may remain incapable of reconciling their conflicting beliefs and values even after a laborious and extended process of scrupulous meditation. In this case, I submit that ambivalent emotions that cohere with significant subsets of the person's subjectively rational values and beliefs may qualify as authentic, quite similarly to cases in which an individual's ambivalent emotions qualify as authentic because they are warranted by incommensurable values of the subject.

An Aristotelian objection to authentic emotional ambivalence

Kristján Kristjánsson (2010) has suggested that authentic ambivalence is in conflict with the ideal of integrity that requires a unified evaluative perspective. Accordingly, he sketches an Aristotelian solution to the problem of emotional ambivalence on the basis of *phronesis*. Kristjánsson does not aim at an exegetically correct interpretation of this central Aristotelian notion. Instead, he applies it to empirical evidence on emotional ambivalence among bicultural individuals. He argues that *phronesis* is a human capacity of critical self-reflection that allows the subject to rationally mediate and adjudicate between her ambivalent emotions.

> [Phronesis] compares the relative weight of competing values and emotions – values that are incompatible but not incommensurable – with *eudaimonia*: the ultimate good and unconditional end of human beings.... This involves reasoning, based on ethical first principles, about one's appropriate and rational combinations of desires and beliefs (Kristjánsson, 2010, p. 507).

Kristjánsson claims that the mediating, overseeing, and prescriptive role of *phronesis* is realized in its role as a second-order intellectual virtue or *meta-emotion* that "incorporates not only true beliefs about what to feel and do, but also includes a motivational component: the desire to adhere to those beliefs; a desire whose satisfaction or frustration, in turn, supplies the affective component of the emotion." (ibid., p. 508).

In the first appearance, an Aristotelian *phronesis* appears very attractive in resolving persistent empirical cases of emotional ambivalence. Unfortunately, the story is not very explicit about how this feat is actually achieved. The most Kristjánsson says is that "*phronesis* first moulds and forms the person's emotional dispositions in order to turn them into emotional virtues; then it stands guard and comes to rescue again if two emotional virtues conflict in a given situation" (ibid., p. 508). This quote hints at a disconcerting conclusion that is confirmed earlier in the text: a person with *phronesis* is understood *by definition* to be capable of "overseeing the virtues and adjudicating the relative weight of each of them in conflict scenarios" (ibid., p. 505). The problem is that if we do not know more about the sophisticated intellectual, conative, and emotional processes through which *phronesis* necessarily rather than contingently succeeds in striking the optimal way to feel, the claim that *phronesis* is the virtue that allows us to solve the problem of emotional ambivalence remains uninformative, especially beyond the context of exegetic Aristotle research where Kristjánsson claims to be operating. Indeed, we should be able to identify *phronesis* not only by its outcomes but also in terms of its operation. Only then can we can claim that something similar to *phronesis* may be guiding biculturals – who unlike the Aristotelian *phronimoi* need not possess "all the [moral] virtues" (ibid., p. 505) – to achieve an integrated rather than compartmentalized identity.

Even if integrity is the ideal, it makes little sense to ask biculturals or members of lesbian, gay, bisexual, transgender and queer groups to abandon or repress one aspect of their identity in order to become wholehearted if this turns out impossible due to incommensurable aspects of their different identities.[12] Something like an

---

12. I agree with Calhoun (1995) who argues that integrity is compatible with ambivalence. Her example is the professor and novelist Maria Lugones, whose two identities, Latina and lesbian, are mutually incompatible in the culture she lives. Lugones' problem is that "within Hispanic culture, lesbianism is an abomination [whereas] within the lesbian community, Hispanic values and ways of living do not have a central value. As a result, 'Latina lesbian' is not a coherent identity." (Calhoun, 1995, p. 239) Calhoun argues that Lugones displays more integrity by resisting the urge to resolve the conflict between her two value structures than by forcing herself to wholeheartedness.

Aristotelian *phronesis* may assist these individuals in reaching a synthesis, however unique and delicate, even in these cases. However, it seems odd to blame these individuals for lacking practical wisdom if they fail to reach a synthesis of their divided identities. When those individuals feel ambivalent emotions, it seems possible that both emotions are true to them albeit on different communal standards. Here we have an intuitive case of authentic emotional ambivalence. Therefore, I conclude that Kristjánsson's Aristotelian proposal fails to provide a plausible resolution of all cases of persistent emotional ambivalence.

Conclusion

I have argued that an integrity view of emotional authenticity is capable of overcoming the anomalies of the sincerity view: recalcitrant emotions and managed emotions. Sincerity is an important virtue in our emotional lives but it must be distinguished from authenticity. Sincerity is a psychological notion that refers to veridical self-knowledge, whereas authenticity is a normative notion that relates to personal authorisation. By the integrity account, authenticity is analyzed as coherence between the evaluative content of emotion and one's subjectively rational values and beliefs. However, sincerity is a necessary condition of authenticity because an authentic emotion must be psychologically real even if it need not emerge spontaneously. Moreover, authenticity is a regulative and open-ended ideal as our spontaneous emotions frequently challenge the coherence of our present emotions, values, and beliefs.

CHAPTER 5

Emotional truth

There is a wide agreement among philosophers, both contemporary and ancient, that emotions are capable of being appropriate and inappropriate or having and lacking warrant. An emotion of fear, for instance, is warranted only if its object is really dangerous for the emoting subject, or if the subject has good reasons to view the object as dangerous. Most contemporary philosophers refer to this kind of warrant by the notion of *appropriateness* or *fittingness* that is often taken to be an analogue of truth in the emotional domain. However, if we allow an analogue between appropriateness and truth, why not go all the way and argue that emotions are capable of being true and false? Many theorists appear to flirt with this idea when they suggest that appropriate emotions "enable us to *get things right*" (Goldie, 2004, p. 99) by "*properly tracking* those properties [funny, shameful, etc.] of which they purport to be perceptions." (D'Arms & Jacobson, 2000a, p. 69) After all, such locutions as 'getting things right' or 'getting the world right' and 'tracking' are usually applied to such discourses where a truth predicate is available. Yet only a few philosophers, most notably Ronald de Sousa (2002, 2004, 2011), have risen to the challenge to offer a plausible account of emotional truth.[1]

There are several reasons for why philosophers have avoided the notion of truth in the emotional domain. One concerns the nature of emotions. Humean philosophical psychology attributes truth value to sentences and propositional attitudes with assertoric content and the mind-to-world direction of fit, such as beliefs, thoughts, and judgments. Therefore, it seems that if emotions are truth-apt, they must be reducible to propositional attitudes. Indeed, hope and fear often figure as examples of propositional attitudes, but such is not the case with many other emotions, including love and hate.

Another prominent worry focuses on the notion of truth. Truth and objectivity are so closely related that it is difficult to see how a domain whose standards of epistemic warrant defy objectivity could qualify as truth-apt. No doubt, evidentially unconstrained truth is beyond the reach of emotions; it would be absurd to suggest that things could, for instance, be funny without an amused human

---

1.   Nussbaum (2001, p. 46) also suggests that emotions are evaluative judgments with the mind-to-world direction of fit and therefore, "like other beliefs, [they] can be true or false". However, she doesn't elaborate this point further.

response to them, whether actual or idealised, as Crispin Wright (1992) points out. However, even an anti-realist account of truth in terms of warranted assertibility of some kind seems unattainable in the emotional domain, because it is hard to make sense of warranted assertibility without invoking irreducibly fragmented communal or personal standards of appropriateness. Therefore, it appears counterintuitive to look for 'objective' affective properties of objects and events.

In this chapter, I attempt to respond to both main concerns about the possibility of emotional truth. Thus I will argue that on an adequate understanding of the nature of emotions, they are truth-apt mental states, even if they cannot be reduced to propositional attitudes. I will also suggest that an anti-realist theory of truth provides a promising model for emotional truth. I start by analysing de Sousa's view of the nature and truth of emotions which I find promising yet insufficient and sketchy as it stands. The ensuing discussion focuses on the problems of de Sousa's view together with my elaborations of it.

De Sousa on emotional truth

Ronald de Sousa has put forward an argument that emotions can be literally true and false. De Sousa rejects strong cognitivism that equates emotions with evaluative judgments. His basic reason is the evidence of groundless emotions, such as fear of flying, that we may experience in spite of contrary, well-founded beliefs. However, de Sousa suggests that perceptions are a form of cognition that is capable of accommodating groundless emotions. The argument is based on an analogy between groundless emotions and visual illusions that may persist in the face of the knowledge that they are illusory. De Sousa admits that emotions differ from sense perceptions by being relatively *opaque*. When you try to describe your visual experience, you end up depicting what you see, whereas the emotional case is quite the reverse: an attempt to describe an emotionally arousing situation may succeed only in portraying the subject's own affective state. Moreover, emotions encompass objects that are accessed in different ways. They often relate to some specific target in the world, but they also represent the subject's bodily state that the former, exteroceptive perception has initiated. Yet de Sousa proposes that the liability of perceptions to assessment in terms of veridicality and illusoriness indicates that they amount to a kind of cognition.

De Sousa argues that emotional truth refers not to semantic satisfaction but to success, which is tied to the correctness of the emotional evaluation. A further distinction can be made between emotions with a propositional object and emotions with a direct object. In the former case, "E(p) is *satisfied* iff p is true, [while] E(p) is *successful* if p actually fits E's formal object," whereas in the latter case, "E(t) is *satisfied* iff *t* exists, [but] E(*t*) is *successful* if *t* actually fits E's formal object" (de Sousa, 2002, p. 72). For instance, the formal object of fear is the property of *dangerous*. A phobic person's fear of spiders is satisfied if spiders exist but it is not successful if spiders are not dangerous. In contrast, if someone is afraid of monsters, his or her emotion is not satisfied if there are no monsters. Yet the emotion may be successful, since monsters would be dangerous if they existed. Emotional truth is thus a matter of *fittingness* of the particular emotional object with the relevant formal object.

The next question is how to evaluate the correctness of emotional evaluations. Here de Sousa introduces his *axiological hypothesis* of emotions as perceptions of value. Values are out there in the world but they are not there independently of our emotional responses, but only by virtue of them. De Sousa calls his view "axiological holism", because it stipulates that we apprehend value only in light of a complex set of factors that include biological facts, social norms, and 'paradigm scenarios' of individual biography. "It is the totality of all these factors – biological, social, personal, and more – that may properly be confronted with one another in the hope of arriving at something like reflective equilibrium" (de Sousa, 2002, p. 74).

Emotional truth

De Sousa's account of emotional truth has two main weaknesses. The first problem is that the truth of an emotion cannot be defined in terms of its success alone. This would entail that my fear of monsters is true insofar as monsters are dangerous, whether or not they exist, which is absurd. The propositional content of one's emotion must also be semantically satisfied or the target of one's emotion must exist.[2] For example, my fear that terrorists will attack my hometown is true only if a terrorist attack would actually be dangerous, and such an attack is actually underway or in preparation. In general, an emotion is true if and only if its actual object fits the formal object of the relevant emotion type, and the propositional content of the emotion is semantically satisfied or the target of the emotion exists or did exist.[3]

---

2. De Sousa (2011, p. 65) purports to evade my argument for the necessary role of semantic satisfaction in emotional truth. Thus he states that "I can happily say that a delusional fear, such as the fear of monsters or of God, is a false fear, on the ground that what doesn't exist isn't really dangerous." Contrary to what de Sousa assumes, I accept this response but I do not see how it helps him, because by invoking existence as a criterion for true and false fears, de Sousa subscribes to my account of emotional truth in which existence figures as the standard of semantic satisfaction for emotions that take a direct object, such as fear of monsters.

3. Andrea Scarantino (2010) has proposed another rival account on the satisfaction condition of emotions. His account is based on the idea that emotions have both cognitive and conative

I can obviously fear that terrorists will attack my hometown for good as well as bad reasons. Intelligence reports generally provide more reliable reasons than an astrologer's prophecy. Yet if the astrologer's prophecy by chance comes true, my fear that was supported by this prophecy may have been true, even if it was not warranted in the first place. Here is an analogy with unwarranted beliefs that can turn out to be true by virtue of epistemic luck. The truth of a belief or an emotion is then independent of its warrant. Nevertheless, the distinction between good and bad reasons is relevant in another respect. For we say that a person *knows* that p if and only if his or her belief or emotion that p is both warranted and true.

The notion of emotional knowledge may sound awkward. After all, we do not have a concept for such an epistemic attitude as emotional knowing as distinct from feeling an emotion. On the other hand, we talk about perceptually knowing that p by sensorially perceiving that p. Insofar as emotions involve evaluative perceptions of actual objects in terms of formal properties, an analogous account may be available for emotions. Thus, roughly speaking, a subject S has emotional knowledge that p is v if and only if (1) S feels e about p (or is disposed to feel e about p in the relevant situations), (2) p is true, (3) v is the formal property of e, and (4) S is warranted in feeling e about p[4]. One reason why we do not have a distinct concept for this epistemic attitude is that emotional knowledge is not about emotions but about *values*. True and warranted emotions give us *axiological* knowledge about those values that emotions represent in their content, namely formal objects, as Kevin Mulligan (2010, p. 485) points out, without subscribing to this view, however. We often express axiological knowledge by the means of evaluative judgments, without feeling the relevant emotion at the time. Even so, emotions

---

representative functions. "On this view, emotions do not *merely* represent formal objects as obtaining, they also represent what is to be made to obtain when formal objects obtain... An emotion is satisfied when what it successfully represents as to be made to obtain fits what it successfully represents as obtaining" (p. 762). Thus, for instance, "we can think of fear as being *satisfied* when it motivates the emoter to avoid dangers, of anger as being *satisfied* when it motivates the emoter to get back at slights, of shame as being *satisfied* when it motivates the emoter to repair failures to live up to an ego ideal, or disgust as being *satisfied* when it motivates the emoter to expel noxious substances, and so on" (ibid). The main problem with this proposal is that the proper emotionally motivated responses depend so much on changing situations that it is impossible to define them even in terms of generic actions. For instance, getting back is not always the proper response to slights, nor is expelling noxious substances to disgust as this emotion can emerge in interpersonal and moral contexts that have nothing to do with bodily contamination. Therefore, I suggest that we limit the satisfaction criteria of emotions to their cognitive representations, while recognising their motivational function as well.

4.   For emotions that take a direct object, the formula is: t is v if and only if (1) S feels e about t (or is disposed to feel e about t in the relevant situations), (2) t exists, (3) v is the formal property of e, and (4) S is warranted in feeling e about t.

may provide primary access to those evaluative properties whose true and warranted ascription amounts to emotional knowledge.

Another problem with my proposed account of emotional truth appears to be that we can never know whether our present fears or hopes – as well as other future-oriented emotions – are true or false because in order to know this, we should know if the feared or hoped-for state of affairs will or has come true. Yet the moment we come to know this, our fear turns either to sadness or terror, and hope to joy, as Robert Gordon (1987) points out. Gordon argues that fear and hope are *epistemic* emotions, because by definition they involve an *uncertain* belief that *p*, whereas terror, sadness, and joy are *factive* emotions, since their subject must believe or rather *know* that *p* in order to feel the emotion.[5] Therefore, it seems that fears, hopes, and other epistemic emotions can never be true except *ex post facto*. This is indeed a disturbing conclusion. Fortunately, it can be avoided, for there is a flaw in the reasoning. It lies in the erroneous equation of epistemic emotions with beliefs having an analogous content.

To believe that *p* is to assert *p* as true. Thus, when I believe that terrorists will attack my hometown, I assert the proposition that terrorists will attack my hometown as true, and this proposition is true if and only if terrorists actually attack my hometown. In like manner, a factive emotion, such as sadness about having my article rejected, asserts that my article has been rejected and that this failing entails a significant loss for me. Both beliefs and factive emotions are thus semantically satisfied if their propositional content is true. In contrast, in feeling an epistemic emotion like fear that terrorists will attack my hometown, I do not assert this proposition as true. Instead, my fear asserts that this event will – more or less – *probably* happen and if it does, it will be frightening. Accordingly, the fittingness of my fear depends on whether a terrorist attack on my hometown would actually be frightening, and whether such an attack is actually as probable as my fear takes it to be. The question about the semantic satisfaction of my fear then turns into a question about *objective* and *subjective* probability of an eventual terrorist attack.

Subjective probability refers to the probability that my fear and its underlying evidence together attribute to the possibility of a terrorist attack, whereas objective probability refers to the probability of such an attack in the light of all relevant evidence. My subjective probability assessment depends on my information about recent terrorist activities in my home country and its status on a proclaimed terrorist target list as well as on my reliance on the national and the international

---

5.   There is an obvious flaw in Gordon's account of factive emotions. For a person must only believe that he or she knows that *p* in order to feel a factive emotion that *p*. If Gordon were right, Romeo could not have mourned Juliet's death because Juliet was not in fact dead at the time Romeo believed this to be true. Other philosophers, such as Roberts (2003, p. 94) and Ben-Ze'ev (2000, p. 543) have made the same point against Gordon.

police, among other things. However, vivid and tormenting memories of the 9/11 terrorist attacks in New York City and Washington DC may raise my subjective probability estimate for a terrorist attack to the point that I become afraid of a possible attack every time I encounter terrorism-related news in the media. Yet if there is no evidence indicating that terrorists are preparing an attack on my hometown, the objective probability for such an attack is not in all likelihood high enough to render my fear fitting.

The determination of the objective probabilities of future events is obviously a difficult if not an insurmountable task, for it requires acquaintance with all relevant evidence concerning the actualisation of those events, and we rarely have such acquaintance. This is because such evidence generally surpasses the evidence that is available for an individual subject at a particular moment. For instance, unbeknownst to me, the CIA or other intelligence agencies may possess information that is relevant for determining the probability of a terrorist attack on my hometown. In this case, my subjective probability assessment does not overlap with the objective probability of the event, even if the assessment is rational by my own standards. But rational warrant is not equal to truth.[6] Indeed, objective probability may be an ideal construct, since no real person may be in the position to assess the probability of a given event in the light of all relevant evidence. Yet it is the closest approximation of truth for the semantic satisfaction of epistemic emotions. Therefore, I propose that a subject S's epistemic emotion E is semantically satisfied if the subjective probability that the emotion ascribes to the actualisation of the future state of affairs x corresponds to the objective probability of the actualisation of x, determined at the moment of S's experiencing the emotion.

It is important to emphasise that there is no fixed degree of objective probability that would render an epistemic emotion satisfied, because the satisfaction depends on the concern involved in the situation. If stakes are high, even a low objective probability may make the emotion fitting. If one takes a medical test for cancer after having discovered a lump in one's body, fear can be a fitting emotion, even if the objective probability for a positive test result were much below 0.5. In contrast, even a high probability of a future event does not make an emotion fitting if the event is not important enough. Such an emotion might be fear of missing one's customary train if the next train leaves within 20 minutes and one's schedule for the day will not be ruined by missing the train. Obviously, the threat of missing one's customary train may merit *some* fear or rather worry, but this must be in proportion to the significance of the event. In general, the probability and the significance of an

---

6.   Recall my distinction between emotional *authenticity* and truth here. If my emotion is warranted by the totality of evidence that is available for me, the emotion is *true to me* even if it may not fit the world. See my discussion on emotional authenticity in Chapter 4.

anticipated event are inversely related when it comes to fittingness and intensity: the more significant the event, the lower objective probability warrants an intense fitting emotion about it, and vice versa. A highly probable but relatively insignificant event warrants only a weak emotion about it, if any. This concludes my discussion on semantic satisfaction as a criterion of emotional truth.

The second main problem of de Sousa's notion of emotional truth is its vagueness. The idea of a wide reflective equilibrium of biological facts, social norms, and individual experience as the standard of fittingness remains overly sketchy. Unfortunately, de Sousa does not give any example of such an equilibrium. Moreover, the notion of a reflective equilibrium does not give us any grounds for adjudicating conflicts between biological, social, and personal factors. Take, for instance, a believer in voodoo who is paralysed on learning that he or she has been cursed. The paralysis is self-inflicted through self-suggestion, but the result still constitutes a significant harm for the subject. Should we conclude that fear of a voodoo curse is true for the believer, even if it is false for a non-believer for whom a similar curse does not constitute a danger?

There is a lively debate about the truth-aptness of moral as well as aesthetic discourses in the contemporary epistemology. Crispin Wright has introduced the property of *superassertibility* as the truth predicate for these discourses. He proposes that superassertibility is "the property of being justified by some (in principle accessible) state of information and then *remaining* justified no matter how that state of information might be enlarged upon or improved" (Wright, 1992, p. 47). Wright applies superassertibility to comic discourse about what is funny. However, I believe that his discussion is applicable to the emotion of amusement whose formal property is the funny, and likewise to other emotions as well. For it seems to me that emotions, properly understood, meet the syntactic and disciplinary requirements of minimally truth-apt states.

Emotions and truth-aptness

There is a well-known argument against the truth-aptness of emotions that focuses on the linguistic structure of emotion-expressive sentences. In this philosophical tradition, emotions are treated as paradigmatic noncognitive states, because their linguistic expressions are best rendered as expressives that lack the truth-aptness of assertoric utterances.[7] Thus York Gunther (2003) has argued that emotions cannot have an assertoric content because they violate against the principle of Force Independence. This principle allows the distinction between the

---

7. For early formulations of this argument, see Stevenson (1947), Ayer (1936).

content and *force* of an utterance, or the distinction between *what* an utterance says and *the way* it is said. The principle of Force Independence states that the content of an utterance can be individuated independently of its illocutionary force. This means that "the same content might be expressed by sentences with different moods, for example, indicative, optative, imperative, or interrogative, or by utterances with different uses: to make an assertion or wish, to issue an order, or to ask a question" (Gunther, 2003, p. 280). The force/content distinction explains how utterances with different illocutionary force connect to each other in a principled way: by having the same content. For instance, the content of the assertion "Gertrude studied psychology" figures also in the question, "Did Gertrude study psychology?" as well as in a conditional, "If Gertrude studied psychology, William was her teacher", where the content is not asserted but merely entertained.

The argument that emotions violate against the principle of Force Independence is based on the assumption that the logical structure of emotions is identical with the logical structure of emotion-expressive sentences. Gunther assumes that the relationship between expressives and emotions parallels the relationship between assertions and beliefs. In the same way as a sincere assertion that *p* presupposes that one has the corresponding belief that *p*, a sincere expressive utterance presupposes that the relevant emotion is experienced by the individual at the moment when he or she utters the expression. Gunther presumes that the content and logical form of an emotion and its sincere utterance coincide in the same way as the content and logical form of a belief and its sincere assertion. If expressive utterances fail to exhibit full logical complexity, the same conclusion applies to the emotional content.

What does it mean that expressive utterances resist full logical complexity? Gunther points out that unlike the assertoric content of beliefs, utterances with emotional content cannot be made disjunctive or conditional. "One cannot thank someone for letting you take their class *or* giving you a passing grade [or] I cannot apologise that *if* I come late, I will make a quiet entrance" (ibid., p. 283). These kinds of expressions are grammatically unsound. Gunther observes that we may attempt to escape the problem by reformulating these utterances. However, even if such logically complex utterances as "I will not take your course or thank you for letting me enrol" or "If I am late, I will apologize" are grammatically sound, Gunther maintains that these utterances are not expressives but utterances *about* emotions. He argues that the same problem haunts such logically complex sentences as "Getrude is happy that if she works hard, she will impress William", or "William is sorry that Gertrude either failed or withdrew from the course". These utterances are not expressions of an actual emotion but ascriptions of *dispositions* to experience emotions of happiness and regret, respectively. Therefore, Gunther rejects such utterances as reliable indicators of the logical structure of emotion.

Gunther admits that there are grammatically sound utterances that express emotion and exhibit an apparent conditional structure. One might say, for example, that "If Gertrude has skipped class again, damn her, she'll fail the course". When used sincerely, this utterance requires that the speaker experiences the requisite emotion. However, the conditional structure of this utterance is not genuine. The problem is that the content of an expressive utterance cannot be entertained in the same way as the content of a belief that is merely entertained in conditional form. There is no such thing as entertaining an emotional content without experiencing it. Rather, the utterance "If Gertrude has skipped class again, damn her, she'll fail the course" requires that the speaker is already irritated about Gertrude's possible misconduct. A similar problem concerns negation. If someone asks William, "Has Gertrude skipped class again, damn her!?", and William replies, "No, she has not skipped class again, damn her!", the reply does not constitute a plausible answer to the question even if the utterance is a sincere expression of William's irritation, because he may be irritated at something else than Gertrude's skipping the class. Therefore, Gunther concludes, "If indeed there are no instances of expressive utterances that exhibit conditional, disjunctive, or genuine negative structure, then I believe there is good reason to suppose that emotions violate Force Independence" (ibid., p. 285).[8]

The plausibility of Gunther's argument depends on whether the logical structure of mental states reliably corresponds to the logical structure of their linguistic expressions. Gunther adopts this assumption of the priority of language over thought from Michael Dummett (1993) who treats it as a central tenet of analytic philosophy. No doubt, the content of a belief is identical with its assertoric content; to believe that *p* is to assert that *p*. However, emotional cognitions are different. Expressive behaviours, facial expressions and other gestures, tone and pitch of voice, and so on, are often more reliable expressions of a subject's present emotion than what he or she explicitly says. Indeed, the same is true about many beliefs if Schwitzgebel (2008) is right. A happy person may express her happiness by exclaiming "I feel good!", but she may do the same by humming her favourite tune, by smiling in a relaxed way, by jumping for joy, by exclaiming "Life is wonderful!", and in several other ways that we are all more or less familiar with. Both verbal and nonverbal expressions count as evidence of an emotion, but in the same way as clinical psychologists do not trust verbal expressions alone in studying their clients' emotions, philosophers should not rely on mere verbal expressions of a certain kind in analysing the logical structure of emotions.

In fact, there are types of emotion-expressive utterances that exhibit the logical complexity of assertoric utterances. These utterances are first-person reports of

---

8.   Yet see Herzberg (2012) who argues that Gunther's examples fail to establish his conclusion.

one's actual emotion such as "I rejoice at my wife's success" or "I resent Gertrude being late". These indicative sentences are expressions of emotion even though they can *also* function as descriptions of my actual emotion or my emotional disposition. Furthermore, it makes perfect grammatical sense to say for instance that "If I rejoice at my wife's success, I am proud of her" or "Either Gertrude is in time today, or I resent her being late". Here we have expressions of emotion that are capable of entering into conditional and disjunctive contexts, albeit without the characteristic affective quality which emotions possess only when they "asserted" in actual emotional experiences. Gunther is then right insofar as the *phenomenal* content and force of an emotion are inseparable. However, this does not preclude emotions from having an assertoric content. Indeed, several theorists of emotion have suggested that the logical *deep structure* of emotions differs from the *surface structure* of their linguistic expressions. One of these theorists is de Sousa.

De Sousa relates the truth-aptness of emotions to their having an evaluative content. The success of an emotion "is tied to the correctness of that evaluation in any particular occurrence of that emotion" (de Sousa, 2011, p. 58). There is an analogy between emotions and beliefs. Just as to assert a belief is to present it as true, to experience an emotion is to present its object as having the relevant formal property. Thus, my belief that snow is white presents the proposition that 'snow is white' *as true*, and it is successful if and only if snow is white. In a like manner, my fear that terrorists will attack my hometown presents – either explicitly or implicitly – the putative state of affairs that terrorist attack my hometown *as dangerous* and it is successful if and only if a terrorist attack would actually be dangerous. Many theorists of emotion agree that an emotional experience puts forward a claim about its own success or warrant, while representing its condition of success in its content. Here is Bennett Helm (2001, p. 64): "The warrant of emotions is intelligible only because the emotion implicitly endorses or assents to the view of the world the emotion presents, for it is that assent, and not the mere appearance, that is evaluated as warranted or not".[9] And since truth is the generic epistemic norm for representational mental states with the mind-to-world direction of fit, emotions are capable of being literally true and false.

Even so, some philosophers think that this argument is too quick. These philosophers argue that emotional content resembles perceptual content in being nonconceptual and therefore it is capable of being *correct* and *incorrect* but not true and false. De Sousa who favours a perceptual view of the emotions baulks at this distinction in developing his account on emotional truth. Sabine Döring, another adherent of the perceptual view, has defended the separation of correctness

---

9.   See also Döring (2007), Pugmire (2005), Goldie (2004), and Roberts (1988) for similar claims.

and truth at length, using it as an argument against the truth-aptness of emotions as well. However, since these arguments are the same as her arguments for the nonconceptual content of emotions that I discussed already in Chapter 2, I will not return to them here, besides recounting the upshot which was that only a minority of human emotions – the evolutionary primitive affect programme responses that we share with higher animals and human infants – possess a nonconceptual content. Instead, the content of most human emotions, unlike perceptual content, is semantically and evidentially related to other states and therefore conceptually structured. These conclusions undermine Döring's arguments against the truth-aptness of human emotions. Nevertheless, I address one more argument of Döring against the truth-aptness of emotions that was not discussed earlier. It focuses on the possibility of experiencing explicitly contrary emotions at the same time.

Döring (2004, pp. 267–269) argues that we can have explicitly contradictory sense perceptions and emotions, whereas this possibility is excluded for beliefs. Thus, one cannot assert both that p and $\sim p$ at the same time as they both cannot be true, whereas one can simultaneously feel contrary emotions about the same object. This appears to be possible: one can feel both happy and sad about the same situation, or hate and love the same person. This suggests that emotions may not have an assertoric content after all. However, if we take a closer look at these cases, they turn out to be more complicated.

In colloquial speech, we often say that a person is both afraid of and delighted about the same object or situation. However, this is a somewhat misleading expression, because it conceals the fact that those emotions can be about distinct *aspects* of the object or situation. For instance, I am both happy that my friend got the job that both she and I applied for and sad about the fact that she, rather than I, got the job. Here I have two conflicting emotions about the same event, my friend's success, evaluated differently by my two emotions. Happiness for my friend's success is warranted by reasons that emerge from our friendship, while sadness about my defeat is warranted by reasons that focus on my personal well-being. The fact that these emotions have different *objects* within the same general situation dispels the problem with their being truth-apt at the same time.

Unfortunately, this solution is not applicable to all cases. Contrary emotions that may have been evoked by different aspects of an object can devolve onto the entire object, as Pugmire (2005) observes. Emotions about persons, such as love, devotion, hate, shame, and forgiveness typically behave in this way. Reasons for these emotions focus on some attributes of the person, but the emotion is still felt towards the person as such. However, it is notoriously difficult to entertain intense and persistent contrary emotions toward the same person. Pugmire explains why this is so, for he suggests that "it may be a condition of ambivalent emotions that they remain inchoate, unconsolidated. That is, they can't arise massively out of the rest of one's relevant mental life (the full body of one's beliefs, imaginings, and related emotions and desires) and survive intact." (Pugmire, 2005, p. 181)[10] The only condition under which emotional contrareity can be sustained is "attenuated engagement" in imagination, remembrance, anticipation, or aesthetic experience. However, emotions that arise in these contexts are not full-bodied, because they do not share the desires, actions, physiological arousal, and general intensity of engaged emotions. This suggests that emotions are analogous to beliefs in their resistance to strict ambivalence. Therefore, I conclude that Döring's objection is not fatal to the truth-aptness of emotions.

The second main condition of a minimally truth-apt discourse is its liability to publicly acknowledged standards of warrant. Wright points out that judgments about comedy whose assertion condition is the emotional experience of amusement are disciplined enough to merit an *is/seems* distinction. However, our practice of criticising emotions for their inappropriateness indicates that emotions meet this condition as well. For instance, joy is inappropriate in danger or upon experiencing a significant loss. Moreover, emotions can be badly informed and open to defeat by better information. I may, for instance, rejoice at winning a million in the lottery until I realize that my coupon was for last week's draw.

But how widely acknowledged standards of warrant do we actually have or can rationally expect to have in the emotional domain? Here we must distinguish between the content of individual emotions and their warrant. Insofar as the constitutive norm for the latter is something like *irreproachability* in the light of *our* sensibility of amusement, fear, shame, or anger, there is demand for convergence, even if not an actual convergence (Wright, 1992, pp. 104–106). And it appears that many standards of emotional sensibilities are at least communal, if not pancultural. Indeed, the fact that very idiosyncratic episodes of fear, shame, anger, and the like – sometimes even joy – are regarded as irrational or disordered and, in the latter case, treated in psychotherapy, suggests that the standards of emotional warrant are communal. This is the case even with seemingly eccentric emotions, such as nostalgia.

We feel nostalgic about events that we do not expect others to find nostalgic, because objects of nostalgia are so intimately connected to our individual life histories and personal values (see Rønnow-Rasmussen, 2011). Yet our *reasons* for nostalgia must be intersubjectively intelligible and plausible for any member of

---

10.   Actually, I think that persistent and warranted emotional ambivalence is possible for an individual who belongs to two or more communities of sensibility whose feeling rules contradict each other. These people often include members of minority groups, whether cultural, ethnic, or sexual. However, this is not a problem for my account of emotional truth because it is cast in terms of warranted assertibility within a community of sensibility. This allows contrary emotions to be true within different communities of sensibility.

our community who takes our point of view. For instance, it may seem that it can never make sense to feel nostalgic about going to the toilet. But we can imagine a possible, or even an actual world, where this is possible. Robert Evans, the protagonist in the documentary film *The Kid Stays in the Picture*, looks back the days of his glory as film producer at Paramount, and feels nostalgic about having had a private toilet with a phone in his office in the late 1960s. Evans may well have felt nostalgic about going to his toilet because a toilet so luxurious symbolised the status and power he once had. And now we have arrived at intersubjectively intelligible reasons for nostalgia that anyone taking Evans' point of view could share.

The relation of emotions and their reasons shows how the notion of superassertibility can be applied to emotions in practice. For emotional perceptions of objects in terms of formal properties cannot be justified by themselves, but only by reasons. These reasons refer to the lower-level property or properties of the particular object that render it fitting for the emotion type.[11] For instance, an object is dangerous if it is capable of inflicting significant harm to the subject. But harmful is a *thick* evaluative concept with a rich descriptive content. Even if harm can be inflicted in many different ways, the result – and the definition – of harm is the same: disruption of the subject's vital biological, psychological, and/or social functions. Thus, the property harmful constitutes the lower-level base on which the formal property of dangerous supervenes.

The supervenience of formal properties on lower-level properties renders ascriptions of the former liable to rational evaluation and criticism. We can ask whether the actual object possesses a lower-level property or properties that warrant the ascription of a certain formal property to it in a particular community of sensibility, or whether a particular lower-level property is capable of warranting the ascription of a distinct formal property in the first place. Since lower-level properties are thick or descriptive, the warrant that they provide for the ascription of formal properties is defeasible in the light of enlarged or improved information. For example, our information about what can significantly harm us may change from time to time, consequently affecting our warranted ascriptions of the property of dangerous. But if such ascription remains warranted, no matter how much our information about what is harmful for us were to be enlarged or improved, it is superassertible. In general, a true emotion is warranted by reasons that remain undefeated no matter how much our information is or will be enlarged or improved.

---

11.   See e.g. de Sousa (1987); Greenspan (1988); D'Arms & Jacobson (2000); and Goldie (2004). I believe that the proposed account of emotional truth is also compatible with a projectivist interpretation of emotional perception insofar as such an interpretation accepts that emotions are warranted by reasons that render the actual object of emotion fitting for the emotional response. See e.g. Gibbard (1990) and Blackburn (1998).

True fears could then, in proper conditions, include fear of radiation or terrorist attack, but also fear of extended unemployment or mental illness, because no further or enlarged information alone, without a social reform, is capable of removing the fact that these things are harmful in contemporary Western societies. This is quite unlike the voodoo case where knowledge about the causal realization of a voodoo curse through self-suggestion is capable of removing the danger of being harmed by the curse, even if this may not happen overnight. Yet it is the improved information as such, instead of eradication of voodoo as a social practice, that is capable of removing the harm of the curse and its warrant as an object of fear.

However, the proposed account may appear too quick, considering that not all disagreements about appropriate emotions are attributable to cognitive factors. In Wright's terms, "emotional discourses" do not satisfy the *Cognitive Command*. But is it then really possible to rationally evaluate and criticise culturally specific reasons for emotions if those reasons do not involve downright false information or distorted reasoning about the lower-level properties of emotional objects? Who are we to say to Asians that dairy products are tasty or to Muslims that pork is perfectly healthy and not at all disgusting? Similar worries arise when we think about fear of eternal damnation, a powerful religious emotion among believers, especially in the Middle Ages, or a Catholic priest's shame of his sexual fantasies.

On the one hand, Wright (1996, p. 10) argues that superassertibility is "a *language-game internal* notion, as it were. [It] is a projection of whatever internal discipline informs the discourse." This suggests that we are not allowed to apply external criteria for evaluating the warrant of religious emotions, for instance. One might argue that there is no such thing as eternal damnation to fear, because we do not have verifiable evidence of life after death. Yet this is probably not a sensible argument for a religious person, because he or she need not be guilty of an ontological mistake or a logical fallacy of reasoning. Nor do we think that the proper – let alone only – way of helping a person who is suffering from this kind of debilitating fear is to turn the person from his or her faith. Rather we – or those people whose help the person would probably seek – may try to persuade the subject to alter his or her of view of the relevant deity by citing scriptures that present the deity as loving and merciful. Likewise, a Catholic priest may learn from his confessor that sexual desire is natural for every healthy adult according to Christianity and that it becomes sinful and shameful for a priest only if he savours it to the extent that he turns away from his calling. These examples indicate that many traditions are rich enough to provide resources for challenging the warrant of emotions that appear unwarranted from an external point of view.

Yet on the other hand, superassertibility involves the idea of warrant that survives "arbitrarily close scrutiny of its pedigree and arbitrarily extensive increments to or other forms of improvement of our information" (Wright 1992, p. 48). This aspect of superassertability appears to be in tension with the language-game internalism, because an *arbitrarily* close scrutiny of pedigree and *arbitrarily* extensive enlargement or improvement of information can apparently involve considerations that are capable of challenging or refuting standards of warrant in entire communities of sensibility. This view is consistent with de Sousa's account of the fittingness of emotions.

De Sousa argues that the semantic content and initial warrant of each emotion dates back to a "paradigm scenario" that involves two aspects: "first, a situation type providing the characteristic *objects* of the specific emotion-type, and second, a set of characteristic or 'normal' responses to the situation, where normality is first a biological matter and then very quickly becomes a cultural one" (de Sousa 1987, 182). An individual emotion is initially warranted if its eliciting situation, meaning structure, and response pattern are relevantly similar to some existing paradigm scenario of the subject. However, an initial warrant may be cancelled by critical scrutiny of the paradigm scenario or by the improvement of our information, as de Sousa admits. A paradigm scenario can be highly idiosyncratic or distorted from a wider social perspective, or a social perspective may itself turn out to be parochial or eccentric from an even more enlightened point of view.

Consider an example of locally warranted racist disdain of certain ethnic groups on the grounds of the supposedly inferior capabilities and endowments of the members of those groups. Critical reflection shows this kind of response to be immature, unimaginative, unsympathetic, and uncultivated, and therefore unwarranted within an anti-realist perspective of truth (Blackburn 1998, 304–310). First of all, such disdain does not survive scientific evidence on human capabilities and endowments. If there are any significant dissimilarities between ethnic groups, they emerge from differences in socioeconomic conditions, education, traditional social stigmas, superstitious beliefs and so on, rather than from biological facts. Moreover, an imaginative and sympathetic emotional response to possible differences, whatever their cause, is compassion for the unfortunate instead of disdain. The example suggests that superassertibility is capable of refuting even widely shared communal standards of warrant if these standards are founded on false, insufficient, biased or otherwise distorted information, or faulty, inconsistent, prejudicial, ideological, or similar reasoning in the processing of information. Obviously, a wide cross-cultural agreement on true emotions may not be forthcoming in practice. Yet the idea of truth as a *focus imaginarius* of a conscientious rational scrutiny is at least imaginable even in the emotional domain.

Emotional truth and appropriateness

The notion of emotional truth might be criticised for being either redundant or too cheap to count as valuable and substantial enough. The former argument is easy to anticipate on the grounds that we already have the notions of appropriateness and rationality for the evaluation of emotions. After all, the fundamental methodological principle of parsimony forbids the introduction of inexpedient theoretical concepts. The latter argument on the cheapness of emotional truth is Adam Morton's response to de Sousa in their joint contribution to the subject. I will discuss it in the next section.

The main problem with defining emotional truth in terms of appropriateness lies in the inextricable ambiguity of this notion. Justin D'Arms and Daniel Jacobson argue that we must distinguish fittingness from other forms of emotional appropriateness. We may ask whether it is prudential, morally right, or all-in reasonable to feel f in a situation s. Nevertheless, none of these considerations is relevant for the fittingness of f to its object. For we may recall or imagine situations, for instance, at funerals and other formal ceremonies where it would be rude or disastrous and therefore all-in unreasonable to be amused by a particular event even if the event really is funny.

So there is a need for a distinct notion of emotional appropriateness as fittingness. True enough, de Sousa defines emotional truth in terms of fittingness but his view that fittingness depends on a wide reflective equilibrium of biological facts, social norms, and individual paradigm scenarios, blurs the distinctions between kinds of emotional appropriateness, analysed by D'Arms and Jacobson. Indeed, 'fittingness' in de Sousa's sense that invokes a wide equilibrium of biological facts, social norms, and individual experience appears to coincide with all-in appropriateness, rather than with the more restricted notion of fittingness that focuses specifically on epistemic warrant, as distinct from prudential, moral, and overall considerations. Instead, D'Arms and Jacobson suggest that the two proper dimensions of fittingness are the *size* and the *shape* of an emotion. An emotion is unfitting on grounds of shape when its object lacks the relevant features. My envy, for instance, is unfitting "if the thing I envy isn't really possessed by my rival, or if it isn't really good – indeed better than mine" (D'Arms & Jacobson, 2000a, p. 73). On the other hand, my envy is unfitting on grounds of its size, if what I have is almost as good as my rival's.

D'Arms and Jacobson correctly focus on the descriptive properties of the actual object that render it fitting for the relevant emotion type. In some cases these appear to be enough: a maggot-infested piece of meat is disgusting or an attacking predator is dangerous, provided that I am the target. However, this is so because well-being and survival are biologically hard-wired concerns for every one of us, and those descriptive properties render the piece of meat disgusting or the predator frightening for virtually every human being. But if I do not share your concerns or values, our emotions or rather their fitting objects differ significantly.

Suppose that I have inherited a World War II pistol from my late grandfather. Being a pacifist, I do not fancy guns but keep the pistol as a memento of my grandfather. My neighbour, in contrast, is a member of the National Rifle Association, an ardent lover and collector of modern firearms, including handguns. My neighbour certainly has a better handgun than I, probably even several of them. But since I do not value guns or the primitive sense of power and security that they bring to their possessor, it does not make sense to suggest that envy of the neighbour's handgun would be a fitting emotion for me, even though his gun is good and better than mine *as a gun*.

Whether envy is a fitting emotion depends then on the value of the envied object, which cannot be determined by its descriptive properties alone, because those properties qualify as reasons for envy only insofar as they render the object valuable. Handguns are valuable for members and sympathisers of the NRA, but hardly for people who detest guns and resent their easy availability in American society. Perhaps it is not possible to determine which of these two emotions toward handguns is objectively more fitting. Each emotion could then qualify as superassertible in the relevant community of sensibility, defined by the members' concern-based values. However, this is not a very probable result of a most careful, informed, and imaginative reflection on the matter. Instead, I presume that a close scrutiny of the reasons for valuing handguns together with enlarged or improved information and imaginative reflection about the availability of handguns, the regularity and consequences of their abuse in criminal activities, school shootings, domestic confrontations, and other acts of violence are capable of removing the warrant of valuing handguns except in strictly controlled police and military use. Accordingly, handguns do not qualify as fitting objects of envy after all. Therefore, I argue that superassertibility provides a more plausible account of fittingness than D'Arms and Jacobson's proposal.[12]

Emotional truth and accuracy

Adam Morton does not deny that emotions are capable of being true. His concern is rather that their truth comes too easily. "My elation that life has many joys and my depression that life is a grim business are both true since life is a grim business with many joys. But there's no philosophical pride to be had from bringing home these

---

12. I discuss and defend this claim in more detail in Chapter 7.

trophies" (Morton, 2002, p. 266). The problem is that such truths are not accurate enough to be interesting and valuable, for it is accuracy that we value in truth, not truth as such. And since the two are independent of each other, as the accuracy of good literary fiction shows, we should focus on accuracy rather than truth.

Morton argues that an accurate emotion contains detailed representations that fit a person's actual situation and its possibilities. For instance, my fear is accurate if I am actually in danger. An accurate emotion hinges on the subject's actual situation and its potentialities for action, whereas an inaccurate emotion misconstrues these things. However, accuracy is not well described as truth, because there are often many accurate depictions of the same situation and its possibilities. For example, Morton suggests that there is not one single, accurate emotional response for the situation of being laid off by one's employer. One may feel relieved, unhappy, or angry, either accurately or inaccurately. An emotion is accurate if it is both elicited by and directed at features of the situation, whereas it is inaccurate if it is only elicited by the situation but directed at a factitious or otherwise irrelevant object. Thus, a laid-off person may become angry at her boss for her unjust treatment and take revenge by pouring a cup of coffee over his head, or she may get mad at American policy in the Middle East and become a fervent campaigner for the internationalisation of Jerusalem. American policy in the Middle East may well be unjust, but it hardly has anything to do with a person's being laid off from her job.

Morton's critique of cheap emotional truth is well-founded, because it is important for the mind-to-world direction of fit of emotions that they latch onto the evidence provided by the emotion-eliciting situation. This is indeed a problem for de Sousa's rendering of emotional truth that focuses on the fittingness or success of an emotion. My proposed account alleviates this problem, since it also requires that the propositional content of a true emotion is semantically satisfied or that the target of such an emotion exists. I admit that truth and accuracy are independent of each other. But we should be interested in both, because emotional truth that depends on both success and satisfaction of emotion is not as cheap as Morton suggests.

Conclusion

Emotions are truth-apt mental states by virtue of having an evaluative content that presents the relevant evaluation of the particular object of emotion as correct or justified. However, an emotion is true if and only if there is an actual fit between the particular object of emotion and its formal object, and the emotion's propositional content is semantically satisfied or the target of the emotion exists. For factive emotions, the standard of semantic satisfaction is truth, whereas an epistemic emotion is semantically satisfied if the subjective probability that the emotion ascribes to the actualisation of the relevant future state of affairs corresponds to the objective probability of the actualisation of that state of affairs. Fittingness between the actual and formal object of emotion is based on the former's lower-level properties whose warrant for ascribing the relevant formal property is superassertible. Moreover, the proposed notion of emotional truth is capable of challenging or refuting even widely shared communal standards of warrant if these are founded on false, insufficient, or otherwise distorted information, or faulty, inconsistent, prejudicial, ideological, or similar reasoning in the processing of information. Finally, emotional truth is distinct from appropriateness and accuracy as a normative standard of emotions. Accordingly, I believe that it provides the best available theoretical account of what it is for an emotion to fit the world.

CHAPTER 6

Authenticity and occupational emotions

In the last two chapters of this book, I move from theoretical issues relating to emotional authenticity and truth to applying these notions; authenticity in the context of occupational emotions, and truth in a metaethical analysis of sentimental values, that is, values whose properties and concepts depend fundamentally on human sensibilities. In this way, I purport to show that the notions of emotional authenticity and truth have important ramifications beyond the narrow domain of emotion theory.

In the first of these more applied chapters, I seek to elucidate conflicting evidence on the relation between emotional labour and worker authenticity by focusing on the concept of emotional authenticity. I first identify a paradox of emotional authenticity, which emerges from the existence of theories that occlude the possibility of authentic emotion management in professional roles even if such emotions are often experienced as authentic. I suggest that this paradox emerges from Arlie Hochschild's (1983) conceptualisations of authenticity and emotional labour that many researchers of emotional labour still either explicitly or implicitly share. I then invoke the theoretical account of emotional authenticity presented in Chapter 4 in arguing that an understanding of authenticity as a regulative ideal of coherence between a person's various roles and their constitutive commitments allows us to see the possibility of authentic emotion work in a professional role whose constitutive commitments are compatible with the worker's other salient epistemic and normative commitments, provided that emotions are managed in proper working conditions. Finally, I analyse nursing as a profession that can meet these criteria.

The problem of emotional authenticity at work

Emotions at work are haunted by a profound dilemma. On the one hand, in many occupations it is part of professional identity genuinely to feel and display emotions that are appropriate to the occupational role. For instance, flight attendants are supposed to feel cheerful and friendly, funeral directors should appear sombre and reserved, and nurses are expected to show empathy and compassion to their patients. These occupation-specific feeling rules may be so important that professionals feel hypocritical if they cannot genuinely feel what they should feel in their professional role. Yet occupational emotions also appear to be inauthentic, since the display and experience of emotion often requires considerable emotional labour, which is associated with experiences of inauthenticity and other negative consequences that are mediated, in part, by a sense of inauthenticity. As Van Maanen and Kunda (1989) summarized, "Managing one's emotions is crucial to successful role performance, yet such self-control raises questions as to what feelings are one's own and what feelings go with the job" (p. 55). The question then is whether it is possible to have authentic occupational emotions, or whether emotional labour always leads to a loss of authenticity, and what does it mean to have an 'authentic emotion' in the first place?

Empirical evidence on the affective consequences of emotional labour is twofold. On the one hand, Arlie Hochschild in her pioneering study, *The Managed Heart* (1983; reprinted 2003), claimed that emotional labour in its both forms of surface acting and deep acting in a corporate context leads to fragmentation of the worker's self. Surface acting of emotional expressions produces emotional dissonance – incongruence between felt and organisationally required emotion – which impairs one's sense of 'true' self. Deep acting, evoking or suppressing of actual emotions through exhortation or trained imagination, in turn, distorts one's spontaneous emotions and thereby engenders alienation from one's 'real' or authentic self. Other negative effects of emotional labour are mediated, in part, by the experience of emotional dissonance or by the sense of inauthenticity, often defined interchangeably. These effects include emotional exhaustion and job dissatisfaction (Hochschild, 2003; Morris & Feldman, 1996; Abraham, 1998; Pugliesi, 1999; Grandey, 2000; Zapf, 2002), stress and distress (Hochschild, 1983; Pugliesi, 1999; Grandey, 2000), depression (Erickson & Wharton, 1997), drug and alcohol abuse, absenteeism and turnovers (Hochschild, 1983; Abraham, 1998), burnout (Wharton, 1993; Erickson & Ritter, 2001; Zapf, 2002), and other health problems (Grandey, 2000; Zapf, 2002; Bolton & Boyd, 2003).

Yet on the other hand, there is evidence that emotion management at work may facilitate job satisfaction, feelings of personal accomplishment, self-efficacy and self-expression (Ashforth & Humphrey, 1993; Tolich, 1993; Wharton, 1993; Erickson & Wharton, 1997; Ashforth & Tomiuk, 2000; Zapf, 2002), and even a sense of authenticity (Ashforth & Humphrey, 1993; Ashforth & Tomiuk, 2000). A common factor behind many of these positive consequences of emotional labour is identification with one's work role. Thus, Ashforth and Humphrey (1993, p. 98) argue that "individuals who regard their [work] roles as a central, salient, and valued component of who they are apt to feel most authentic when they are conforming to role expectations, including display rules". This suggests that it is not emotional labour itself but emotional dissonance that is responsible for the negative consequences associated with emotional labour. Identification with the work role is a double-edged sword, because it may exacerbate the psychological impact of job stressors and performance failures. Yet if everything goes well, identification can function as a source of emotional well-being, providing a sense of belonging, empowerment, and meaningfulness.

Poignant questions about emotional authenticity emerge from these seemingly conflicting findings. If emotional labour engenders experiences of inauthenticity as if by default, how can it also associate with quite opposite feelings of authenticity and being true to oneself? Here we face the paradox of emotional authenticity that constitutes the focus of this chapter Ashforth and Tomiuk have attempted to solve this paradox by distinguishing between *surface authenticity* and *deep authenticity*. Surface authenticity refers to congruence between actual experience and expression of emotion, whereas in deep authenticity, expression of emotion is consistent with the display rules of a role that one has internalised as a reflection of the self, regardless of whether the expression reflects one's present feelings. However, the concept of deep authenticity merely redescribes the paradox, for we can plausibly ask, how is it possible to feel authentic while managing emotions in an occupational role, provided that existing theories identify emotional labour, in part, in terms of experiences of emotional dissonance and inauthenticity. I believe that we can make headway in solving the paradox by looking at how the notion of emotional authenticity has been understood in recent research.

Emotional authenticity for Hochschild and beyond

In Chapter 4 I pointed out that most contemporary researchers, both philosophical and empirical, conceptualise authenticity in emotions in terms of sincerity and spontaneity. An authentic or genuine emotion is the subject's actual psychological state, and it is expressed sincerely, without suppression, inflation, or other modification of the underlying emotional state. Sincerity associates with the lack of emotional dissonance: there is no incongruence between the felt and the expressed emotion.

A sincere emotion can be either spontaneous or managed; the main thing is that it is a real emotion, not an empty expression. All spontaneous emotions are sincere, but the opposite is not true, because some actual emotions emerge through management that contributes to the formation of the emotion. When this happens, there is no emotional dissonance, because the expression and the experience are consistent with each other. However, the problem with successful emotion management is that emotional dissonance can be suppressed had the subject not felt the way he or she does without management, or if "to manage feeling is to actively try to change a preexisting emotional state", as Hochschild (2003, p. 229) believes. This is the reason why Hochschild thinks that deep acting, by suppressing spontaneous emotions, leads to estrangement from one's 'real' or authentic self even if it does not involve surface acting, which is the paragon of emotional inauthenticity.

Researchers have widely embraced Hochschild's worry about the inescapability of inauthenticity in emotional labour. The idea that emotional labour involves faking in either bad or good faith (Rafaeli & Sutton, 1987) implies that authentic emotions are those that are not faked or acted: the spontaneous and sincere ones. In the studies where job-related emotional inauthenticity has been measured, it has been operationalised with questions about faking emotions in a work role, on the one hand, and with questions about experiences of inauthenticity or emotional dissonance, on the other hand. Thus, Erickson and Wharton (1997, p. 197), asked their respondents, how often they "had felt (a) that they could not be themselves while at work and (b) that they had to fake how they really felt at work". Erickson and Ritter (2001) added questions on emotional hardening and numbness to their scale of inauthenticity, but questions on faking and emotional dissonance still constituted the core of their inventory. In a like manner, Ashforth and Tomiuk defined their notion of surface authenticity by the lack of emotional dissonance. Their deep authenticity is a different kind of notion, because it allows emotional dissonance. Yet, insofar as deep authenticity involves *faking* in good faith, the paradigm of authenticity is surface authenticity, which is free from faking and emotional dissonance.

The most important reason for the wide acceptance of the sincerity view of emotional authenticity, however, associates with the conceptualisation and operationalisation of emotional labour itself. For insofar as emotional labour is defined, at least in part, in terms of emotional dissonance, the notion of emotional inauthenticity is built into emotional labour as emotional dissonance and inauthenticity are defined interchangeably. This is the case with most theories of emotional labour including Hochschild's. Thus, Morris and Feldman (1996) propose that emotional labour consists of four dimensions: frequency of interactions, attentiveness, variety of emotions required to be expressed, and emotional dissonance – a mismatch between genuinely felt and organisationally required emotions. Grandey (2000), in turn, identifies emotional labour in terms of deep and surface acting. Abraham (2000, pp. 229–30) argues that emotional dissonance is "a facet rather than a consequence of emotional labour". Some researchers have proposed even more inclusive definitions of emotional labour in terms of emotional dissonance. For instance, Kruml & Geddes (2000) suggest that the two dimensions of emotional labour are emotive effort and emotive dissonance. Therefore, even if several researchers have emphasised the need to move on from Hochschild, their conceptualisation of emotional labour partly in terms of emotional dissonance, which is used as the measure of emotional inauthenticity, has kept them from making progress towards solving the paradox of authentic emotion management at work. Fortunately, Hochschild herself provides cues to solving this paradox.

In some passages of *The Managed Heart*, Hochschild writes as if the authentic heart were an unmanaged one, 'natural' and spontaneous. Thus, she observes that "the value placed on authentic or 'natural' feeling has increased dramatically with the full emergence of its opposite – the managed heart" (Hochschild, 2003, p. 190). However, there are reasons for putting 'natural' within quotation marks here, for as a social constructionist, Hochschild does not believe that there are natural emotions in social life. All human emotions are influenced by social and cultural interpretations and norms, including feeling rules. These rules guide emotion management both in our private and public lives by setting criteria for the appropriateness of emotion in particular situations and roles.

From this perspective, the main problem is not emotion management itself, but *who*, ultimately, manages our emotions: we ourselves as autonomous individuals and as members of commitment-based groups, or some external authority through its feeling and display rules that we are required to follow at the risk of organisational sanctions. At stake here are the *origin* and the *purpose* of those rules that guide our emotion management. In private life, feeling rules are part of the subject's internalised social fabric and negotiable with other members of one's community, and emotion management serves interpersonal gift exchange, which "has as its ostensible purpose the welfare and pleasure of the people involved. [However], when this emotional system is thrust into a commercial setting, it is transmuted. A profit motive is slipped in under acts of emotion management, under the rules that govern them, under the gift exchange." (Hochschild, 2003, p. 119). Hochschild admits that this transmutation is "a delicate achievement and potentially an important and beneficial one" (ibid.). Yet she believes that even if the transmutation succeeds, there is a cost to be paid that outweighs the benefits: diminished control over the guidelines of one's work, acceptance of uneven rules of social exchange, and exposure to the detrimental consequences of emotional labour; ultimately, fragmentation of one's self.

The main criticism against Hochschild has focused on her way of using the dichotomies between a true and false self and between a private and public self interchangeably. Tracy and Trethewey (2005, p. 174) remark that "this point of view presumes that emotion is more authentic and pristine before it enters the realm of organizations, where it is 'transmuted' and thus 'processed, standardised' for organisational ends". On the one hand, Hochschild suggests that if we are able to identify with our work roles without being fused with them, it may be possible to reconcile the public self and the private self without feeling inauthentic. Yet on the other hand, she assumes that the fact that emotional labour is paid for entails it always being commercialised and motivated by profit. However, this assumption appears to be false for there are several forms of emotion management in the workplace that do not involve a profit motive. Indeed, Bolton (2005) argues that Hochschild overemphasised the divide between public and private emotion management by using the terms 'public' and 'commercial' interchangeably, thus creating an oversimplified dichotomy. She observes that for Hochschild, "there is no distinction between emotion management as part of the capitalist labour process, emotion management due to professional norms of conduct, or emotion management during normal social interaction in the workplace" (Bolton, 2005, p. 63). By introducing these distinctions between different types of emotion management, we can make room for authentic emotion management at the workplace. But does this typology still allow authentic emotion management *in a professional role*?

Bolton's typology of emotion management at work

In her *Emotion Management in the Workplace* (2005), Sharon Bolton proposes a distinction between four types of emotion management: *pecuniary, prescriptive, presentational,* and *philanthropic.* Parallel though not overlapping with this typology is the distinction between four types of feeling rules: *commercial, organisational, professional,* and *social.* While pecuniary emotion management is governed by commercial feeling rules, and prescriptive emotion management associates with organisational and professional feeling rules, both presentational and philanthropic emotion management draw on non-institutional social feeling rules. This distinction between feeling rules is Bolton's primary reason for dividing types of emotion management into two main groups: pecuniary and prescriptive emotion management in accordance with an organisation's feeling rules, on the one hand, and presentational and philanthropic emotion management along with "the implicit traffic rules of social interaction" (ibid., p. 133), on the other hand.

The demands of pecuniary and prescriptive emotion management fall on us as organisational actors with specific roles and obligations. Yet there are significant differences between these two types of emotion management. Pecuniary emotion management according to commercial feeling rules can be most readily equated to emotional labour in Hochschild's sense with profit-seeking, instrumental motivation, cynical performance, externally imposed identity, and alienating consequences for the worker. Prescriptive emotion management according to organisational or professional feeling rules widens the motivational basis of emotion management from instrumental reasons to altruistic and status-related reasons. This difference in motivation allows identification with one's work role and involvement with one's organisation or professional body, which, in turn, favour sincere performance of emotion work. This is the case especially with professional feeling rules that are not primarily imposed by the employer but learned and internalised during a secondary socialisation into the profession. The distinction between pecuniary and prescriptive emotion management is also relevant to the consequences of emotion management. Bolton and Boyd (2003) showed that the negative effects of emotional labour, such as stress, alienation, job dissatisfaction, and health problems, emerge largely from pecuniary emotion management, with material working conditions and lack of work autonomy being other main causes of those effects.

In spite of these differences between pecuniary and prescriptive emotion management, Bolton reserves authenticity to presentational and philanthropic emotion management in accordance with social feeling rules that derive from our basic socialisation. These forms of emotion management aim to offer a sense of stability and ontological security to the participants of interaction. At the workplace, presentational and philanthropic emotion management operate in 'spaces' that employees create in order to escape from organisationally imposed feeling rules. Such 'spaces' are used for resistance and misbehaviour, gift exchange, humour, the creation and maintenance of occupational communities, violations, as well as for the maintenance and creation of identity. Authenticity is associated especially with philanthropic emotion management as a gift, which Bolton repeatedly sets against pecuniary emotion management or commercial feeling rules, and only rarely against prescriptive emotion management or professional feeling rules – for a good reason, I believe.

One of those rare passages where Bolton contrasts philanthropic and prescriptive emotion management is where she laments that the time when nurses, teachers, and social workers "could offer their authentic self to patients, pupils and clients has been restricted" (ibid., p. 159) and fears that if these professionals "were to withdraw their *philanthropic emotion management* and only perform *prescriptive emotion management* half-heartedly, then clearly this would be of great cost to the consumer" (ibid., p. 160). This is a curious statement, for it appears to imply that prescriptive emotion management is half-hearted *as if by default*. However, this assumption conflicts with Bolton's own observation that professionals may identify with their work roles so strongly that they "attain a new dimension to their identity; they give sincere performance and become committed to the feeling rules of a profession" (ibid., p. 101). Of course, individual professionals may follow their professional feeling rules half-heartedly, or fail to follow such rules altogether, but when this happens, "often the system is the villain, rather than the individual professional, as undue pressures prevent the adherence to professional feeling rules", as Bolton (ibid., p. 125) points out. The problem of half-hearted or cynical emotion management in organisations concerns then primarily organisational and commercial feeling rules, not professional feeling rules. So why not then accept professionally managed emotions as authentic?

Bolton seems to think that emotions controlled by professional feeling rules cannot be authentic because these rules restrain rather than support the actor's emotional expression. Thus, she argues that professional feeling rules have a twofold protective function. They act as a shield that protects the worker's self from the emotional demands of the job, and they protect the 'right' image or façade of a professional. Image management may be hard work, but Bolton suggests that professionals can be so attached to the image of the professional and its associated benefits that the effort involved in maintaining the image is hardly experienced as work. Still, sometimes keeping the face becomes a burden. Bolton claims that nurses "cannot truly share their feelings whilst at work as they must always maintain the professional face" (ibid., p. 140). Here again the enactment of professional feeling rules is set against authentic caring as a gift. However, this is an exaggerated dichotomy, for their professional feeling rules do not require nurses to keep a stiff upper lip either. Professional feeling rules of nurses – or other professionals– are not merely, or even primarily, about offering "the detached face of a professional carer" (Bolton, 2000, p. 584). Instead, these rules prescribe an affective, empathic concern for the patient's health and well-being, which manifests itself in medically informed, compassionate emotions (Omdahl & O'Donnell, 1999).

Problems with Bolton's analysis of professional emotion management suggest that her typology of emotion management is not a plausible standard of emotional authenticity. The view of authenticity as a phenomenon that belongs exclusively to the domain of non-institutional social interaction, from which it leaks "into even those performances which adhere completely to organisational prescribed feeling rules" (Bolton, 2005, p. 150) is suspicious as it seems to share Hochschild's misgivings about all institutional forms of emotion management. However, these suspicions are ill-founded, for professionals are very sensitive to the distinction between professionally, organisationally, and commercially motivated display and feeling rules. They willingly commit themselves to the professional feeling rules but protest and violate against the commercial and the organisational feeling rules when such rules are inconsistent with the professional ones (ibid., pp. 128–135). Occupational stories about violations against commercial feeling rules also testify to an acute sensitivity to the distinction between professionally and commercially required emotion management (Ashforth & Humphrey, 1993; Bolton & Boyd, 2003). But how can we accommodate the authenticity of professionally managed emotions?

Authenticity as regulative ideal of coherence

I believe that in order to make conceptual room for the authenticity of professionally managed emotions, we must go back to the scant existing theoretical discussion on emotional authenticity. Rebecca Erickson, a leading sociological researcher of inauthenticity at work, proposes a conceptualisation of authenticity in terms of commitment to self-values. Drawing from Trilling, Berman, and Goffman, she argues that there is an emotionally grounded, transsituational self, whose felt identity "is an individual's *subjective sense* of his or her own situation and the continuity and character that an individual comes to have as a result of his or her various social experiences" (Erickson, 1995, p. 126). Felt identity is constituted through commitments to various role-identities, such as teacher, parent, or volunteer, which themselves are social and implicate certain values. Values that persist as salient self-meanings across one's various role-identities constitute the person's self-values. It is the commitment to those identities which enable us to express our most important self-values that constitutes the core of authenticity. Accordingly, "It is our emotional reaction to the maintenance of such commitments that comprises the heart of our feelings of relative authenticity, and our reaction to their violation – feelings of relative inauthenticity" (ibid., p. 127, see also Gecas, 2000).

Erickson highlights a sense of unity and coherence as a regulative ideal of authenticity. Yet she emphasizes that "the particular self-values that are implicated in any two situational contexts or relationships may differ" (ibid., p. 139), thus, arriving at a more context- and relationship-relative view of authenticity. Still, for the subject, the challenge of "integrating these increasingly complicated and contradictory fragments of identity" (ibid.) within one's biographic self and one's more transsituational set of self-values remains. And since the task of integrating identities comes down to integrating their constitutive value commitments, authenticity becomes a matter of reaching coherence, however unique, among one's values, commitments, and emotions. This explication of authenticity is compatible with the more detailed *normative* account of emotional authenticity that I have presented above in Chapter 4.

A normative understanding of authenticity provides us a deeper insight into the relation of identity and authenticity by showing that it is not identification with the work role as such but commitment to the constitutive beliefs, values and norms of this identity and their compatibility with the person's other central, either private or social, beliefs, values and norms that renders emotion management in the work role authentic. Indeed, Ashforth and Mael (1989, p. 29) support this interpretation by pointing out that "it is not the identities *per se* that conflict, but the values, beliefs, norms, and demands inherent in the identities". Conversely, when two or more role-identities are compatible, it is the values, beliefs, norms, and demands inherent in those identities that are compatible with each other. Such compatibility may be attainable only after an arduous process of "juggling and synthesising" one's multiple identities, as Bolton suggests. But then again, this is why authenticity is a regulative ideal rather than a readily attainable state.

An authentic emotion coheres then with the constitutive epistemic and normative commitments of the agent's various identities, both private and professional. Moreover, an authentic emotion must be sincere, because otherwise it does not qualify as a real *emotion*. However, spontaneity is not necessary for emotional authenticity, because authentic emotions may emerge either spontaneously or through emotion management, either private or professional.

The value-based understanding of authenticity provides an explanation for conflicting observations on felt authenticity at work. The model proposes that people can feel authentic when performing emotion work if they can find a way of reconciling the normative and epistemic commitments of their work roles with the commitments of their other private and social identities. In part, compatibility is achieved by organising different identities into a hierarchy in terms of salience and commitment to the identity (e.g. Hogg, 1992). However, some role or identity conflicts are too deep to be resolved through subordination or negotiation. For example, if one values politeness and tact, it is difficult to accept the occupational feeling rule of debt collectors that requires the employee to intimidate debtors. Even people adept at "juggling and synthesising" may at times experience emotional exhaustion when managing their emotions according to professional feeling rules. However, the value-based account of authenticity suggests that there need not be anything *inherently alienating* about managing emotions at work, provided that the epistemic and normative commitments of the work role are compatible with the worker's other salient commitments. If emotion management according to professional feeling rules is nevertheless experienced as inauthentic more than occasionally, it is possible that the causes of this experience lie elsewhere.

It is a well-known fact that unfavourable working conditions have the capacity to erode or vitiate the authenticity of emotion management in accordance with professional feeling rules. Even highly motivated and committed professionals who strongly identify with their work roles are bound to burn out if they have to work under a constant overload without autonomy in a socially unsupportive and authoritatively managed organisation (Ashforth & Humphrey, 1993; Wharton, 1993; Morris & Feldman, 1996; Abraham, 1998; Pugliesi, 1999; Grandey, 2000; Zapf, 2002; Bolton & Boyd, 2003)[1]. For this reason, the compatibility of a person's

---

1.   Felt inauthenticity at work must also be distinguished from moral distress that workers experience when they know the ethically appropriate action in a particular situation but are constrained from taking it, often for organisational reasons (see Jameton, 1984). Moral distress is in fact an expression of emotional authenticity at work as it emerges from the worker's commitment to the service ideal of his or her profession, see below pp. 135–6.

professional and other beliefs, values, and norms can render an occupational emotion merely *prima facie* authentic. However, it is important to distinguish between different types of causes of inauthenticity: the ones emerging from a conflict between the values, norms, and demands of one's various identities, and the ones based on working conditions. This distinction is significant because it suggests that the professional context need not render emotion management inauthentic by default. On the contrary, professions may provide an important source of self-values to their members.

Professional values, virtues, and emotions

In this last part of my article, I will outline a philosophical argument that purports to show that certain emotions in certain occupational roles can be authentic. I realise that the argument requires empirical evidence for its support, but since I cannot provide it here, I will refer to some recent studies of nursing. The argument begins from a philosophical account of professions as practices that are justified by their inherent commitment to distinct value-based service ideals, such as health, well-being, security, justice, and autonomy. It continues with an account of professional virtues that facilitate and support the service of professional values. Professional virtues, in turn, cannot be realised without appropriate emotions. The *prima facie* authenticity of professional emotions is based on the compatibility of professional service ideals with the values of any rational person. However, this is only a necessary condition of authentic emotion work, because it requires authenticity-supporting working conditions as well.

In his article in *Encyclopedia of Applied Ethics*, Timo Airaksinen (1998) presents an elaborate philosophical theory about professions. Building on sociological definitions of the professions, Airaksinen argues that "profession" is a normative concept that can be understood in terms of *expertise, authority*, and a *value-based service ideal*. This definition distinguishes professions from other occupations that do not qualify as professions in the *normative* sense.[2] The theory does not then purport to cover all occupations, nor does it purport to give an *empirical* definition of all occupations called professions in everyday life. Still, examples of generally undisputable professionals include physicians, nurses, teachers, lawyers, social workers, and psychologists. Science-based education provides professionals with

---

2.   For sociological discussion on distinctions between professions and other occupations, see e.g. Freidson 1994. For a sociological account of values as constitutive of personal identities, see e.g. Gecas, 2000, who also points out that many role identities are associated with specific values, the identities of such professionals as physicians and professors among them.

the expertise and the social status that distinguish them from charlatans, on the hand, and from semi- or paraprofessionals who "lack the autonomy or the socially recognised depth of knowledge to become part of the established professions" (Bolton, 2005, p. 124), on the other hand. Yet expertise and social status alone are insufficient to justify the authority of professionals because both expertise and status can be abused. Professional authority can be justified only by reference to a service ideal. For instance, doctors have committed themselves to health as their service ideal and are not, therefore, supposed to require more medical tests than are necessary in order to determine our disease. Other examples of profession-specific service ideals include human growth for teachers, justice for lawyers, autonomy for psychologists, and welfare for social workers.

Unlike classic functionalists in the sociology of professions, Airaksinen does not entertain a naïve picture of professionals as altruistic servants of their practice-internal values. On the contrary, he observes that the real functions of professions often diverge from their ideals. Yet the justification of professional power and authority requires that professionals aim to meet the service ideal of their profession. Everyone in the contemporary world works for money and success, but a professional should not work for *mere* profit and success, either private or corporate. The lack of a service ideal explains, in part, why we hesitate to qualify low-status, low-paid, poorly educated front-line service agents as professionals. However, many occupations are not so easy to classify because their service ideals are intertwined with the pursuit of corporate profit. Flight attendants provide a good example, because passenger safety and well-being are their genuine professional service ideals. Yet their friendly service is also a competitive advantage for airlines that try to prescribe and capitalise on it.

Service ideals give rise to profession-specific virtues that facilitate and support the realisation of professional values. Virtues, in philosophical sense, are dispositions or traits that enable their possessor to act well in his or her position or role. Thus, a good parent is loving and supportive, a good friend is loyal and helpful, and a good superior is fair and concerned about his or her subordinates. Professional virtues differ to some extent between professions. For instance, a good police officer is courageous and resolute, whereas a good nurse is emphatic and compassionate. Likewise, enthusiasm and perseverance are a teacher's virtues, whereas honesty and uprightness are important for a civil servant.

The final step in the argument from professional values and virtues to professional emotions is founded on Aristotle's classic theory of virtues. Aristotle argued that emotional sensitivities are necessary for appropriate perception of significant events and features in one's environment. Thus, we need anger in order to perceive that we have been slighted, and fear to detect danger. Moreover, emotion motivates us to act in an appropriate manner in the situation: to seek retribution for slights and to escape danger, for instance. When the emotion is an appropriate response to a given situation, i.e. when we have been conspicuously slighted or we face a real danger, the emotion also justifies the action it elicits. This tripartite – epistemic, motivational, and justificatory– role of emotion renders it indispensable in Aristotelian moral psychology. Even if one could somehow grasp salience without emotion, this way of seeing would still be defective and imperfect; for unlike emotional perception, it would fail to motivate the person to act on his or her seeing, which implies that the person had not fully understood and embraced salience in the first place (Aristotle, 1954, 1146b30–1147a24; Sherman, 1989, pp. 45–48).

Aristotle associates virtue with both action and emotion. In modernised terms, we can perhaps characterise Aristotle's view by saying that virtue involves the capacity to regulate one's emotions so as to feel and act in an appropriate manner in the situation. Aristotle's famous general principle of appropriateness is his doctrine of the Golden Mean, which states that virtue is an intermediate position between excessive and defective emotion and action. Thus,

> for instance, both fear and confidence and appetite and anger and pity and in general pleasure and pain may be felt both too much and too little, and in both cases not well; but to feel them at the right times, with reference to the right objects, towards the right people, with the right motive, and in the right way, is what is both intermediate and best, and this is characteristic of virtue (Aristotle, 1954, 1106b16–23).

An essential aspect of Aristotle's theory of virtue is its functionalism. The virtues of a being or an artefact can be derived from its function. For instance, the function of a knife is to cut well, and therefore, its virtue is sharpness. In a like manner, Aristotle thought that the general function of all humans is to live in accordance with reason, and such virtues as courage, temperance, fairness, friendliness, and generosity make this possible. However, the functional view of virtues allows their ascription to social roles as well. Thus, for instance, a virtuous soldier is courageous, whereas a virtuous merchant is fair. Since virtue is first and foremost learned through emulation and habit, the acquisition of virtue requires instructors who must be virtuous themselves. Moreover, the instruction of virtue requires time, because virtue must become internalised as a second nature, and this is not possible without a long learning process.

That fact that we moderns doubt the universalist and rationalist aspects of Aristotle's virtue theory should not prevent us from seeing the usefulness of this model in the context of professions, whose functions are tied to their service ideals. Professional virtues are dispositions that help professionals in their service work. These virtues are realised, in part, through emotions that are regulated in accordance with professional feeling rules. Thus, emotion regulation at work may be motivated and justified by standards internal to one's professional identity. Obviously, one must recognise the professional role as an important and valuable aspect of one's identity in order to feel the pressure of its professional feeling rules. However, it is important to realise that in proper professions, the process of adopting the professional role begins already during one's education and training into the profession.

The *prima facie* authenticity of emotions managed in accordance with professional feeling rules emerges from the compatibility of the worker's professional and private identity, or rather from the compatibility of the normative and epistemic commitments of these identities. It seems to me that professions have an edge on other occupations in this respect because they serve objective values, such as health, well-being, security, justice, and autonomy that are compatible with the values of any rational person.[3] One such profession is nursing.

A case study: Authentic emotional labour in nursing

Nursing is one of the most demanding and stressful occupations when it comes to emotion management. It scores high in studies of burnout, stress, and other negative consequences of emotional labour (Maslach, 1982; Smith, 1992; McVicar, 2003). Therefore, if we can establish that emotional authenticity is possible in such a demanding job as nursing, it may be possible in other, emotionally less exhaustive professions as well, although this possibility must be established for each profession individually.

Nursing has undergone a profound change in recent decades. The traditional task-oriented view of nursing was focused on meeting patients' biological needs through various treatments, whose techniques, procedures, and informational basis constituted the core of the profession. This core is obviously still there, but it has become equally clear that nursing care cannot be defined in terms of mere treatment, however skilfully administered. Patients are people in need, and insofar as nursing attempts to remove or relieve their suffering and restore their health and well-being, nurses must treat patients as whole persons.

The holistic and patient-oriented view of nursing emphasises the role of empathy and compassion in the nurse-patient relationship. Empathy is necessary for understanding the meaning and implications of illness from the patient's perspective. It involves appreciative and imaginative receptivity to another person's inner reality, to his or her thoughts, emotions, and needs, and thereby conveys vital information for the determination of appropriate therapeutic intervention. However,

---

3.   I abstract from non-normative psychological factors, such as temperament, in the consideration of compatibility between a person's different identities. For instance, my values are compatible with the service ideal of medical professions, but if seeing blood makes me feel sick, those professions are psychologically incompatible with my personality.

empathy is not enough because it must be accompanied by compassion, willing participation in another person's suffering that introduces solidarity with the other person and an altruistic motive to help him or her. It is compassion that leads the nurse to initiate informed actions and treatments that purport to empower the patient. Indeed, nursing has been characterised as an inherently moral practice by virtue of its commitment to care and the essential role of empathy and compassion in the service of this value (Benner & Wrubel, 1989; Gastmans, 1999; Benner, 2000; Bolton, 2000; von Dietze & Orb, 2000; Reynolds, Scott, & Austin, 2000; Scott, 2000).

Empathy and compassion are examples of professional virtues that manifest themselves as appropriate emotions and actions at work. Only an emotionally sensitive nurse is capable of effective nursing, since he or she can take the patient's perspective, recognise the patient's needs, and respond in an appropriate manner. Without these emotional propensities, the perception of complex situations vis-á-vis the patient's condition is likely to be clouded and the therapeutic interventions chosen less than optimal (Benner & Wrubel, 1989; Nordtvedt, 1998; Staden, 1998; Benner, 2000; von Dietze & Orb, 2000; Reynolds, Scott, & Austin, 2000; Scott, 2000; Henderson, 2001; McQueen, 2004). For "a sympathetic, compassionate or kind person is not only apt to perform beneficent acts, but also characteristically perceives more situations as warranting beneficent actions when this is in fact the case, than would a person lacking in sympathy, compassion, or kindness," as Justin Oakley (1992, p. 51) remarks.

In addition to their vital role in nursing care, professional empathy and compassion are delicate skills exemplifying the Aristotelian principle of the Golden Mean. A nurse who faces suffering on a regular basis must learn to cope without losing his or her sensibilities. Thus, nurses must continuously strike and maintain a balance between two dysfunctional opposites regarding affective engagement, the Scylla of detachment and the Charybdis of overinvolvement, for it is the mean that represents functionality (Carmack, 1997) – and professional virtue. To quote Gleichgerrcht and Decety (2012, 254): "In training for empathy, the main objective should be to achieve the optimal balance between being empathic without suffering the costs that come from overstimulating negative emotional arousal." In spite of the rise of holistic and patient-oriented nursing, this balancing skill still seems to belong to the tacit knowledge of nursing; practicing nurses often complain that their professional training did not properly prepare them for the emotional labour of nursing (Smith, 1992; Henderson, 2001). Yet this deficiency is no great surprise if balancing is a virtue in the Aristotelian sense, for virtues are learned only in practice under the tutelage of senior colleagues.

Nevertheless, balancing affective engagement can be learned, given time and experience. Betty Carmack (1997) suggested that having the potential to affect outcomes without needing to control them constitutes the core of this ability. Self-care and self-monitoring, as well as setting limits and boundaries on one's emotional labour also contribute to effective balancing. Omdahl and O'Donnell (1999), in turn, distinguished between emotional contagion and empathic concern in empathy. They found that emotional contagion was positively correlated with burnout, whereas empathic concern, which relates to an affective concern for the well-being of another without sharing emotion, was negatively correlated with burnout. These results are consistent with empirical evidence on down-regulation of empathy that comes with experience in medical settings (e.g. Decety, Yang, and Cheng, 2010). Thus, Gleichgerrcht and Decety (2012, 253) point out that "caregivers' down-regulation of the emotional response dampens their emotional arousal in response to the pain or distress of others and may thus have beneficial consequences in freeing up cognitive resources necessary for being of assistance and expressing empathic concern." Empathic concern manifests then *regulated* rather than contagious empathy. The role of experience in learning emotion regulation in a professional role suggests that it is a skilful capacity requiring careful observation of many "rights," determined by one's professional feeling and display rules.

Finally, there is some evidence that nurses may experience their emotion work in accordance with professional feeling and display rules as authentic even if this work requires considerable amount of emotion management. An emphatic nurse who perceives that his or her patient is anxious about a forthcoming operation and engages in a reassuring conversation with the patient is a case in point. The nurse's compassionate support of the patient complies with her professional feeling rules. A professional role may become a second nature to a seasoned nurse, who need not engage in conscious manoeuvring in order to evoke and maintain the relevant occupational emotions. However, the nurse still feels those emotions *qua* professional as his or her emphatic interest in the patient typically differs in its range and depth from the similar interest of a close relative or friend. Yet the differences between private and professional empathy do not render the latter inauthentic, as Louise de Raeve (2002) remarked. Instead of modelling authenticity on the intensity and spontaneity of some private emotions, we should rather see the two "worlds", private and professional, as distinct and meaningful in their own right. This view is consistent with the idea that our identities consist of various private and social roles whose feeling and display rules we have internalised as a part and parcel of those roles.

Nothing said above denies that the professional emotion management of nurses can be hard work – demanding, exhaustive, even sorrowful, as Nicky James (1989) showed in her studies on nursing the dying. However, the argument implies that exhaustiveness *alone* does not render emotion management in a professional role inauthentic any more than the occasional arduousness of managing emotions in private life. The main problem with emotionally exhaustive jobs seems to be that they must "be designed to be flexible enough to accommodate emotional labour" as James (1989, p. 34) argued. This requires, above all, that emotion work is recognised as a vital aspect of nursing and other professional work. Moreover, organisational mechanisms must be introduced to support coping with the negative effects of professional emotion work. Even so, we may not be able make this work easy. However, if we can show that emotions managed in our professional roles can cohere with our commitments, both private and professional, then we have presented a case for the authenticity of these emotions.

Conclusion

I have rejected Hochschild's and Bolton's view that limits authenticity to spontaneous emotions or emotions managed in accordance with non-institutional social feeling rules as insufficient. Instead, I have argued that the proper, a normative understanding of authenticity as a regulative ideal of coherence between a person's various roles and their constitutive commitments allows us to make conceptual room for the authenticity of emotions managed in a professional role, provided that the constitutive values, virtues, and beliefs of the role are compatible with the worker's other salient epistemic and normative commitments, and that emotions are managed in proper working conditions that include considerable autonomy, participative management style, social support, and a reasonable workload.

This resolution of the paradox of emotional authenticity challenges the prevalent view of emotional dissonance or inauthenticity as a defining aspect of emotional labour. Emotion management in accordance with professional virtues qualifies as emotional labour even if it need not involve experiences of inauthenticity. Moreover, professional emotion management in proper working conditions suggests itself as that benign type of emotional labour whose existence previous empirical research has indicated, without being able to specify it. This hypothesis appears plausible, given the evidence surveyed in this article. However, its testing is a topic for an interdisciplinary rather than merely philosophical study.

CHAPTER 7

From true emotions to sentimental values

The challenges of neosentimentalism

There is a popular research program in contemporary metaethics that purports to explicate value concepts and value properties in terms of appropriate or fitting emotions and other pro-attitudes.[1] Theories that focus on emotions in this task are known as *neosentimentalist* theories of value as they follow the classic sentimentalism that was initiated, among others, by David Hume and Adam Smith and developed by Franz Brentano and A.C. Ewing. Contemporary neosentimentalists include Justin D'Arms and Daniel Jacobson (2006a,b, 2000a, b, 2010; O'Arms, 2005); Simon Blackburn (1998), Allan Gibbard (1990), Julien Deonna (2006), John McDowell (1997a, b); Kevin Mulligan (1998), Ronald de Sousa (2004), Holmer Steinfath (2002), Christine Tappolet (2011), and David Wiggins (1997). In spite of their disagreements on the metaphysical status of value and the cognitive or noncognitive nature of value judgments, these theorists agree on a certain basic idea that justifies their classification into the same theoretical approach. This idea is that values and their concepts depend fundamentally on human sensibilities as they can be analysed or explicated in terms of appropriate (fitting, merited, correct, justified, warranted) sentiments or emotions.[2] Accordingly, neosentimentalism comes in two closely associated versions, conceptual and metaphysical.

---

1.   The general approach that purports to analyze values in terms of correct or fitting pro-attitudes, whether conative or affective, is known in recent metaethical literature as the 'buck-passing' account of value, thanks to T.M. Scanlon (1998), who coined this view. It maintains that to be good or valuable is to have properties that give us a reason to take up a certain pro-attitude towards the bearer of those properties. Neosentimentalist theories are a subclass of the 'buck-passing' view as they invoke fitting or appropriate emotions in their analysis of value. Accordingly, I will focus on neosentimentalist theories of value and discuss problems of the more general 'buck-passing' account only as far as they concern neosentimentalist theories as well. The most important case is the problem of the wrong kind of reasons, raised by Justin D'Arms and Daniel Jacobson (2000b) as "the conflation problem" for neosentimentalist theories in particular, and by Wlodek Rabinowicz and Toni Rønnow-Rasmussen (2004) for all 'buck-passing' accounts of value.

2.   I speak about emotions rather than sentiments in this chapter, even though some adherents of sentimentalism stick to this traditional notion, mainly to widen the scope of affective states that may ground values, as far as I can see. Since I am not a native English speaker, I am not the

The conceptual version of neosentimentalism seeks to analyse or explicate value concepts in terms of appropriate or fitting sentiments. Sentimentalist analyses have typically been proposed for *thick* value concepts such as *admirable, funny, enviable, shameful, disgusting,* and *offensive* that have a one-to-one connection with distinct emotions – admiration, amusement, envy, shame, disgust, and anger, respectively. For concepts of this kind, D'Arms and Jacobson (2000b, p. 729) formulate the following "response-dependency thesis":

> RDT: to think that X has some evaluative property Φ is to think it appropriate to feel F in response to X.

Value judgments are then, essentially, judgments about appropriate/correct/warranted emotions.

In contrast, the metaphysical version of neosentimentalism defines or identifies value properties by means of appropriate or fitting sentiments. The responses are the same as in the conceptual version but instead of concepts, we talk about properties. Rephrasing the response-dependency thesis of D'Arms and Jacobson for value properties, we have

> RDT*: for X to have some evaluative property Φ is for X to be such that it is appropriate to feel F in response to X.
> Or, more briefly,
> RDT**: X has some evaluative property Φ if feeling F is appropriate in response to X.

In what follows, I shall focus on the metaphysical version of neosentimentalism because I believe that it suffers from less serious problems than its conceptual cousin.

Neosentimentalist theories of value face two major problems. The first problem concerns the relation between evaluative concepts and the associated emotional responses. It seems that in order to avoid a vicious circle, we must deny that emotional responses involve those evaluative concepts that we purport to analyse

---

right person to determine the correct meaning of "sentiment". However, if we assume, with some theorists that employ this concept, that "sentiments" include all affective phenomena – emotions as well as feelings, moods, affective dispositions and traits, pleasures and pains, etc. – emotions are still the most promising candidates among sentiments to ground values. Unlike feelings and moods, emotions are intentional states directed at particular objects that they present in a certain evaluative light. By virtue of these characteristics, emotions can be assessed in terms of their appropriateness or rationality. No doubt, we sometimes talk about irrational feelings (of fear or guilt, for example) or moods (of happiness or anxiety, for instance). However, it seems to me that when we do so, we ascribe to these states a representational content and a direction of fit. Whether or not other affective states besides emotions possess those qualities is a theoretical problem that I cannot address here.

or explicate in terms of the relevant responses. For instance, if we claim that amusement contains the concept of being funny, we cannot analyse this concept in terms of the emotion of amusement, because grasping the sentiment already requires an understanding of the concept of being funny that is part of the emotion. Many sentimentalists, both traditional and contemporary, have tried to avoid this problem by adopting a noncognitive view of the emotions. Unfortunately, this theory is unappealing on independent grounds, as I have argued in previous chapters of this book. Noncognitivism is particularly implausible in the case of such emotions as pride, shame, guilt, indignation, admiration, and gratitude, which emerge late in ontogenetic development and are not merely caused but felt for reasons.

Neosentimentalists sympathetic to cognitivism about emotions have purported to defend themselves against the circularity objection in two main ways. The first strategy is to admit the circularity but argue that it is not vicious because the elucidation of value concepts requires an epistemologically indispensable detour through sentiments that cannot be identified and understood without the relevant concepts (e.g. Wiggins, 1997; McDowell, 1997a, b). The detour is benign and informative because it allows us to explicate the application criteria of those value concepts in our evaluative practices in spite of remaining circular. The second strategy is to argue that emotional content can be evaluative even if it does not involve concepts. A nonconceptual view of emotions purports to alleviate the circularity worry by suggesting that emotions "involve a pre-judgmental or nonconceptual representation of values" (Tappolet, 2011, p. 129). Even so, the solution is not entirely satisfactory insofar as emotions still are or involve appraisals that – either nonconceptually or functionally – represent their formal objects, such as danger (fear), loss (sadness), or offence (anger). It does not matter if the content of emotional appraisal is conceptual or nonconceptual insofar as this content is identified or explicated in terms of the same evaluative concept that is defined by reference to the emotional content. To quote Michael Brady (2008, p. 471),

> If a subject wants to know about the content of the evaluative judgment that something is dangerous, it does not help for her to be told that something is dangerous if it is correct to appraise it as dangerous. That is something that she already knows.... Insofar as evaluative judgments concern the accuracy of such appraisals, then the resulting sentimentalist account of evaluative judgment will be at best circular and at worst vacuous.[3]

---

3. Brady also applies this argument against noncognitive theories of emotion such as D'Arms and Jacobson (2003) and Prinz (2004), who maintain that emotions are functionally or involve appraisals. However, their possible circularity, which concerns the semantic project of defining value concepts rather than the metaphysical task of determining value properties, is not my worry here because I have rejected these theories of emotion on independent grounds elsewhere in this book.

Therefore, the combination of emotional cognitivism and metaethical sentimentalism appears to be a dead end right from the outset (see Svensson, 2004, for a particularly thorough discussion of this problem).

However, it is important to observe that the circularity problem focuses on the possibility of analysing value concepts in terms of appropriate emotional responses. If we do not read the response-dependency thesis as a conceptual or semantic claim but instead as a metaphysical claim about the nature of value properties, then the thesis may retain its appeal. The idea is that a particular joke is, for instance, funny if amusement is an appropriate response to hearing the joke for the first time. It may be possible to track value properties by the means of appropriate emotions that ascribe the same properties to particular objects and events even if a definition of value concepts in terms of such responses would be circular or vacuous. The main challenge for this proposal is how to fix the relevant notion of appropriateness. Unfortunately, this task has turned out to be notoriously difficult, amounting to the second main problem for neosentimentalist theories of value.

The conflation problem refers to the difficulty of distinguishing between reasons that are relevant and irrelevant for the appropriateness or warrant of emotions. D'Arms and Jacobson (2000a) coined this problem as the "conflation problem", whereas Rabinowicz and Rønnow-Rasmussen (2004) analysed a similar, "wrong kind of reason" problem in all buck-passing theories of value. The problem is that insofar as neosentimentalist theories of value are incapable of discriminating between reasons that are relevant and irrelevant for the appropriateness or warrant of emotions or other pro-attitudes, they conflate these reasons together. Prudential, strategic, moral, and all-in reasons may often repudiate an emotion even though evidential reasons render it appropriate or warranted. We may recall or imagine situations, for instance, in funerals and other formal ceremonies, where it would be rude and imprudent and therefore all-in unreasonable to be amused by a particular event, even though the event is actually funny. Rabinowicz and Rønnow-Rasmussen (2004) focus on contrary cases, in which we have seemingly good reasons to have an emotion or another pro-attitude even though the object intuitively lacks the evaluative property that our pro-attitude ascribes to it. Their prime example is a demon who wants us to admire him for his malicious set of mind and threatens to punish us if we don't admire him. This seems like a psychologically viable reason for admiration, although we intuitively think that this kind of malicious mind does not merit admiration. However, insofar as we are unable to discriminate between relevant and irrelevant reasons for appropriate emotions, the neosentimentalist program is seriously flawed or at least incomplete.

In what follows, I focus on the conflation problem in neosentimentalist theories that restrict the scope of relevant values to those with a one-to-one relationship with some particular sentiment or emotion, such as fear, anger, shame, pride, embarrassment, and amusement. It is an open question as to whether or not other values allow a sentimentalist explication, but I do not engage in that study here as it has not been the aim of most neosentimentalist theories. Instead, I introduce the conflation problem in existing neosentimentalist theories in more detail. I then proceed to D'Arms and Jacobson's solution to this problem in terms of fitting reasons. I am sympathetic to their way of defining reasons of fit on the basis of each emotion's characteristic concern as well as to their strategy of examining actual emotions piecemeal in order to find the criteria of fitting responses. However, I argue that their project has not yielded plausible results. In general, D'Arms and Jacobson exaggerate the agent-relativity of reasons of fit for such emotions as fear and envy and the objectivity of those reasons for amusement and disgust. This suggests that we need an alternative account of reasons of fit. As such an account I investigate Danielsson and Olson's distinction between content-reasons and holding-reasons in which the former kind of reasons bear on correctness of emotional evaluation. Unfortunately, content-reasons prove to be as uninformative as D'Arms and Jacobson's reasons of fit. Finally, I introduce a proposal that emerges from my account of emotional truth, presented in the previous chapter.

The conflation problem

The conflation problem emerges from the ambivalence of such notions as "appropriate", "rational", and "warrant" to which neosentimentalist theories have referred in their analyses of value concepts or properties in accordance with different versions of the response-dependence thesis – conceptual and metaphysical. Several criteria appear to be relevant when we appraise the appropriateness or warrant of particular emotions, such as amusement, envy, or shame. However, some criteria are more relevant than others, some of which can be even quite irrelevant. Neosentimentalist theories are aware of this problem as they maintain that it is possible to rank sensibilities "according to whether there are better *reasons* for one sensibility's responses than another's", as McDowell (1997a, p. 220) points out. Even so, D'Arms and Jacobson argue that these theories are notoriously unclear about what kind of reasons qualify as better than others and how the relevant reasons are to be found and differentiated from other reasons.

 Both McDowell and Blackburn maintain that we can improve our sensitivity to Φ properties (a general term for response-dependent properties). Thus, Blackburn (1984, p. 79) writes, "My attitudes ought to be formed from qualities I admire – the proper use of knowledge, real capacity for sympathy, and so on". In a like manner, McDowell (1997a, p. 221), in discussing reasons for preferring the deliverances of one sensibility over another, suggests that "there is no reason not to appeal to all the resources at our disposal, including all the ethical concepts that we can lay hands on, so long as they survive critical scrutiny". However, D'Arms and Jacobson remark that it is not obvious that every kind of improvement of sensibility constitutes an increased sensitivity to the response-dependent property Φ. An increase in sympathy may refine one's sense of humour, thus constituting a rational improvement. Yet if the new, morally refined sense of humour is less sensitive to the funny, then the refinement is founded on the wrong kind of reason and does not constitute an improvement of the right kind. D'Arms and Jacobson observe that McDowell is aware of the danger of bringing moral considerations to bear on the merit of amused responses. Even so, his advice to appeal to all ethical recourses at our disposal in deciding whether or not a response is merited, together with his adherence to the unity of the virtues suggests that he is not able to ward off comic moralism, which constitutes a decrease in sensitivity to the funny.

Next D'Arms and Jacobson consider the neosentimentalist theory of Wiggins. He purports to avoid the conflation problem by means of working from within evaluative practices. Wiggins eschews reasons talk and appeals to the relevant sensibilities themselves. Even so, his manner of talking about "marks" of Φ properties which are "made for" the associated emotional responses suggests that those "marks" figure in the account as reasons for the correct ascription of Φ properties to objects. Wiggins offers a speculative account of the social evolution of evaluative properties and responses in human practices, which sheds some light on the "made-for" relation between responses and Φ properties as well as on the descriptive "marks" of the latter, identified by way of our responses. No reduction of Φ properties to their "marks" is available or forthcoming, but ascriptions of Φ properties can be criticized and refined partly by appeal to the "marks" of property and partly by appeal to the nature of the shared responses.

D'Arms and Jacobson argue that Wiggins is vague and abstract when it comes to determining what a given sentiment is made for. "This much is clear: different cultures find different things funny, disgusting, shameful, and so on. Their differing histories of reflection and refinement, driven by social pressures imposed by the feelings and judgments of a community, inevitably establish disparate standards of shameful" (D'Arms & Jacobson, 2000b, p. 737). Yet it is obvious that communal standards do not settle questions about the correct ascription of those properties. Shame need not be an appropriate response to homosexuality, for instance, even if prevailing standards of one's community are adamant about the matter. Wiggins appreciates this point by emphasising that the "marks" of evaluative properties must be essentially contestable in order for these properties to serve their function in normative discourse. D'Arms and Jacobson do not object, but they point out that "simply to adduce essential contestability without further explication and at such a high level of abstraction threatens to undermine the suggestion that we can understand the appropriateness of a sentiment by appeal to what it is made for – a suggestion that itself needed support" (ibid., p. 738). Therefore, they conclude that Wiggins has not made any headway towards the solution of the conflation problem.

The most promising neosentimentalist theory in D'Arms and Jacobson's view is Gibbard's. He suggests that we should understand the question of whether an emotion is rational as a question of its warrant. Thus, Gibbard distinguishes *evidential* reasons for feeling a given emotion from strategic, moral, and all-in reasons, and maintains that "what is rational to feel about something settles what to feel" (Gibbard, 1990, p. 49), while judgments of rationality are identified with a thin, flavourless endorsement. However, the problem is that "the warranted feeling is not always what to feel, all things considered", as D'Arms and Jacobson (2000b, p. 743) point out. Bad consequences of being ashamed of one's academic inabilities, for instance, may trump considerations of warrant that render those inabilities shameful. There is a conflict between warranting and prudential reasons here, which Gibbard accommodates by distinguishing between the rationality of an attitude, either belief or emotion, and the rationality of wanting to have this attitude. "Rationally *feeling* or *believing* something is distinct from rationally *wanting* to feel or believe it", Gibbard (ibid., p. 37) writes. Unfortunately, this distinction is not very helpful for a person who endorses both feeling shame for evidential reasons and the desire not to feel ashamed for prudential reasons, because it leads him to an impasse: "he would feel counterproductive shame while vainly desiring not to feel it" (D'Arms and Jacobson, 2000b, p. 744). This impasse shows that endorsement may not settle what it is rational to feel.

D'Arms and Jacobson argue that it would be more plausible to let the subject endorse not feeling ashamed of his inabilities after weighing all the reasons, while also thinking that shame is warranted in the situation. This shows that the question of whether X is Φ is different from whether it is rational to feel F in response to X. More importantly, however, the question of whether X is Φ is also different from whether anyone is warranted in feeling F at X. This is because "whether someone is warranted in feeling an emotion depends upon the evidence he has about the circumstance, but whether the circumstance is Φ may not depend on any such thing" (D'Arms & Jacobson, 2000b, p. 745). People may be unaware of some relevant evidence or, worse still, their evidence may be systematically misleading. In such cases, the subjects are warranted in feeling F even if the object of their emotion is not Φ. Therefore, D'Arms and Jacobson (ibid.) conclude that "judgments that X is Φ are not judgments about the warrant of the relevant sentiments".

D'Arms and Jacobson emphasize that their criticism is not that sentimentalist theories "*must* fall prey to the conflation of relevant and irrelevant reasons to feel, but that they *do*" (D'Arms & Jacobson, 2000b, p. 736, original italics). Since I agree with this criticism, I do not attempt to defend the theories that D'Arms and Jacobson discuss. Instead, my primary interest lies in their proposed solution of the conflation problem.[4] I shall next focus on this proposal, which turns out to be seriously incomplete as it stands.

Reasons of fit

D'Arms and Jacobson share the basic neosentimentalist intuition that the search for the right kind of reasons must start from within, from the sensibilities themselves. They argue that we need a specific and limited form of appropriateness which does not collapse into strategic, moral, evidential, or all-in reasons to feel an emotion. They postulate that *fittingness* constitutes this specific kind of rational assessment of emotions. "Reasons of fit are those reasons that speak directly to what one takes the emotion to be concerned with, as opposed to reasons that speak to the advisability or propriety of having that emotion" (D'Arms & Jacobson, 2006a, p. 108). For instance, the characteristic concerns of fear are *threats*, whereas sorrow focuses on *losses*, disgust on *contamination*, and shame on *social disabilities*. All these concerns are deep, and they have a wide psychological role in almost all humans, which renders them plausible candidates for human values. Accordingly, fitting reasons for fear are those reasons that speak to whether or not something is a threat, whereas fitting reasons for sorrow focus on whether or not some event constitutes a loss.[5] In the same way, each emotion has a generic evaluative presentation that our glosses are capable of capturing only in a rough-and-ready and disputable manner.[6]

So far, the proposed account of fittingness is uncontroversial. It is compatible with the well-known argument from *formal objects*, which states that for each emotion there is a characteristic evaluative category, a formal object, that constitutes

---

4.   Rabinowicz and Rønnow-Rasmussen (2004) discuss several possible solutions to the wrong kind of reason problem, but eventually reject them all. Accordingly, they are pessimists about the solvability of the problem.

5.   In a like manner, Rabinowicz and Rønnow-Rasmussen (2004, p. 421) point out that "reasons for an attitude are of the right kind only if they speak to the attitudes' characteristic concern".

6.   In contrast to D'Arms and Jacobson, Roberts (2003) offers detailed analyses of emotion-specific construals. He argues that emotional content is expressible in terms of utterances with propositional content even in those cases where the content does not causally depend on concepts. I agree with Roberts that it is possible to provide detailed descriptions of the content of typical adult human emotions. However, such descriptions may be metaphorical at best in the case of pre-linguistic human and animal emotions whose content I have argued to be nonconceptual in Chapter 2.

the general representational content and the standard of fittingness for individual emotions of that type (see e.g. Kenny, 1963; de Sousa, 1987; Goldie, 2004; Teroni, 2007). Typical examples of formal objects are dangers or threats for fear, losses for sorrow, slights for anger, contamination for disgust and so on. D'Arms and Jacobson's glosses of emotion-specific concerns figure thus as formal objects of emotions. The problem is how to flesh out the notion of fittingness in a substantial and informative manner.

Considering D'Arms and Jacobson's sensitivity to the shortcomings of other neosentimentalist theories in solving the conflation problem, they are surprisingly brief about the nature of their own reasons of fit. True enough, they argue at length that those deep and wide concerns that underlie our emotions impose constraints on the tenability of norms of fittingness. This argument is directed mainly against perfectionist theories, such as Stoicism or Christianity, which deny the legitimacy of some or all emotional concerns and, hence, the fittingness of some emotions, such as envy and anger, *tout court*. Important as this question may be, it is nevertheless distinct from the one that concerns the nature of reasons of fit. All we learn about the latter question is that almost all humans, when they are in the right context, have such reasons, and that the right context for each emotion depends on whether the emotion's characteristic concern is being impinged upon.[7] Thus, for instance, in order to have fitting reasons for fear, one must be in danger. But this is hardly news to anybody. We all know that reasons of fit are context-relative in this sense.

A more interesting claim about reasons of fit is that "anyone in the right context has reason to feel F, irrespective of his values and emotional propensities" (D'Arms & Jacobson, 2006a, p. 114). Again, this is not a substantial claim about reasons of fit, but it is nevertheless highly important because it implies that the same things have, in the right context, the same value to all humans. This is a bold claim, but D'Arms and Jacobson are ready to bite the bullet at least in the case of some emotions, such as amusement, shame, and disgust. Prudential emotions, such as fear, grief, and envy, whose characteristic concerns have to do with what is good or bad for the agent, have more relational reasons of fit. Thus, even if the death of every human individual is a loss to someone, it is not a loss to those people who had no tangible relation with the deceased. This is obvious even though the relationality appears to concern fitting objects of emotion rather than reasons of fit themselves, which are the same for all individuals whose concerns are impinged upon in the relevant situations.

---

7.   D'Arms and Jacobson specify that the excluded group includes "some autistics, sociopaths and other outliers" who may lack the emotional capacities necessary for being sensitive to sentimental values.

Although D'Arms and Jacobson's general description of reasons of fit is mea-gre, this is not an entirely surprising outcome, given their earlier statement that reasons of fit can be discovered by examining our actual emotions piecemeal, by articulating "differences in how each emotion presents some feature of the world to us when we are in its grip" (D'Arms & Jacobson, 2000b, p. 746). In accordance with this strategy, D'Arms and Jacobson provide detailed analyses of envy and amusement and their fitting reasons. In what follows, I focus on these analyses as examples of the general plausibility of D'Arms and Jacobson's proposal.

D'Arms and Jacobson point out that "the paradigm cases of envy concern goods that contribute to determining an agent's social position" (D'Arms & Jacob-son, 2006a, p. 120). A typical example is one's colleague's promotion, which con-stitutes a cost to one's own relative position. However, all goods that can function as assets in interpersonal comparison and competition may become positional goods, whose distribution plays an important role in people's self-esteem and wel-fare. Indeed, D'Arms and Jacobson maintain that all pursuit of excellence in various endeavors from scholarship to the arts, industry, and sports, however in-trinsically motivated, also manifests a stake in positional goods, not least because the standards of excellence are defined as a function of the performance of others, at least within a local comparison class. Even those who do not pursue excellence manifest interest in positional goods by trying to avoid falling to the bottom of their reference group, by dropping down a league, if necessary. Thus, D'Arms and Jacobson conclude: "Once it is granted that positional goods matter for human flourishing, then it follows that envy is sometimes fitting, because the success of rivals can be bad for an agent in the way envy suggests: it marks a comparative loss" (ibid., pp. 123–124).

The main problem with D'Arms and Jacobson's account of fitting envy emerg-es from what I call their "sociological conception of rivalry". D'Arms and Jacobson observe, correctly, that people affiliate to various reference groups whose charac-teristic practices involve them in the pursuit of positional goods, whose posses-sion constitutes the standard of success or excellence and, hence, status within the group. I call this conception of rivalry sociological because it takes rivalry within the various practices as a social fact, without raising the question about the inde-pendent value of those goods that constitute the objects of rivalry. However, this question appears to be relevant when we think which objects are *truly* enviable, rather than *de facto* enviable for members of actual groups. True enough, having or lacking some highly esteemed positional good may affect the agent's self-es-teem and subjective well-being, which renders the good *prima facie* enviable. Yet if the value of being enviable derives ultimately from human flourishing, which is a more objective notion than subjective well-being,[8] we should perhaps require that the positional goods whose possession warrants fitting envy are valuable also on some independent grounds, in addition to their being positional goods in social rivalry.

To illustrate this argument, let us go back to the example of the members of the National Rifle Association, gun lovers who take pride in their possession of modern firearms: handguns, assault rifles, machine pistols, and whatnot. The members of this organization may proudly present these weapons to each other in their meetings at shooting clubs. Accordingly, these articles constitute positional goods whose possession defines, at least in part, one's social status in the local branch of the organization. Thus, when one member presents an especially fine specimen of the (in)famous Kalashnikov AK-47 assault rifle at the shooting club, other members find the rifle enviable. According to D'Arms and Jacobson's sociological conception of rivalry, these people's envy is fitting in this context if their lack of this gun inflicts a loss to their self-esteem and welfare that are relevant for their flourishing. However, if we think about the intrinsic value of guns for human flourishing, their value is actually a *disvalue*, for it is hard to imagine circumstances where guns, and assault rifles in particular, would promote human flourishing. The only exception is their strictly controlled police and military use, where the value of guns is purely instrumental, not positional.

The example indicates that reasons of fit for prudential emotions are not as agent-relative as D'Arms and Jacobson think. Another way to put the point in their own terms is to say that what is good or bad for the agent, or what is in his or her

---

8.   D'Arms and Jacobson speak about human flourishing without relating this notion to any specific theory about the ultimate end or *telos* of human beings that constitutes the framework for traditional accounts of human flourishing. Instead, they give examples of endeavors with internal standards of excellence that contribute to human flourishing. These endeavors include the arts, industry, scholarship, and athletics. This approach resembles the strategy of Alasdair MacIntyre (1981), who advocates a teleological theory of ethics without a metaphysical *telos*. For MacIntyre, human flourishing relates to virtuous striving of excellence within the practices of one's community. However, he argues that flourishing also requires an overarching *telos* beyond internal goods achieved through excellence within practices. Such *telos* emerges from a narrative unity of life spent seeking for the good life for oneself and humans in general within a particular moral tradition together with others. MacIntyre's communitarian account of human *telos* has been criticized for its vagueness and conformist implications (e.g. Kymlicka, 1990). Yet its lesson is that D'Arms and Jacobson's allusions to human flourishing require some normative framework that would explicate how the various endeavors with internal standards of excellence contribute to human flourishing. And even if they do not provide such a framework, it is obvious that flourishing understood as excellence in such inherently social endeavors as the arts, industry, scholarship and athletics has more objective standards than subjective well-being that is generally defined in terms of experienced positive and negative affect and cognitively evaluated life satisfaction (e.g. Diener, 2000).

interests, does not depend on the agent's actual judgment. If goodness or badness for an agent depends on the agent's own judgment in the first place, it must depend on an ideally well-informed, rational judgment rather than on an actual one. True enough, not getting something one thinks is good for oneself when some relevant other gets it may undermine one's relative social position and, thus, perceived self-esteem and subjective well-being. However, the previous example suggests that these effects do not provide sufficient criteria for the object's being enviable, because this would imply that anything can qualify as a fitting object of envy insofar as it functions as a positional good in some human practice. But since the status of being a positional good cannot turn an intrinsically worthless thing into a valuable one, we must maintain that a fitting object of envy must be independently valuable on moral, aesthetic, epistemic, eudaemonistic, pragmatic, or similar grounds, or it must be instrumentally valuable in the service of some intrinsic value, in addition to being valuable as a positional good. Indeed, D'Arms and Jacobson's examples of endeavours in which positional goods are distributed include scholarship, the arts, industry, and sports, where intrinsic values of different kinds are pursued, but not for instance organised crime, counterfeiting, or torture even if some standards of 'excellence' are conceivable in these intrinsically immoral practices as well. These examples indicate that D'Arms and Jacobson presuppose some view of human flourishing that encompasses endeavors whose internal goods are intrinsically valuable and rules out inherently immoral endeavors, even if they do not explicate this view.[9]

The alternative view about fitting envy that emerges from this discussion falls between D'Arms and Jacobson's sociological view and the equally radical Stoic view that envy is systematically unfitting, which they criticise. However, the Stoic view is clearly a straw man, and D'Arms and Jacobson have not provided an argument to

---

9.   Fabrice Teroni (oral communication) is worried that my view of truly enviable objects that requires them to have an intrinsic value of some kind besides being positional goods in social rivalry is overly stringent. He maintains that people flourish or not as a function of their obtaining positional goods and anticipates that I have a hard time trying to convince many of my readers that social inclusion, prestige, and the like are irrelevant for human flourishing. Fortunately, I do not defend such a claim. I recognize the importance of prestige and social inclusion for flourishing, but I am more optimistic than Teroni about the contexts in which such positional goods are typically pursued. That excellence in an endeavor qualifies as a positional good in a community already requires that the endeavor and its internal good enjoy wide social esteem. This indicates that the internal good is regarded as intrinsically valuable at least within the relevant community. Of course, there may be communities whose views of intrinsically valuable endeavors are immoral from a more enlightened perspective, such as terrorist cells or criminal organizations. However, I do not believe that many of my readers derive their flourishing from prestige and inclusion in such communities or think them as viable contexts for deriving positional goods that are conducive to human flourishing.

show that their sociological view about envy is preferable to an account which maintains that fitting objects of envy must have intrinsic value on some further ground or grounds, in addition to being positional goods in a social practice.

A contrary problem haunts D'Arms and Jacobson's view that certain sentimental values are universal, that is, independent from the agent's values and emotional propensities. D'Arms and Jacobson see the hardness of the bullet they are willing to bite. They discuss in passing the conditions in which a Chinese peasant who speaks no English has reason to be amused at the witticisms of Oscar Wilde, which they present as examples of truly amusing jokes. D'Arms and Jacobson (2006a, p. 114) suggest that the right context for having a fitting reason to be amused at a joke "requires at least that one have heard the joke and understood it".[10] Yet these are clearly just minimal conditions because they are obviously insufficient, especially in the case of Wilde and the Chinese peasant. Hearing and understanding a literal translation of a joke from an entirely different culture rarely conveys the point of the joke, unless the point is about some very general theme pertaining to the universal human condition. We typically need some background knowledge about the cultural context from which a joke originates in order to be able to share and appreciate its point. This is clearly the case with D'Arms and Jacobson's other example of the truly funny: the early Woody Allen movies, whose humour, apart from their physical comedy, emerges from the sexual and other neuroses of contemporary urban liberal-minded intellectuals.

These examples suggest that the value of being amusing that emerges from our responses of amusement is culturally relative, even though the borders between cultures can in some cases be transcended, which creates the impression of a universal value. The same objection applies to disgust, which D'Arms and Jacobson also present as a sensibility in which "anyone in the right context has reason to feel F, irrespective of his values and emotional propensities". Yet the property of being disgusting, even in its evolutionarily original gustatory context, is so dependent on individual and communal preferences that it is difficult to comprehend how D'Arms and Jacobson can argue to the contrary.[11] In a like manner,

---

10. In a more recent article, D'Arms and Jacobson (2010) discuss the instability of affective responses as a problem for the determination of stable sentimental values. Accordingly, they are somewhat more specific about the conditions in which, for instance, jokes can reliably track the property of being funny than in the earlier article. However, the instability problem relates only indirectly to the problem of fitting reasons, which is not discussed in the relevant article.

11. Rozin, Haidt, and McCauley (2008) argue that variety in disgust sensibility is present even at biologically early stages of disgust whose organising principle is oral rejection of bad-tasting or contaminating items, let alone at the later stages of interpersonal and moral disgust. To focus on contamination, which D'Arms and Jacobson regard as the characteristic concern of disgust, "most cultures value some kind of decayed/fermented food that is disgusting in most other

moral disgust relates to transgressions against a perceived natural order that depends on culturally varying metaphysical and religious beliefs (Prinz, 2007). Different forms of disgust may constitute an evolutionary continuum on which concerns of contamination were first applied to the body and later to the soul as well. Yet individual and cultural differences in disgust sensitivity are so wide that "there is no overarching abstract definition of the class of disgust elicitors", as Rozin, Haidt, and McCauley (2008, p. 771) argue. This conclusion is in sharp contrast with that of D'Arms and Jacobson who exaggerate the agent-relativity of reasons of fit for such emotions as fear and envy and the objectivity of those reasons for amusement and disgust.

Therefore, I conclude that D'Arms and Jacobson fail to provide a plausible account of emotional fittingness that is capable of solving the conflation problem. Their general description of reasons of fit, which emphasises the right context, is overly abstract, as this context is defined in terms of each emotion's characteristic concern. Worse still, their characterization of reasons of fit in terms of our having them in the right context is uninformative without independent criteria for determining when the characteristic concerns or sentimental values are at stake. Feeling an emotion suggests to the subject of the emotion that the relevant concern is at stake; indeed emotions serve as heuristic detectors of such concerns (Prinz, 2004). However, the impression can be deceptive because emotions can be misplaced. Sometimes we feel afraid when we are not in danger, or angry when we have not been offended. Therefore, D'Arms and Jacobson's recommended strategy to locate reasons of fit by articulating "differences in how each emotion presents some feature of the world to us when we are in its grip" (D'Arms & Jacobson, 2000b, p. 746) is unsatisfactory. Being in the grip of emotion does not guarantee that the subject is "in the right context with respect to the value in question" (D'Arms & Jacobson, 2006a, p. 114). Indeed, this seems to be the case only when the emotion is felt for reasons of the right kind. But if the right context and reasons of fit can be identified only interchangeably, the account remains uninformative and circular, or "elliptical" as D'Arms and Jacobson (ibid.) put it.

---

cultures, but such food varies quite a bit", as Rozin at al. (ibid., p. 766) point out. To support this view with some anecdotal evidence, the traditional Swedish dish of *surströmming* (sour Baltic herring) tastes awful (rotten) to non-Swedes, and many foreigners are so disgusted at the feces-like appearance of the traditional Finnish Easter dessert *mämmi* – which tastes like sweet malt – that they cannot even taste it. The Scottish *haggis*, including the idea of its contents, also raises nausea in many. Finally, fermented dairy products such as yoghurt and cheeses that Westerners generally enjoy arouse disgust in many Asians.

Appropriateness as correctness

Another prospective solution to the wrong kind of reasons problem has been inspired by Franz Brentano's distinction between truth and correctness as analogous epistemic standards for beliefs and pro-attitudes, respectively. Sven Danielsson and Jonas Olson (2007) have invoked this distinction in suggesting that pro-attitudes can be correct or incorrect in the same way that beliefs can be true or false.[12] In the same way as the right kind of reasons for beliefs bear on the truth of beliefs, rather than on the beneficiality of having the belief, so too the right kind of reasons for pro-attitudes bear on the correctness of those attitudes rather than on the beneficiality of having the attitude. Accordingly, Danielsson and Olson introduce a distinction between two types of reasons, *content-reasons* and *holding-reasons*. Content-reasons provide arguments for the correctness of a pro-attitude, whereas holding-reasons are reasons for having the relevant attitude. Content-reasons also give rise to defeasible holding-reasons for attitudes. "Just as we ought in most cases, to have true beliefs or at least avoid having false beliefs, we ought in most cases to have correct conative attitudes or at least avoid having incorrect attitudes" (ibid., p. 519). Such holding-reasons derived from content-reasons also qualify as reasons of the right kind. For instance, if we have a content-reason to admire a talented artist, we also have a holding-reason to have that correct attitude. However, the opposite is not the case: holding-reasons do not give rise to content-reasons. We have a holding-reason to admire the evil demon in the problem case because he threatens to punish us if we don't admire him, but this reason does not render the demon admirable even if it may warrant this emotional attitude from an all-things-considered perspective in spite of its incorrectness in such an abnormal and bizarre case.

The distinction between content-reasons and holding-reasons seems capable of providing plausible responses to hard cases. We have holding-reasons to admire the evil demon, but these reasons do not render his malevolence admirable because they do not provide reasons for the correctness of this attitude. However, the distinction remains insufficient insofar as we attempt to identify value properties in terms of sentiments that are warranted by content-reasons. The problem is that the analogy between the truth of beliefs and the correctness of pro-attitudes breaks

---

12. Danielsson and Olson point out that Brentano originally made the distinction between judgments ('Urteile') and conative attitudes ('Gemütsbewegungen', 'Lieben und Hassen'), conceived as psychological attitudes. Beliefs are indisputable examples of judgments that are capable of being true and false, whereas the contemporary term of pro-attitudes refers to conative and evaluative attitudes for which correctness may qualify as an analogue of truth. However, Danielsson and Olson do not aspire to historical accuracy in their interpretation of Brentano,

down on a closer analysis as there is an important distinction in their respective truth and correctness conditions. To quote Jennie Louise (2009, p. 352),

> Truth predicated of belief is not primitive, but rather rests upon the truth of the proposition that is believed. But the point of the normative-priority account is to *deny* the analogous claim about correct pro-attitudes: the truth-analogues for conative attitudes would be evaluative predicates, so that the correctness of admiration would depend on the admirability of the thing that is admired. Normative priority says that there are no analogues to propositional truth in the case of pro-attitudes. The normative-priority account of correct attitudes therefore has a different structure to that of true belief.

Since pro-attitudes are correct if and only if there are reasons for their correctness, the content of pro-attitudes cannot provide a correctness condition for them in the same way as the content of beliefs provides the truth condition for beliefs. Consequently, Danielsson and Olson and other normative neosentimentalists cannot appeal to evaluative properties as the basis for correct attitudes.[13] They can appeal only to the descriptive properties of objects that provide content-reasons for the pro-attitudes in terms of which the relevant evaluative properties are explicated. Thus, for instance, 'x is admirable if and only if it has properties that provide content-reasons for admiring x'; which amounts to the same as 'x is admirable if and only if it has properties which make admiration of x correct'.[14]

The main problem with this account is that it is uninformative. It provides *formal* criteria for those emotional responses that are relevant for the identification of corresponding evaluative properties. Even so, we should know more about the correctness conditions of emotions and other pro-attitudes. To quote Deonna and Teroni (2012, p. 48):

---

13. For the distinction between normative and descriptive neosentimentalist theories of value, see Tappolet (2011). Descriptive theories suggest that emotions are perceptual experiences of value and correct when they represent objects accurately as these are. Accordingly, for these theories, the correctness of an emotion is distinct from its justification and therefore does not depend on its warranting reasons but on the epistemic accuracy of its evaluative content. Yet the problem of distinguishing value-tracking emotional responses from incorrect ones remains for these theories as well, even if the problem is framed in different terms that highlight the purported analogy between emotion and perception. However, there are reasons to suspect the solvability of this problem, as for instance Brady (2011) and Salmela (2011) have argued. Therefore, I do not discuss this version of neosentimentalism here.

14. The former formulation is adapted from Danielsson and Olson's (2007, p. 520) claim that x is good means that x has properties that provide content-reasons to favor x, whereas the latter is adapted from Louise's (2009, p. 353) rendering of the same claim as x is good means that x has properties which make favouring x correct.

> Without further specification of the nature of these correctness conditions, we are left with the hardly informative claim that the reasons relevant for the F[itting] A[ttitude]-analysis of evaluative properties are those reasons that make the content of the relevant response correct. This looks more like a way of restating the problem than a way of resolving it.

Therefore, Danielsson and Olson's notion of content-reasons for the correctness of pro-attitudes does not make any headway from D'Arms and Jacobson's proposal in which reasons of fit speak to the characteristic concerns of emotions, defined in terms of formal objects of emotion. In both cases we know that a particular object of emotion has the relevant response-dependent value property if the emotional response is warranted by either content-reasons or reasons of fit, respectively. Yet both accounts are formal as they do not aim at specifying those descriptive properties of particular objects that provide content-reasons or reasons of fit for the relevant emotional responses to those objects. This problem leaves the task of fixing response-dependent value properties by means of corresponding appropriate emotions seriously incomplete.

Appropriateness as truth

In the previous chapter I proposed and defended my account of emotional truth and argued that it offers the best available theoretical account of what it is for an emotion to be true to the world. Truth resembles correctness as an epistemic standard for the right sort of appropriateness of emotional evaluations. Unlike descriptive neosentimentalist theories, however, my anti-realist account of emotional truth does not invoke evaluative properties of objects as the basis for true emotions. True emotions represent evaluative properties that supervene on the descriptive properties of particular objects of emotion. Metaphysically, evaluative properties do not exist independently of emotional responses but are constituted only on the basis of the latter. The supervenience thesis is metaphysically neutral as it merely states that there cannot be a difference in the evaluative properties of two objects without some difference in the descriptive properties of those objects. However, the supervenience thesis does not imply that descriptively dissimilar objects could not have the same evaluative property. The reason is that evaluative properties are multiply realizable as they can supervene on dissimilar descriptive properties. For instance, smells and flavours of different kinds can be disgusting, but if two flavours differ in terms of their disgustingness, there must be some phenomenal difference in their taste as well, whereas indistinguishable tastes are similar also in terms of their disgustingness.

But how can we tell on which descriptive properties of particular objects evaluative properties supervene in specific cases? Like other neosentimental theories, my proposal seeks to elucidate these properties in terms of our appropriate, or in this case, true emotions. To recapitulate, an emotion is true if and only if there is an actual fit between the particular object of emotion and its formal object, and the emotion's propositional content is semantically satisfied or the target of the emotion exists. In addition to fittingness, the proposal also invokes semantic satisfaction in the explication of value-grounding descriptive properties. This is an important amendment because it addresses the problem that D'Arms and Jacobson have with identifying the cases that we should study in attempting to articulate reasons that are and are not relevant for the fittingness of emotions. D'Arms and Jacobson suggest that we should engage in this task when we are in the grip of emotions, but I believe that we should focus on those cases where the propositional content of emotion is semantically satisfied or the target of emotion exists. This means, for instance, that the loss I mourn has actually occurred instead of being merely imagined or anticipated, or that the object of my envy exists, or that the outcome I fear is as probable as my fear takes it to be.

In the case of factive emotions such as joy and grief, the semantic satisfaction of the emotional content and the existence of an emotional target seem trivial requirements. Psychologically, it may be difficult to avoid anticipated grief for an inevitable future loss such as the death of one's terminally ill parent, and such emotion may have important adaptive value in preparing the subject for the upcoming loss. Even so, it is obvious that we should focus on already befallen setbacks rather than anticipated or imagined ones in articulating the features of events that qualify as losses that merit grief instead of mere annoyance. In contrast, with epistemic emotions such as fear and hope, there is no easy way of determining to what extent the probability estimate of the emotion corresponds to the objective probability of the outcome – other people's assessment may be more reliable than one's own when experiencing the emotion. Even so, this criterion is particularly important for the situational appropriateness of epistemic emotions. Of course, semantic satisfaction alone does not make an emotion true, since its particular object must also have properties that render it a fitting object to the relevant emotion type. Yet, it makes more sense to articulate reasons that make emotions fitting on the basis of cases in which our emotions are consistent with non-normative facts than whenever we are in the grip of emotions.[15]

---

15. Obviously, there is another established and popular manner of refining one's sensibilities besides articulation of emotions in which one is directly involved. Empathy allows us to experience vicarious emotions in response to other people's destinies and their emotions in these situations. In literature, empathy is capable of operating in both fiction and non-fiction, but fiction has the edge of offering even more detailed depictions of the protagonists' internal space of

How does my proposed account of fit between the particular and formal object of emotion improve previous neosentimentalist accounts of fittingness discussed above? The first impression is that it doesn't: 'reasons of fit' and 'content-reasons' are coextensive with those reasons that are relevant for whether the particular object of emotion fits the formal object of the emotion type. Similarly to these accounts, mine invokes lower-level, descriptive properties of particular objects that provide reasons for emotional evaluations. Without specifying those properties, which must be done by studying emotional responses piecemeal, as D'Arms and Jacobson suggest, my account nevertheless provides a general characterization of those descriptive properties. They are properties that warrant the ascription of the relevant formal property to the actual object of emotion in a particular community of sensibility and this warrant remains undefeated no matter how much the status of information and understanding in the relevant community is or will be enlarged or improved through a critical, conscientious, imaginative, and sympathetic reflection and discussion.[16]

According to this semi-idealized account of justification, members of the community may not in their reflection and discussion neglect or ignore counter-evidence that is conceivably available to them. Understandable limitations to available evidence include historical, cultural, and social limitations. Historical limitations concern information that is not available to a community because no one has discovered it yet. The shape of the Earth as a globe is such a fact that influenced, for instance, the warrant of fear of falling off the edge of the world for

---

reasons than most genres of non-fiction, with memoirs and in-depth interviews excluded perhaps. In suggesting that we should focus on cases in which the evaluative content of emotion is satisfied or the target of emotion exists when articulating the reasons that render emotions fitting, I do not wish to deny or downplay the role of empathic understanding in the refinement of our emotional sensibilities. However, I surmise that the capacity of fictive works to arouse our empathic fellow-feelings, insofar as these works have this capacity, emerges from the non-fictive roots of fiction in emotional experiences of real people that the author has been capable of combining and restructuring in an original yet psychologically credible manner.

16. Joshua Gert (2012, p. 101) argues that "it is the *social purposes* of the practice of admiring and talking of who to admire that have determined – in conjunction with other contingencies in the development of the concept of the admirable – what counts as admirable and therefore which instances of admiration count as fitting and which do not". This recent Wiggins-style solution to the problem of the wrong kind of reasons eschews reasons-talk and emphasises the role of linguistic practices in determining the criteria of accurate value ascriptions. My proposal is similar to Gert's in invoking communities of sensibility whose evaluative practices provide initial warrant to ascriptions of sentimental values. Yet my account differs from Gert's in being both backward- and forward-looking in terms of warrant. The latter aspect is necessary in order to ward off value ascriptions that are warranted within existing communities of sensibility due to systematic bias, distortion of evidence, irrational reasoning, or other epistemic deficiencies.

centuries. Cultural limitations to available evidence are relevant if communities are geographically or linguistically so isolated from each other that information found in one community does not travel to the other communities. The Japanese culture that was isolated from Western influences until mid-19th century might be an example. However, mere ideological isolation does not qualify as an acceptable limitation, because counterevidence would have been available if the relevant society's members had sought it. This is even more so in the case of social limitations to available evidence. Only a few social arrangements, such as hierarchical class societies in which mobility between classes is non-existent or minimal, group boundaries are sharp, and these boundaries are enforced by violence if necessary, may qualify as societies where social limitations to available evidence bar entire communities of sensibility access to information that could otherwise be available to them. For it is sufficient that individual members have access to counterevidence that is relevant for the continuous warrant of specific value ascriptions in their relevant communities. It can be argued that it is an epistemic duty of the other group members to give the evidence presented by individual members its proper due in the critical, conscientious, imaginative, and sympathetic reflection and deliberation of the community (Mathiesen, 2006).

Accordingly, the evaluative properties of being funny, enviable, admirable, shameful, regrettable, and so on, can be determined in terms of the respective true emotions: amusement, envy, admiration, shame, regret, and so on within the evaluative perspective of the relevant community of sensibility. Emotional experiences ascribe these evaluative properties to their particular objects, but the objects have the relevant properties if and only if the emotion is true in the sense of being both fitting to its actual object by virtue of its descriptive properties, and either having a semantically satisfied content or an existing target.

The main question is whether my proposal is capable of making any headway in the conflation problem. If the reasons that warrant an emotion in a particular community of sensibility are such that this warrant survives an "arbitrarily close scrutiny of its pedigree and arbitrarily extensive increments to or other forms of improvement of our information" (Wright, 1992, p. 48), nothing substantial about the *type* of these reasons seems to have been said. With reference to Danielsson and Olson, these reasons could be characterized as *content reasons* as distinct from *holding reasons* for having the relevant emotion for some strategic or instrumental reasons. However, it is important to notice that several kinds of reasons – moral, aesthetic, and eudaemonistic reasons in addition to the more specifically 'fitting' reasons in D'Arms and Jacobson's sense – may qualify as content-reasons as they can be relevant to the fittingness of emotional evaluations to their objects.

For instance, even if moral considerations are not the primary criteria in our sense of humour, they may on some occasions override purely aesthetic standards if the particular joke is too coarse for its racist or sexist overtones to be truly funny. D'Arms and Jacobson, who oppose comic moralism, claim that "the wrongness of feeling an emotion never, in itself, constitutes a reason that the emotion fails to be fitting" (D'Arms and Jacobson, 2000a, p. 87). Thus, they believe that many racist jokes are actually funny but we refuse to be amused because we also judge them to be coarse and morally objectionable. The point here is that wrongness does not prevent or reduce the joke's amusingness even if it may speak against feeling amused by the joke. However, I doubt that this interpretation rings true to our experience. It would be odd to suggest that those people who find racist or sexist jokes funny in spite their unsavouriness possess a more refined sense of humour than other people who find some jokes of this kind coarse or offensive and therefore not funny. Instead of finding racist or sexist jokes funny *but* coarse and therefore objectionable all-things-considered, the coarseness of jokes with racist or sexist overtones may in some extreme cases be so blatant that it annuls the amusingness of these jokes in the first place, especially if the person who tells the joke is not ironic, sarcastic, or otherwise detached from the content. Jordan and Patridge (2012, p. 93) claim that in those cases, "moral considerations play the role of silencing or disabling *any* reason that an agent might otherwise have to be amused". On this account, moral considerations can be *fit-relevant*, which implies that amusement has a moral shape after all.[17] This conclusion can be generalized to other sensibilities and their fit-relevant reasons. "If what we are concerned about is judging correctly case by case, then judging correctly will involve countenancing considerations of all kinds – prudential and aesthetic, as well as moral" (Jordan & Patridge, 2012, p. 90).

Humour is not the only sensibility where several types of reason may influence the fittingness of emotional evaluations. The sensibility of envy discussed above is an apt example. D'Arms and Jacobson attempt to analyse reasons of fit for envy in terms of positional goods in social status competition. Yet their sociological conception of rivalry relativises enviable objects conspicuously in allowing anything to qualify as a fitting object of envy insofar as it functions as a positional good in some human practice with internal criteria of excellence. But since the status of

---

17. Jordan and Patrigde suggest that the joke-telling context is crucial in silencing reasons that would otherwise count in favour of amusement. One of their examples is Bill Clinton telling a dead baby joke at the United Nation's Special Session on Children. Jordan and Patridge maintain that "dead baby jokes, while providing reasons for amusement in many contexts, when told before the United Nation's Special Session on Children by Bill Clinton simply do not" (p. 92). While accepting the importance of context, I believe that reasons related to the content of jokes may silence reasons for amusement as well. Contrary to Jordan and Patridge, I think that jokes about dead babies, for instance, may qualify as jokes that are *not* funny in *most* contexts because of their gross content.

being a positional good in social rivalry cannot turn an intrinsically worthless thing into a valuable one, as I have argued above, a fitting object of envy must be independently valuable on some other grounds, in addition to being valuable as a positional good. As in the case of humour, fit-relevant reasons for envy may include moral, aesthetic, eudaemonistic, or prudential considerations. Examples of this kind indicate that our sensibilities are not immune to moral and other reasons even if those reasons do not figure as central in these sensibilities.

I suggest then that an actual object of emotion x has the evaluative property Φ if and only if x has a descriptive property or properties that warrant the ascription of Φ to x in the particular community of sensibility and this warrant remains undefeated no matter how much the status of information and understanding in the community is or will be enlarged or improved through a critical, conscientious, imaginative, and sympathetic reflection and discussion. In contrast to D'Arms and Jacobson, I emphasise that different kinds of reasons are capable of contributing to the fittingness of emotions as the previous examples suggest. I favour piecemeal examination of actual emotional responses in finding relevant reasons for emotional evaluations as much as D'Arms and Jacobson, but I do not believe that such an examination is capable of yielding just one type of reason that would capture the essence of fittingness. Danielsson and Olson's notion of content-reasons fares better, but only because many kinds of considerations are capable of providing content-reasons for emotional evaluations. This conclusion is also compatible with the view of Gibbard insofar as his evidential reasons that warrant emotions may involve several kinds of reasons. Reasons that emerge from the characteristic concern of the emotion-type may in some cases be silenced by moral, aesthetic, eudaemonistic, or prudential reasons that in those cases bear on the fittingness of the emotional response to its particular object. This kind of proposal appears to solve the conflation problem by *dissolving* as much as resolving it. In a way, this is my conclusion. My proposal offers a theoretical account of how to distinguish between reasons that are and are not relevant to the fittingness of emotional evaluations, but it does not identify any *single* type of fitting reasons because there are no such reasons for emotional sensibilities, except within distinct emotional episodes perhaps.

The proposed account of sentimental value properties is relativistic as it is cast in terms of semi-idealised epistemic warrant in particular communities of sensibility. However, it is only moderately relativistic because the susceptibility of sentimental values to rational standards of warrant reduces the scope of relativism from what we see to be the case in our world. Indeed, many past or actual communally warranted ascriptions of sentimental values are or have been maintained by means of culpable ignorance or negligence of counterevidence to those value ascriptions that is or would have been available to members of the relevant community. For instance, racist disdain of other ethnic groups or sexist denigration of women fail to qualify as warranted ascriptions of sentimental values, because these emotions are not fitting in light of evidence that is available to racists and sexists, respectively. Indeed, these sentimental values may have never been warranted even though people in some ages and societies have regarded such emotions and the corresponding value ascriptions warranted insofar as members of those communities have not engaged in a critical, conscientious, imaginative, and sympathetic reflection and deliberation of the matter. This view is consistent with the philosophical and common sense intuition that there is progress in the realm of values: old values are being rejected and new values are being established. My sentimentalist theory explains this development in terms of warrant that is cancelled when the state of information and capacities of reflection in a community of sensibility are being enlarged upon or improved. Blackburn, McDowell, and Wiggins have proposed similar views of the development of sentimental values along with the refinement of sensibilities. However, I believe that my account provides a more solid theoretical foundation for this approach.

Conclusion

I believe that my sentimentalist account of values in terms of true emotions is capable of solving the conflation problem that has troubled previous neosentimentalist theories of value. My solution suggests that reasons of the right kind for the fittingness of emotions to their actual objects are those reasons that are relevant to the emotion's characteristic concern and remain undefeated no matter how much our information and understanding is or will be enlarged or improved through a critical, conscientious, imaginative, and sympathetic reflection. Unlike D'Arms and Jacobson's fitting reasons, fit-relevant reasons in my sense cover several types of reasons, with the exception of strategic and instrumental reasons, which means that my solution of the conflation problem dissolves as much as resolves it.

This is bad news for semantic neosentimentalism that purports to define value concepts in terms of appropriate emotions of the right kind. If it is not possible to specify the right kind of reasons, the project of defining value concepts in terms of appropriate emotions remains seriously incomplete. However, the metaphysical project that seeks to identify value properties survives with less severe damage, as the determination of value properties may still proceed on the basis of true emotions. The main limitation of this account is that it is capable of providing a sentimentalist explication of only those value properties that have a one-to-one relation to the associated emotions. Hard questions of whether or not it is possible to give other seemingly response-dependent values, such as elegance, grace, or prettiness, a neosentimentalist explication, and how this can be done, if it can be done, thus remain open. However, since neosentimentalist theories have usually settled for the more limited task, I am satisfied if my proposal from true emotions can make headway in this task, as I believe it can.

CHAPTER 8

Concluding remarks

This book focused on three major philosophical questions about human emotions: what emotions really or *truly are*; what does it mean for an emotion to be *true to the self*; and what does it mean for an emotion to be *true to the world*? I started from the first question, which is fundamental regarding the other two. It does not make much sense to ask whether or how emotions can be true to the self if they have a life of their own at another level of information processing than a person's beliefs, desires, and values that we also take to be central to the self. In a like manner, the question about the truth of emotions to the world presupposes that emotions have a representational content that presents the world as being in some way.

Foundational questions about the nature of emotions – itself one key issue in interdisciplinary emotion research – were dealt with in Chapters 2 and 3 of this book. There I studied the role of cognition in the structure and dynamics of emotion at the functional and algorithmic levels of analysis, using some evidence from the implementational level to support my argumentation at the other two levels of analysis. At the functional level of analysis, all emotions of human and higher animals were found to involve cognition as they include mental representations that mediate between perceptions of emotion-eliciting stimuli and emotional responses. However, this conclusion was uninformative given differences between human and (other) animal emotions and between human emotions of a dissimilar kind – biologically hard-wired, pathological, and ordinary non-pathological. Therefore, I also discussed cognition in emotion at the algorithmic level of processes and types of representation, dividing emotional content into conceptual and nonconceptual, with subdoxastic, logical, and phenomenological subtypes of the latter. Each type of representation was found to fit some human emotions, but none of them was capable of accommodating all or even most human emotions. Moreover, instances of pure types were found to be rare as most human emotions have contents that mix properties of conceptual and nonconceptual content, being more or less conceptual or nonconceptual on a continuum from strongly conceptual to more nonconceptual.

This conclusion calls into question the applicability of dual process models of information processing to human emotions. Many dual-process theorists in cognitive psychology such as Slovic et al. (2004) and Kahneman (2011) agree with the neurophysiologist Damasio (1994, 1999) in associating emotion categorically with fast heuristics that operates on somatic gut feelings with certain valence and intensity rather than on conscious, semantic judgments. Most emotion theorists disagree, suggesting instead that human emotions involve processes of different types, both implicit, associative, and automatic Type 1 processes with nonconceptual content, and explicit, rule-based, and flexible Type 2 processes with conceptual content. These theorists are correct in claiming that both types of processes and representations are involved in ordinary human emotions. However, this does not mean that human emotions can be divided into two radically different kinds as Griffiths (2004) suggests. This is because different types of processes and representations normally operate together in appraising the relevance of the eliciting situation and producing an adaptive emotional response to it. Dual-process theories call such models "default-interventionist". I have preferred this model to the other, parallel-competitive model of dual processing that fits human emotions even worse. However, the default-interventionist model does not fully characterize the nature of interaction between levels of processing in ordinary human emotions either.

Default-interventionist models place the two levels of processing into a certain causal order. A fast intuitive Type 1 processing always precedes a slower analytic Type 2 processing that has at least some opportunity to approve or modify the results of the fast processing. In some cases, such as pre-linguistic infant human emotions; biologically hard-wired adult human emotions like fear of heights; and some pathological human emotions (e.g. post-traumatic stress disorder but not for instance depression and anxiety disorders as these involve distorted cognitions as well), lower level processing is capable of producing full-fledged emotional responses on its own. Yet in ordinary adult human emotions, the appraisal process only begins at the lower level and is completed at the higher level, as both process-oriented appraisal theories and psychological constructionists maintain. Or it begins from a higher level appraisal of the relevance of sensory or conceptual information which recruits the lower level only later, as in Robinson's example of fright over an economic loss. The fact that appraisals of this kind can become automatic and implicit upon learning does not change the role of conceptual cognition in these emotions because the content of the emotion is still cognitive. These considerations indicate that the two levels of processing cooperate in the production of ordinary human emotions to the extent that even the default-interventionist view on the relation of two levels remains overly schematic.

The involvement cognition in ordinary human emotions at the algorithmic level of processing made it possible to distinguish between two important senses of emotional authenticity: descriptive and normative. In the descriptive sense, authenticity coincides with sincerity in emotions. A sincere emotion is a veridical expression of one's actual affective state that is not being suppressed, inflated, or modified by other means. Emotions could enjoy authenticity in this sense even if they were purely noncognitive affects and feelings. However, the other, normative, sense of authenticity is possible for emotions only insofar as they can be evaluated within a wider context of the person's identity, which is inextricably interwoven with his or her conceptions of the good. Authenticity in this sense requires that emotions have a content that is in an inferential relation to our beliefs and values, being capable of having or lacking coherence with the latter. Ordinary human emotions were found to meet this criterion.

The need to distinguish between the two senses of emotional authenticity emerges in several domains, including clinical psychology, sociology of occupations, and gender studies. In this book, I focused on emotional authenticity in occupational life, but a similar account could be given on the transformation of clients' emotions in several psychotherapies. Indeed, the robust involvement of cognition in adult human emotions explains the efficacy of cognitive-behavioural therapies in the treatment of many affective disorders. However, instead of authenticity, existing therapies rely on the terminology of "functional" and "dysfunctional" or "adaptive" and "maladaptive" in evaluating clients' emotions. Functionality and adaptiveness in turn are understood in relation to the subject's goals or needs in a certain environment. Accordingly, these criteria focus on the *consequences* of having a specific emotion in a particular situation.

An adaptive emotion can become maladaptive in two ways: either by a change in the subject's needs and goals, or by a change in his or her circumstances. For instance, a little boy's fear of his father is adaptive if the father is generally hostile to him and rejects the son whenever he feels insecure and seeks protection from the father. However, the emotional schema becomes maladaptive later in the child's life when he generalizes the fear to other senior male figures irrespective of their actual behaviour and thereby fails to form satisfying reciprocal relations with them. Yet the core problem with maladaptive emotions of this kind does not seem to lie in their consequences but instead in their lack of fittingness to the eliciting situation from the subject's more enlightened perspective. Indeed, in his emotion-focused therapy Leslie Greenberg maintains that the adaptiveness of an emotion depends on its coherence with the person's wants, needs, and "other conscious goals, plans, values, and realistic assessments of the situation" (Greenberg, 2002, 175). Greenberg's view is congenial to my notion of emotional authenticity in its normative sense that defines in more detail what it means for an emotion to cohere with the subject's rational epistemic and evaluative attitudes. Accordingly, I put forward the notion of emotional authenticity in both senses, as sincerity and integrity, as a viable conceptual tool for psychotherapeutic theorizing (see Salmela, 2008).

While authenticity represents the truth of an emotion to the self, the notion of emotional truth extends the problem of the fittingness of emotions to an external perspective, namely truth to the world. The evaluative content of emotions is a necessary condition for literal truth to make sense of them, but it is not sufficient because the content of emotions must also have an assertoric logical structure. Thus, I argued that to experience an emotion is to present its particular object as having the formal property of the relevant emotion type, quite in the same way as to believe that p is to present p as having the formal property of beliefs, namely truth. Moreover, I claimed contrary to de Sousa that the truth of an emotion does not depend solely on the fittingness of its evaluative content with the formal object of the emotion type. The propositional content of one's emotion must also be semantically satisfied, or the target of one's emotion must exist. For factive emotions such as joy and sadness, the standard of semantic satisfaction is the truth of the proposition, whereas an epistemic emotion such as hope and fear is semantically satisfied if the subjective probability that the emotion ascribes to the actualisation of the relevant state of affairs corresponds to the objective probability of the actualisation of that state of affairs. Finally, I suggested that the fittingness of an emotion can be understood in terms of an idealised communal warrant such as Crispin Wright's property of superassertibility. This proposal focuses on justificatory reasons for ascriptions of evaluative properties to particular objects in emotions. The criteria of justificatory reasons are communal even if the particular objects of evaluative attitudes vary between individuals, such as in the case of sadness and nostalgia. Therefore, I suggest that justifying reasons for emotional evaluations can also be specified for communities of sensibility rather than merely individually.

Nevertheless, one may wonder, what is the relation between emotional authenticity and truth? If authenticity is presented as an ideal for an individual's emotions, what is the relevance of truth from this perspective? Can and should one aim at truth in one's emotions, in addition to aiming at their authenticity? Or is truth in the world-related sense a plausible standard for emotions in the first place. After all, emotions are so personal and intimately related to the self that truth in this literal sense may not seem to make much sense even if the theoretical question can be formulated and debated. I take this objection seriously as I believe that theoretical notions should have practical relevance for our actual emotional lives.

The relation between emotional authenticity and truth is more harmonious than the first impression may suggest. The notions are cast in somewhat dissimilar terms: authenticity as coherence among one's cognitive and evaluative attitudes, including emotions, and truth in terms of idealised communal warrant by reference to justifying reasons that remain undefeated no matter how much our information is or will be enlarged or improved. However, the distinction between internal and external justification does not mean that in aiming at the former, authenticity, the subject could not simultaneously aim at the latter, truth, from his or her particular point of view. Rather, this is the default mode. This can be seen when we understand authenticity and truth as two complementary perspectives on the situational fittingness or appropriateness of emotions. The normative notion of emotional authenticity views the fittingness of emotions from an individual's epistemic and evaluative perspective in which coherence is a plausible ideal, whereas the notion of emotional truth focuses on the problem of fittingness from a wider, communal perspective in which most careful, informed, imaginative, and sympathetic reflection of the matter and the situation provides a procedural standard of warrant. Indeed, the distinction between authenticity and truth can be framed in terms of the amount and quality of evidence that the subject possesses to evaluate the warrant of an emotion. An emotion is authentic if it is internally justified by the total body of evidence that is conceivably available to the subject even though the emotion may not be justified in a more global sense that is associated with the notion of emotional truth. The ideally enlightened communal warrant that is associated with emotional truth is external to both individual persons and actual human communities but not to human sensitivities as such.

In the final two chapters, I argued that the notions of emotional authenticity and emotional truth can be applied to other debates where these notions can help us to make headway in solving important problems concerning the authenticity of occupational emotions and the constitution of sentimental values, respectively. In the former context, I argued that my distinction between two senses of authenticity allows us to remove the paradox of authenticity from emotions experienced in a work role. I also explicated some conditions, both internal and external, on which occupational emotions may qualify as authentic in the normative sense. In the latter, metaethical context I suggested that the notion of emotional truth best captures the sentimentalist idea of fitting emotions that are based on reasons of the right kind. Unlike many other proposals, mine does not present reasons of any privileged type as the right kind of reasons. Instead, it allows reasons of several types, with the exception of strategic and instrumental reasons, to qualify as fitting in particular situations. The notion of emotional truth provides a procedural standard for specifying the reasons which come out as fitting at the end of the day, i.e. after an ideally critical, conscientious, imaginative, and sympathetic reflection and discussion. This proposal may seem as formal as the ones I rejected for their emptiness. However, I believe that it does better justice to our actual justificatory practices in relation to judgments about values that ontologically depend on human sensibilities.

"True emotion" is then an ambiguous notion and indeed a nexus of several core problems in the philosophy of emotions. I hope that this book has been able to illuminate and refine these problems, some of which have been discussed under different headings in other contexts. My main aim has been to show how these problems relate to each other and together form a plausible area of research. If the volume succeeds in bringing these questions closer to the forefront in philosophical and interdisciplinary emotion research, it has served its purpose. Together with introducing three problems of "true emotions", I have sketched my own solutions to these problems. The jury is out on their plausibility within the community of critical, conscientious, imaginative and – hopefully also – sympathetic emotion researchers.

References

Abraham, R. (2000). The role of job control as a moderator of emotional dissonance and emotional intelligence-outcome relationships. *Journal of Psychology*, 134, 169–185. DOI: 10.1080/00223980009600860

Abraham, R. (1998). Emotional dissonance in organizations: Antecedents, consequences, and moderators. *Genetic, Social & General Psychology Monographs*, 124, 229–247.

Airaksinen, T. (1998). Professional ethics. In R. Chadwick (Ed.), *Encyclopedia of applied ethics*, Vol 3 (pp. 671–682). San Diego: Academic Press.

Aristotle. (1954). *The Nicomachean ethics*. Translated by W.D. Ross. London: Oxford University Press.

Armon-Jones, C (1991). *Varieties of affect*. London: Harvester Wheatsheaf.

Ashforth, B.E. & Humphrey, R.H. (1993). Emotional labour in service roles: The influence of identity. *The Academy of Management Review*, 18, 88–115.

Ashforth, B.E & Mael, F. (1989). Social identity theory and the organization. *The Academy of Management Review*, 14, 20–39.

Ashforth, B.E. & Tomiuk, M.A. (2000). Emotional labour and authenticity. Views from service agents. In S. Fineman (Ed.), *Emotions in organizations* (pp. 184–203). London: SAGE. DOI: 10.4135/9781446219850.n10

Aue, T., Flyht, A., & Scherer, K. (2007). First evidence for differential and sequential efferent effects of stimulus relevance and goal conduciveness appraisal. *Biological Psychology*, 74, 347–357. DOI: 10.1016/j.biopsycho.2006.09.001

Aue. T. & Scherer. K. (2008). Appraisal-driven somatovisceral response patterning: Effects of intrinsic pleasantness and goal conduciveness. *Biological Psychology*, 79, 158–164. DOI: 10.1016/j.biopsycho.2008.04.004

Aue, T. & Scherer, K. (2011). Effects of intrinsic pleasantness and goal conduciveness appraisals on somatovisceral responding: Somewhat similar, but not identical. *Biological Psychology*, 86, 65–73. DOI: 10.1016/j.biopsycho.2010.10.008

Averill, J.R. (1982). *Anger and aggression: an essay on emotion*. New York: Springer. DOI: 10.1007/978-1-4612-5743-1

Averill, J.R. (2005). Emotions as mediators and as products of creative activity. In J. Kaufman & J. Baer (Eds.), *Creativity across domains: Faces of the muse* (pp. 225–243). Mahwah, NJ: Erlbaum.

Averill, J.R. & Nunley, E.P. (1992). *Voyages of the heart*. New York: The Free Press.

Averill, J.R., Hahn, D.W., & Chon, K.K. (2001). Emotions and creativity. *Asian Journal of Social Psychology*, 4, 165–183. DOI: 10.1111/1467-839X.00084

Ayer, A.J. (1936). *Language, truth, and logic*. London: Victor Gollancz.

Bargh, J.A. & Williams, L.E. (2007). The nonconscious regulation of emotion. In J.J. Gross (Ed.), *Handbook of emotion regulation* (pp. 429–445). New York: The Guilford Press.

Barrett, L.F. (2006a) Are emotions natural kinds? *Perspectives on Psychological Science*, 1, 28–58. DOI: 10.1111/j.1745-6916.2006.00003.x

Barrett, L.F. (2006b). Solving the emotion paradox. Categorization and the experience of emotion. *Personality and Social Psychology Review*, 10, 20–46. DOI: 10.1207/s15327957pspr1001_2

Barrett, L.F. (2009). Variety is the spice of life. A psychological construction approach to understanding variability of emotion. *Cognition and Emotion*, 23, 1284–1306. DOI: 10.1080/026999 30902985894

Barrett, L.F., Ochsner, K.N., & Gross, J.J. (2007). On the automaticity of emotion. In J.A. Bargh (Ed.), *Social psychology and the unconscious: The automaticity of higher mental processes* (pp. 173–217). New York: The Psychology Press.

Beer, J.S. & Lombardo, M.V. (2007). Insights into emotion regulation from neuropsychology. In J.J. Gross (Ed.), *Handbook of emotion regulation* (pp. 69–86). New York: The Guilford Press.

Benner, P. (2000). The roles of embodiment, emotion and lifeworld for rationality and agency in nursing practise. *Nursing Philosophy*, 1, 5–19. DOI: 10.1046/j.1466-769x.2000.00014.x

Benner, P. & Wrubel, J. (1989). *The primacy of caring*. Menlo Park, CA: Addison-Wesley.

Ben-Ze'ev, A. (2000). *The subtlety of emotions*. Cambridge, MA.: The MIT Press.

Bermudez, J. (2008). Nonconceptual mental content. *Stanford encyclopedia of philosophy*. Downloaded May 6, 2010.

Blackburn, S. (1984). *Spreading the word*. Oxford: Oxford University Press.

Blackburn, S. (1998). *Ruling passions*. Oxford: Clarendon Press.

Bluhm R. (2007). Beyond the basics: The evolution and development of human emotions. In L. Faucher & C. Tappolet (Eds.), *The modularity of emotion. Canadian Journal of Philosophy* Supplementary Volume 32, 73–94.

Bolton, S.C. (2005). *Emotion management in the workplace*. Basingstoke: Palgrave Macmillan.

Bolton, S.C. (2000). Who cares? Offering emotion work as a "gift" in the nursing labour Process. *Journal of Advanced Nursing*, 32, 580–586. DOI: 10.1046/j.1365-2648.2000.01516.x

Bolton S.C. & Boyd, C. (2003) Trolley dolly or skilled emotion manager? Moving on from Hochschild's *Managed Heart. Work, Employment, and Society*, 17, 289–308.

Brady, M. (2008). Value and fitting emotions. *The Journal of Value Inquiry*, 42, 465–475. DOI: 10.1007/s10790-008-9134-8

Brady, M. (2011). Emotions, perceptions, and reasons. In C. Bagnoli (Ed.), *Morality and the emotions* (pp. 135–149). Oxford: Oxford University Press. DOI: 10.1093/acprof:oso/97801 99577507.003.0007

Brosch, T. & Sander, D. (2013). Comment: The appraising brain: Towards a neuro-cognitive model of appraisal processes in emotion. *Emotion Review*, 5, 163–168. DOI: 10.1177/17540 73912468298

Bzdok, D., Laird, A.R., Zilles, K., Fox, P.T., & Eickhoff, S.B. (2013). An investigation of the structural, connectional, and functional subspecialization in the human amygdala. *Human Brain Mapping*, 34, 3247–3266. DOI: 10.1002/hbm.22138

Calhoun, C. (1995). Standing for something. *The Journal of Philosophy*, 92, 235–260. DOI: 10.2307/2940917

Carmack, B.J. (1997). Balancing engagement and detachment in caregiving. *Image: the Journal of Nursing Scholarship*, 29, 139–143. DOI: 10.1111/j.1547-5069.1997.tb01546.x

Charland, L.C. (1996). Feeling and representation. Computational theory and the modularity of affect". *Synthese*, 105, 273–301. DOI: 10.1007/BF01063560

Charland, L.C. (1997). Reconciling cognitive and perceptual theories of emotion: A representational proposal, *Philosophy of Science*, 64, 555–579. DOI: 10.1086/392572

Christman, J. (1991). Autonomy and personal history. *Canadian Journal of Philosophy*, 21, 1–24.

Clore, G. & Ortony, A. (2000). Cognition in emotions: Always, sometimes, or never? In R.D. Lane & L. Nadel (Eds.), *Cognitive neuroscience of emotion* (pp. 24–61). New York & Oxford: Oxford University Press.

Crane, T. (1992). The nonconceptual content of experience. In T. Crane (Ed.), *The contents of experience* (pp. 136–157). Cambridge: Cambridge University Press. DOI: 10.1017/CBO978 0511554582.007

Darlow, A.L. & Sloman, S.L. (2010) Two systems of reasoning; architecture and relation to emotion. *Wiley Interdisciplipnary Reviews: Cognitive Science*, 1, 382–392. DOI: 10.1002/wcs.34

D'Arms, J. & Jacobson, D. (2000a). The moralistic fallacy: On the "appropriateness" of emotions. *Philosophy and Phenomenological Research*, 61, 65–90. DOI: 10.2307/2653403

D'Arms, J. & Jacobson, D. (2000b). Sentiment and value", *Ethics*, 110, 722–748. DOI: 10.1086/233371

D'Arms, J. & Jacobson, D. (2003). "The significance of recalcitrant emotion (Or: anti-quasijudgmentalism). In A. Hatzimoysis (Ed.), *Philosophy and the emotions* (pp. 127–146). Cambridge: Cambridge University Press. DOI: 10.1017/CBO9780511550270.009

D'Arms, J. (2005). Two arguments for sentimentalism. *Philosophical Issues*, 15, 1–21. DOI: 10.1111/j.1533-6077.2005.00050.x

D'Arms, J. & Jacobson, D. (2006a). Anthropocentric constraints on human value. In R. Schafer-Landau (Ed.), *Oxford studies in metaethics*: Vol. 1 (99–126). Oxford: Clarendon Press.

D'Arms, J. & Jacobson, D. (2006b). Sensibility theory and projectivism. In D. Copp (Ed.), *The Oxford handbook of ethical theory* (pp. 186–218). Oxford/New York: Oxford University Press.

D'Arms, J. & Jacobson, D. (2010). Demystifying sensibilities. Sentimental values and the instability of affect. In P. Goldie (Ed.), *The Oxford handbook of philosophy of emotion* (pp. 585–613). Oxford: Oxford University Press.

Damasio, A. (1994) *Descartes error. Emotion, reason, and the human brain*. New York, Putnam.

Damasio, A. (1999). *The feeling of what happens*, New York: Harcourt.

Damasio, A. (2003). *Looking for Spinoza. Joy, sorrow, and the feeling brain*. Orlando: Harcourt.

Danielsson, S. & Olson, J. (2007) Brentano and buck-passers. *Mind*, 116, 511–522. DOI: 10.1093/mind/fzm511

Darwin, C. (1965[1872]). *The expression of the emotions in man and animals*. Chicago: University of Chicago Press.

Davidson, D. (1980). *Essays on actions and events*. Oxford: Oxford University Press.

Davidson, R.J., Fox, A., & Kalin, N.H. (2007). Neural bases of emotion regulation in nonhuman primates and humans. In J.J. Gross (Ed.), *Handbook of emotion regulation* (pp. 47–68). New York: The Guilford Press.

DeAraujo, I.E.T, Rolls, E.T., Velazco, M.I., Margot, C., & Cayeux, I. (2005). Cognitive modulation of olfactory processing. *Neuron*, 46, 671–679. DOI: 10.1016/j.neuron.2005.04.021

Decety, J., Yang, C-Y., & Cheng, Y. (2010). Physicians down-regulate their pain empathy response: An event-related brain potential study. *NeuroImage*, Doi: 10.1016/j.neuroimage.2010.01.025

Deigh, J. (1994). Cognitivism in the theory of emotions. *Ethics*, 104, 824–854. DOI: 10.1086/293657

Deigh, J. (2004). Primitive emotions. In R.C. Solomon (Ed.), *Thinking about feeling*. (pp. 9–27). Oxford & New York: Oxford University Press.

Deigh, J. (2008). *Emotions, values, and the law*. Oxford: Oxford University Press.

Deonna, J.A. (2006). Emotion, perception, and perspective. *Dialectica*, 60, 29–46. DOI: 10.1111/ j.1746-8361.2005.01031.x

Deonna, J.A. & Scherer, K.R. (2010). The case of a disappearing intentional object. Constraints on a definition of emotion. *Emotion Review*, 2, 44–52. DOI: 10.1177/1754073909345544

Deonna, J.A. & Teroni, F. (2012). *The emotions. A philosophical introduction.* London: Routledge.

Diderot, D. (2002[1762]). *Rameau's nephew.* Translated by Ian C. Johnston. http://www.mala. bc.ca/~johnstoi/diderot/rameau_E.htm

Diener, E. (2000). Subjective well-being: The science of happiness and a proposal for a national index. *American Psychologist*, 55, 34–43. DOI: 10.1037/0003-066X.55.1.34

von Dietze, E. and Orb, A. (2000). Compassionate care: A moral dimension of nursing. *Nursing Inquiry*, 7, 166–174. DOI: 10.1046/j.1440-1800.2000.00065.x

Dillon, R.S. (1997). Self-respect: Moral, emotional, political. *Ethics*, 107, 226–249. DOI: 10.1086/ 233719

Dilman, I. (1989). False emotions. *Proceedings of the Aristotelian society*, Supplementary Volume 63, 287–295.

Dobson, K.S. (ed.) (2001), *Handbook of cognitive-behavioural therapies.* New York: The Guilford Press.

Döring, S.A. (2003). Explaining action by emotion. *The Philosophical Quarterly*, 53, 214–230. DOI: 10.1111/1467-9213.00307

Döring, S.A. (2004). *Gründe und Gefühle. Rationale Motivation durch emotionale Vernunft.* Habilitationschrift, Universität Essen-Duisburg.

Döring, S.A. (2007). Seeing what to do: Affective perception and rational motivation. *Dialectica*, 61, 363–394. DOI: 10.1111/j.1746-8361.2007.01105.x

Döring, S.A. (2009). The logic of emotional experience: Noninferentiality and the problem of conflict without contradiction. *Emotion Review*, 3, 240–247. DOI: 10.1177/1754073909103592

Dretske, F. (1981). *Knowledge and the flow of information*, Cambridge, MA: The MIT Press

Dummett, M. (1993). *The origins of analytic philosophy.* London: Duckworth.

Ekman, P. (1977). Biological and cultural centre countries to body and facial movement. In S. Blacking (ed.), *Anthropology of the body* (pp. 34–84). London: Academic press.

Ekman, P. (1992). An argument for basic emotions. *Cognition & Emotion*, 6, 169–200. DOI: 10.1080/02699939208411068

Ekman, P. (1999). Basic emotions. In T. Dalgleish & M.J. Power (Eds), *Handbook of cognition and emotion* (pp. 45–60). Chichester: John Wiley & Sons.

Ekman, P. (2003). *Emotions revealed.* New York: Owl Books.

Ellsworth, P.C. (1991). Some implications of cognitive appraisal theories of emotion. In K.T. Strongman (Ed.), *International review of studies of emotion*, vol. 1 (pp. 143–161). New York: Wiley.

Ellsworth, P.C. (1994). William James and emotion: Is a century of fame worth a century of misunderstanding? *Psychological Review*, 101, 222–229. DOI: 10.1037/0033-295X.101. 2.222

Ellsworth, P.C. & Scherer, K.R. (2003). Appraisal processes in emotion. In R.J. Davidson, K.R. Scherer, & H. Hill Goldsmith (Eds., *Handbook of affective sciences* (pp. 572–595). Oxford. Oxford University Press.

Epstein, S. (1994). Integration of the cognitive and psychodynamic unconscious. *American Psychologist*, 49, 709–748. DOI: 10.1037/0003-066X.49.8.709

Erickson, R. (1995). The importance of authenticity for self and society. *Symbolic Interaction*, 18, 121–144. DOI: 10.1525/si.1995.18.2.121

Erickson, R. & Wharton, A. (1997) Inauthenticity and depression. *Work and Occupations*, 24, 188–213. DOI: 10.1177/0730888497024002004

Erickson, R. & Ritter, C. (2001) Emotional labour, burnout, and inauthenticity: Does gender matter? *Social Psychological Quarterly*, 64, 146–163. DOI: 10.2307/3090130

Evans, J. St.B. (2008). Dual-processing accounts of reasoning, judgment, and social cognition. *Annual Review of Psychology*, 59, 255–278. DOI: 10.1146/annurev.psych.59.103006.093629

Evans, J. St.B. (2009). How many dual-process theories do we need? One, two, or many? In J. St.B. Evans & K. Frankish (Eds.), *In two minds: Dual processes and beyond* (pp. 33–54). Oxford: Oxford University Press. DOI: 10.1093/acprof:oso/9780199230167.003.0002

Faucher, L. & Tappolet, C. (eds.) (2007). *The modularity of emotion. Canadian Journal of Philosophy* Supplementary Volume 32.

Fodor, J. (1983). *Modularity of the mind*. Cambridge, MA: The MIT Press.

Folkman, S. & Lazarus, R.S. (1990). Coping and emotion. In N.L. Stein, B. Leventhal, & T. Trabasso (Eds.), *Psychological and biological approaches to emotion* (pp. 313–332). Hillsdale: Lawrence Erlbaum.

Freidson, E. (1994). *Professionalism reborn. Theory, prophecy, and policy*. Cambridge: Polity Press.

Frijda, N. (1986). *The emotions*. Cambridge: Cambridge University Press.

Frijda, N. (1993). The place of appraisal in emotion. *Cognition and Emotion*, 7, 357–387. DOI: 10.1080/02699939308409193

Frijda, N.H. & Zeelenberg, M. (2001). Appraisal: What is the dependent? In K.R. Scherer, A. Schorr, & T. Johnstone (Eds), *Appraisal processes in emotion* (pp. 141–155). Oxford and New York: Oxford University Press.

Furtak, R.A. (2010). Emotion, the bodily, and the cognitive. *Philosophical Explorations*, 13, 51–64. DOI: 10.1080/13869790903318508

Gastmans, C. (1999). Care as a moral attitude in nursing. *Nursing Ethics*, 6, 214–23.

Gecas, V. (2000). Value identities, self-motives, and social movements. In S. Stryker, T.J. Owens, & R.W. White (Eds), *Self, identity, and social movements* (pp. 93–109). Minneapolis: The University of Minneapolis Press.

George, J.M. (2002). Affect regulation in groups and teams. In R.G. Lord, R.J. Klimoski & R. Kanfer (Eds), *Emotions in the workplace* (pp. 183–217). San Francisco: Jossey-Bass.

Gert, J. (2012). *Normative bedrock*. Oxford: Oxford University Press. DOI: 10.1093/acprof:oso/9780199657544.001.0001

Gibbard, A. (1990). *Wise choices, apt feelings*. Cambridge, MA: Harvard University Press.

Giddens, A. (1989). *Modernity and self-identity*. Cambridge: Polity Press.

Gleichgerrcht, E. & Decety, J. (2012). The costs of empathy among health professionals. In J. Decety (Ed), *Empathy: from bench to bedside* (pp. 245–261). Cambridge, MA: The MIT Press.

Goldie, P. (2000). *The emotions*. Oxford: Oxford University Press.

Goldie, P. (2002). Emotions, feelings, and intentionality. *Phenomenology and the Cognitive Sciences*, 1, 235–254. DOI: 10.1023/A:1021306500055

Goldie, P. (2004). Emotion, feeling, and knowledge of the world. In R.C. Solomon (Ed.), *Thinking about feeling* (pp. 91–106). Oxford & New York: Oxford University Press.

Goldie, P. (2009). Getting feelings into emotional experience in the right way, *Emotion Review*, 3, 232–239. DOI: 10.1177/1754073909103591

Golomb, J. (1995). *In search of authenticity*. London: Routledge.

Gordon, R. (1987). *The structure of emotions*. Cambridge: Cambridge University Press.

Grandey, A. (2000). Emotion regulation in the workplace. *Journal of Occupational Health Psychology*, 5, 95–110. DOI: 10.1037/1076-8998.5.1.95

Green, O.H. (1992). *The emotions*. Dordrecht/Boston/London: Kluwer Academic Publishers.

Greenberg, L.S. (2002). *Emotion-focused therapy*. Washington DC: American Psychological Association.

Greenspan, P.S. (1988). *Emotions and reasons*. New York/London: Routledge.

Griffiths, M. (1997). *Feminisms and the self*. London: Routledge.

Griffiths, P.E. (1997). *What emotions really are?* Chicago: Chicago University Press. DOI: 10.7208/chicago/9780226308760.001.0001

Griffiths, P.E. (2004). Is emotion a natural kind? In R.C. Solomon (Ed.), *Thinking about feeling* (pp. 233–249). Oxford & New York: Oxford University Press.

Gross, J.J. (1998). Antecedent- and response-focused emotion regulation: Divergent consequences for experience, expression, and physiology. *Journal of Personality and Social Psychology*, 74, 224–237. DOI: 10.1037/0022-3514.74.1.224

Gross, J.J. (Ed.), (2007). *The handbook of emotion regulation*. New York: The Guilford Press.

Gross, J.J. & Barrett, L.F. (2011). Emotion generation and emotion regulation: One or two depends on your view. *Emotion Review*, 3, 8–16. DOI: 10.1177/1754073910380974

Gross, J.J. & Thompson, R. (2007). Emotion regulation: Conceptual foundations. In J.J. Gross (Ed.), *The handbook of emotion regulation* (pp. 3–24). New York: Guildford Press.

Gunther, Y. H. (2003). Emotion and force. In Y. Gunther (Ed.), *Essays on nonconceptual content* (pp. 279–288). Cambridge, MA: The MIT Press.

Gunther, Y.H. (Ed.) (2003). *Essays on nonconceptual content*. Cambridge, MA: The MIT Press.

Hamlyn, D.W. (1989). False emotions. *Proceedings of the Aristotelian society*. Supplementary Volume 63, 275–286.

Hatfied, E., Cacioppo, J.T., & Rapson, R.L. (1994). *Emotional contagion*. Cambridge, MA: Cambridge University Press.

Healy, D. (1990). *The suspended revolution*. London: Faber & Faber.

Heidegger, M. (1962). *Being and time*. Translated by John Macquarrie & Edward Robinson. Oxford: Basil Blackwell.

Helm, B. (2001). *Emotional reason*. Cambridge: Cambridge University Press. DOI: 10.1017/CBO9780511520044

Henderson, A. (2001). Emotional labour and nursing: An under-appreciated aspect of caring work. *Nursing Inquiry*, 8, 130–138. DOI: 10.1046/j.1440-1800.2001.00097.x

Herzberg, L. A. (2012). To blend or to compose: A debate about emotion structure. In P. Wilson (ed.): *Dynamicity in Emotion Concepts. Lódz Studies in Language*, Vol. 27 (pp. 73–94). Frankfurt-am-Main: Peter Lang.

Hochschild, A.R. (2003). *The managed heart. Commercialization of human feeling. With a new afterword*. Anniversary 20th edition. Los Angeles: University of California Press.

Hogg, M.A. (1992). *The social psychology of group cohesiveness: From attraction to social identity*. Hemel Hampstead: Harvester Wheatsheaf.

Hollis, M. & Lukes, S. (Eds.) (1982). *Rationality and relativism*. Oxford: Basil Blackwell.

Hume, D. (1985[1739–40]). *A treatise on human nature*. London: Penguin Books.

Illouz, E. (2008). *Saving the modern soul. Therapy, emotions and the culture of self-help*. Berkeley: University of California Press.

Jaggar, A. (1997). Love and knowledge. Emotion in feminist epistemology. In A. Garry & M. Pearsall (Eds), *Women, knowledge and reality* (pp. 129–155). Boston: Unwin Hyman.

James, N. (1989). Emotional labour: Skill and work in the social regulation of feelings. *Sociological Review*, 37, 15–42. DOI: 10.1111/j.1467-954X.1989.tb00019.x

James, W. (1884). What is an emotion? *Mind*, 9, 188–204. DOI: 10.1093/mind/os-IX.34.188

Jameton. A. (1984) Nursing practice: Ethical issues. London: Prentice-Hall.

John, O.P. & Gross, J.J. (2004). Healthy and unhealthy emotion regulation: Personality processes, individual differences, and lifespan development. *Journal of Personality*, 72, 1301–1334. DOI: 10.1111/j.1467-6494.2004.00298.x

John, O.P. & Gross, J.J. (2007). Individual differences in emotion regulation. In J.J. Gross (Ed.), *The handbook of emotion regulation* (pp. 351–372). New York: Guildford Press.

Johnstone, T., van Reekum, C., & Scherer, K.R. (2001). Vocal expression correlates of appraisal processes. In K.R. Scherer, A. Schorr, & T. Johnstone (Eds), *Appraisal processes in emotion* (pp. 271–284). Oxford and New York: Oxford University Press.

Jones, K. (2007) Modularity and the pro-emotion consensus. In L. Faucher & C. Tappolet (Eds), *The modularity of emotion. Canadian Journal of Philosophy* Supplementary Volume 32, 3–27.

Jordan, A. & Patridge, S. (2012). Against the moralistic fallacy: A modest defence of a modest sentimentalism about humour. *Ethical Theory and Moral Practice*, 15, 83–94. DOI: 10.1007/s10677-011-9268-9

Kahneman, D. (2011). *Thinking, fast and slow*. New York: Farrar, Straus, and Giroux.

Kaiser, S. & Wehrle, T. (2001). Facial expressions as indicators of appraisal processes. In K.R. Scherer, A. Schorr, & T. Johnstone (Eds), *Appraisal processes in emotion* (pp. 285–300). Oxford and New York: Oxford University Press.

Kenny, A. (1963). *Action, emotion, and will*. London: Routledge & Kegan Paul.

Knuuttila, S. (2004). *Emotions in ancient and medieval philosophy*. Oxford: Clarendon Press. DOI: 10.1093/0199266387.001.0001

Kristjánsson, K. (2010). The trouble with ambivalent emotions. *Philosophy*, 85, 485–510. DOI: 10.1017/S0031819110000434

Kruml, S.M. & Geddes, D. (2000). Exploring the dimensions of emotional labour. *Management Communication Quarterly*, 14, 8–49. DOI: 10.1177/0893318900141002

Kymlicka, W. (1990). *Contemporary political philosophy*. Oxford: Clarendon Press.

Laird. J.D. (2007) *Feelings. The perception of self*. New York: Oxford University Press.

Lambie, J.A. & Marcel, A.J. (2002). Consciousness and emotion experience: A theoretical framework, *Psychological Review*, 109, 219–259. DOI: 10.1037/0033-295X.109.2.219

Lanctôt, N. & Hess, U. (2007) The timing of appraisals. *Emotion*, 7, 207–212. DOI: 10.1037/1528-3542.7.1.207

Lazarus, R.S. (1982). Thoughts on the relation between emotion and cognition. *American Psychologist*, 37, 1019–1024. DOI: 10.1037/0003-066X.37.9.1019

Lazarus, R.S. (1984). On the primacy of cognition. *American Psychologist*, 39, 124–129. DOI: 10.1037/0003-066X.39.2.124

Lazarus, R.S. (1991). *Emotion and adaptation*. New York/Oxford: Oxford University Press.

Lazarus, R.S. & Alfert, E. (1964). Short-circuiting of threat by experimentally altering cognitive appraisal. *The Journal of Abnormal and Social Psychology*, 69, 195–205. DOI: 10.1037/h0044635

Lazarus, R.S. & Folkman. S. (1984) *Stress appraisal and coping*. New York Springer

Leahy, R.L. (ed.) (2004). *Contemporary cognitive therapy. Theory, research, and practice*. New York and London: The Guilford Press.

LeDoux, J. (1995). *The emotional brain*. New York: Simon & Schuster.

Levenson, R.W. (1988). Emotion and the autonomic nervous system: A prospectus for research on autonomic specificity. In H. L. Wagner (Ed.), *Social psychophysiology and emotion: Theory and clinical applications* (pp. 17–42). Hoboken, NJ: John Wiley & Sons.

Levenson, R.W. (2003). Autonomic specificity and emotion. In R.J. Davidson, K.R. Scherer, & H.H. Goldsmith (eds.), *Handbook of affective sciences* (pp. 212–224). New York: Oxford University Press.

Leventhal, H. & Scherer, K.R. (1987). The relationship of emotion to cognition: A functional approach to a semantic controversy. *Cognition and Emotion*, 1, 3–28. DOI: 10.1080/02699 938708408361

Lewis, M.D. (2005). Bridging emotion theory and neurobiology through dynamic systems modelling, *Behavioural and Brain Sciences*, 28, 169–245.

Lieberman, M.D. (2003) Reflexive and reflective judgment processes: A social cognitive neuroscience approach. In J.P. Forgas, K.D. Williams, & W. von Hippel (Eds.), *Social judgments*. Cambridge: Cambridge University Press.

Lindquist, K.A, Wager, T.D, Kober, H., Bliss-Moreau, E., & Barrett, L.F. (2012). The brain basis of emotion. *Behavioural and Brain Sciences*, 35, 121–202. DOI: 10.1017/S0140525X11 000446

Logue, A. W., Ophir, I, & Strauss, K.E. (1986) Acquisition of taste aversions in humans. *Behavioural Research and Therapy*, 19, 319–333. DOI: 10.1016/0005-7967(81)90053-X

Louise, J. (2009). Correct responses and the priority of the normative. *Ethical Theory and Moral Practice*, 12, 345–364. DOI: 10.1007/s10677-009-9177-3

Lycan, W. (1994). Functionalism. In S. Guttenplan (Ed.), *A companion to the philosophy of mind* (pp. 317–323). Oxford: Blackwell.

MacIntyre, A. (1981). *After virtue*. London: Duckworth.

Magai, C. & Haviland-Jones, J. (2002). *The hidden genius of emotion*. Cambridge: Cambridge University Press. DOI: 10.1017/CBO9780511509575

Markus, H.R. and Kitayama S. (1991). Culture and self: Implications for cognition, emotion, and motivation. *Psychological Review*, 98, 224–253. DOI: 10.1037/0033-295X.98.2.224

Maslach, C. (1982). *Burnout: The cost of caring*. Englewood Cliffs: Prentice Hall.

Mathiesen, K. (2006). The epistemic features of group belief. *Episteme*, 2, 161–175. DOI: 10.3366/ epi.2005.2.3.161

Matsumoto, D., Keltner, D., Shiota, M.N., O'Sullivan, M., & Frank, M. (2008). Facial expressions of emotion. In M. Lewis, J. Haviland-Jones, & L.F. Barrett (Eds.), *Handbook of emotions*. 3rd edition. (pp. 211–234). New York. The Guilford Press.

McDowell, J. (1997a). Projection and truth in ethics. Reprinted in S. Darwall, A. Gibbard, & P. Railton (Eds.), *Moral discourse and practise* (pp. 201–214). New York & Oxford: Oxford University Press.

McDowell, J. (1997b). Values and secondary qualities. Reprinted in S. Darwall, A. Gibbard, & P. Railton (Eds.), *Moral discourse and practise* (pp. 215–226). New York & Oxford: Oxford University Press.

McDowell. J. (2009). *Having the world in view: Essays on Kant, Hegel, and Sellars*. Cambridge, MA: Harvard University Press.

McIntyre, A. (1990). Is akratic action always irrational? In O. Flanagan & A. Oksenberg Rorty (Eds.), *Identity, character, and morality* (pp. 379–400). Cambridge, MA & London: The MIT Press.

McQueen, A.C.H. (2004). Emotional intelligence in nursing work. *Journal of Advanced Nursing*, 47, 101–108. DOI: 10.1111/j.1365-2648.2004.03069.x

McVicar, A. (2003). Workplace stress in nursing: A literature review. *Journal of Advanced Nursing*, 44, 633–642. DOI: 10.1046/j.0309-2402.2003.02853.x

Moors, A. (2007). Can cognitive methods be used to study the unique aspect of emotion: An appraisal theorist's answer. *Cognition and Emotion*, 21, 1238–1269. DOI: 10.1080/026999 30701438061

Moors. A. (2009). Theories of emotion causation: A review. *Cognition and Emotion*, 23, 625–662. DOI: 10.1080/02699930802645739

Moors, A. (2010). Automatic constructive appraisal as a candidate cause of emotion. *Emotion Review*, 2, 139–156. DOI: 10.1177/1754073909351755

Moors, A. (2012). Comparison of affect program theories, appraisal theories, and psychological construction theories. In R.D. Ellis & P. Zachar (Eds), *Categorical vs. dimensional models of affect. A seminar on the theories of Panksepp and Russell.* (pp. 257–78). *Consciousness & Emotion Book Series*, Vol. 7. Amsterdam/Philadelphia: John Benjamins. DOI: 10.1075/ceb.7.13moo

Moors, A., Ellsworth, P.C., Scherer, K.R. & Frijda, N.H. (2013). Appraisal theories of emotion: State of the art and future development. *Emotion Review*, 5, 119–124. DOI: 10.1177/175 4073912468165

Morgan, C. & Averill, J.R. (1992). True feelings, the self, and authenticity: A psychosocial perspective. In D.D. Franks & V. Gecas (Eds), *Social perspectives on emotion*, Vol. 1 (pp. 95–123). Greenwich, CT: JAI.

Morris, J.A. & Feldman, D.C. (1996). The dimensions, antecedents, and consequences of emotional labour. *The Academy of Management Review*, 21, 986–1010.

Mulligan, K. (1998). From appropriate emotions to values. *The Monist*, 81, 161–188. DOI: 10.5840/monist199881114

Mulligan, K. (2009). Was sind und was sollen die unechen Gefühlen? In U. Amrein (Hsg.), *Das Authentische. Referenzen und Repräsentationen* (ss. 225–248). Zürich: Chronos Verlag.

Mulligan, K. (2010). Emotions and values. In P. Goldie (Ed.), *The Oxford handbook of philosophy of emotion* (pp. 475–500). Oxford: Oxford University Press.

Neu, J. (1977). *Emotion, thought, and therapy*. Berkeley and Los Angeles: University of California Press.

Nordtvedt, P. (1998). Sensitive judgment: An inquiry into the foundations of nursing ethics. *Nursing Ethics*, 5, 385–392.

Nussbaum, M.C. (1993). *The therapy of desire: Theory and practice in Hellenistic ethics*. Princeton: Princeton University Press.

Nussbaum, M.C. (2001). *Upheavals of thought*, Cambridge: Cambridge University Press. DOI: 10.1017/CBO9780511840715

Oakley, J. (1992). *Morality and the emotions*. London: Routledge.

Ochsner, K.N. & Gross, J.J. (2005). The cognitive control of emotion. *TRENDS in Cognitive Sciences*, 9, 242–249. DOI: 10.1016/j.tics.2005.03.010

Ochsner. K.N. & Gross, J.J. (2007). The neural architecture of emotion regulation. In J.J. Gross (Ed.), *Handbook of emotion regulation* (pp. 87–109). New York: The Guilford Press.

Ochsner, K.N., Ray, R.R., Hughes, B., McRae, K., Cooper, J.C., Weber, J., Gabrieli, J.D.E., & Gross, J.J. (2009). Bottom-up and top-down processes in emotion generation. Common and distinct neural mechanisms. *Psychological Science*, 20, 1322–1331. DOI: 10.1111/j.1467-9280.2009.02459.x

Öhman, A. & Wiens, S. (1994). The concept of evolved fear module and cognitive theories of anxiety. In A.S.R. Manstead, N. Frijda, and A. Fischer (Eds.), *Feelings and Emotions. The Amsterdam symposium* (pp. 58–80). Cambridge: Cambridge University Press.

Omdahl, B.L. & O'Donnell, C. (1999). Emotional contagion, empathic concern and communicative responsiveness as variables affecting nurses' stress and occupational commitment. *Journal of Advanced Nursing*, 29, 1351–1359. DOI: 10.1046/j.1365-2648.1999.01021.x

Panksepp, J. (1998). *Affective neuroscience.* New York: Oxford University Press.

Panksepp, J. (2012). In defence of multiple core affects. In R.D. Ellis & P. Zachar (Eds), *Categorical vs. dimensional models of affect. A seminar on the theories of Panksepp and Russell.* (pp. 31–78). *Consciousness & Emotion Book Series*, Vol. 7. Amsterdam/Philadelphia: John Benjamins DOI: 10.1075/ceb.7.02pan

Parkinson, B. (1997). Untangling the appraisal-emotion connection. *Personality and Social Psychology Review*, 1, 62–79. DOI: 10.1207/s15327957pspr0101_5

Parkinson, B. (2001). Putting appraisal in context. In K.R. Scherer, A. Schorr, & T. Johnstone (Eds.), *Appraisal processes in emotion* (pp. 173–186). Oxford and New York: Oxford University Press.

Parkinson. B. & Manstead, A.S.R. (1992) Appraisal as a case of emotion. In Margaret S. Clark (ed.), Emotion. *Review of personality and social psychology*, no 13 (pp. 122–149). Thousand Oaks, CA: Sage publications

Parkinson, B, Fischer, A.H., & Manstead, A.S.R. (2005). *Emotion in social relations.* New York. The Psychology Press.

Parrott, W.G. (2007). Components and the definition of emotion. *Social Science Information*, 46, 419–424. DOI: 10.1177/05390184070460030109

Peacocke, C. (1992). Scenarios, concepts, and perception. T. Crane (Ed.), *The contents of experience: Essays on perception* (pp. 105–135). Cambridge: Cambridge University Press. DOI: 10.1017/CBO9780511554582.006

Pecchinenda, A. (2001). The psychophysiology of appraisals. In K.R. Scherer, A. Schorr, & T. Johnstone (Eds.), *Appraisal processes in emotion* (pp. 301–315). Oxford and New York: Oxford University Press.

Pessoa, L. (2008) On the relationship between emotion and cognition. *Nature Reviews Neuroscience*, 9, 148–158. DOI: 10.1038/nrn2317

Pessoa. L. (2010) Emotion and cognition and the amygdala: from "what is it?" to "what's to be done?" *Neuropsychologic*, 48, 3416–3429.

Pessoa, L. & Adolphs, R. (2010). Emotion processing and the amygdala: from a 'low road' to 'many roads' of evaluating biological significance. *Nature Reviews Neuroscience*, 11, 773–782. DOI: 10.1038/nrn2920

Power, M. & Dalgleish, T. (2007). *Cognition and emotion. From order to disorder.* 2nd revised edition. Hove: The Psychology Press.

Prinz, J.J. (2004). *Gut reactions. A perceptual theory of emotion.* Oxford & New York: Oxford University Press.

Prinz, J.J. (2007). *The emotional construction of morals.* Oxford & New York: Oxford University Press.

Pugmire, D. (1998). *Rediscovering emotion.* Edinburgh: Edinburgh University Press.

Pugmire, D. (2005). *Sound sentiments.* Oxford: Oxford University Press. DOI: 10.1093/0199276897.001.0001

Pugliesi, K. (1999). The consequences of emotional labour: Effects on work stress, job satisfaction, and well-being. *Motivation and Emotion*, 23, 125–154. DOI: 10.1023/A:10213291 12679

Rabinowicz, W. & Rønnow-Rasmussen, T. (2004). The strike of the demon: On the fitting pro-attitudes and value. *Ethics*, 114, 391–423. DOI: 10.1086/381694

de Raeve, L. (2002). The modification of emotional responses: A problem for trust in nurse-patient relationships? *Nursing Ethics*, 9, 465–471. DOI: 10.1191/0969733002ne536oa

Rafaeli, A. & Sutton, R.I. (1987). Expression of emotion as part of the work role. *The Academy of Management Review*, 12, 23–37.

Reynolds, W., Scott, P.A., & Austin, W. (2000). Nursing, empathy and perceptions of the moral. *Journal of Advanced Nursing*, 32, 235–242. DOI: 10.1046/j.1365-2648.2000.01440.x

Roberts, R.C. (1988). What an emotion is: A sketch. *Philosophical Review*, 97, 183–209 DOI: 10.2307/2185261

Roberts, R.C. (2003). *Emotions*. Cambridge: Cambridge University Press. DOI: 10.1017/CBO9780511610202

Robinson, J. (2005). *Deeper than reason*. Oxford: Clarendon Press. DOI: 10.1093/01992636 55.001.0001

Rolls, E. (2013). *Emotion and decision-making explained*. Oxford: Oxford University Press. DOI: 10.1093/acprof:oso/9780199659890.001.0001

Rønnow-Rasmussen, T. (2011). *Personal value*. Oxford: Oxford University Press. DOI: 10.1093/acprof:oso/9780199603787.001.0001

Rozin, P., Haidt, J, & McCauley, C.R. (2008). Disgust. In M. Lewis, J. Haviland-Jones, & L.F. Barrett (Eds), *Handbook of emotions* (pp. 757–776). New York: The Guilford Press.

Russell, J. A. (2003). Core affect and the psychological construction of emotion. *Psychological Review*, 110, 145–172. DOI: 10.1037/0033-295X.110.1.145

Russell, J.A. (2009). Emotion, core affect, and psychological construction. *Cognition and Emotion*, 23, 1259–1283 DOI: 10.1080/02699930902809375

Russell, J.A. (2012a). Final remarks. In R.D. Ellis & P. Zachar (Eds), *Categorical vs. dimensional models of affect. A seminar on the theories of Panksepp and Russell.* (pp. 279–300). *Consciousness & Emotion Book Series*, Vol. 7. Amsterdam/Philadelphia: John Benjamins. DOI: 10.1075/ceb.7.14rus

Russell, J.A. (2012b). From a psychological constructionist perspective. In R.D. Ellis & P. Zachar (Eds), *Categorical vs. dimensional models of affect. A seminar on the theories of Panksepp and Russell.* (pp. 79–118). *Consciousness & Emotion Book Series*, Vol. 7. Amsterdam/Philadelphia: John Benjamins. DOI: 10.1075/ceb.7.03rus

Sabini. J. & Silver. M. (1998) *Emotion. character, and responsibility*. New York: Oxford University Press.

Salmela, M. (2002). Intentionality and feeling – A sketch for a two-level account of emotional affectivity. *SATS (Nordic Journal of Philosophy)*, 3, 56–75.

Salmela, M. (2005). Emotional feelings as twofold representations. In Å. Carlson (Ed.), *Philosophical aspects of emotions* (pp. 275–294). Stockholm: Thales.

Salmela, M. (2008). How to evaluate the factual basis of emotional appraisals? In L.C. Charland & P. Zachar (Eds), *Fact and value in emotion* (pp. 35–52). *Consciousness & Emotion Book Series*, Vol. 5. Amsterdam/Philadelphia: John Benjamins. DOI: 10.1075/ceb.4.03sal

Salmela, M. (2011). Can emotion be modelled on perception? *Dialectica*, 65, 1–29. DOI: 10.1111/j.1746-8361.2011.01259.x

Samuels, R. (2009). The magical number two, plus or minus: Dual-process theory as a theory of cognitive kinds. In J. St.B. Evans & K. Frankish (Eds.), *In two minds: Dual processes and beyond* (pp. 129–146). Oxford: Oxford University Press. DOI: 10.1093/acprof:oso/9780199 230167.003.0006

Sartre, J.-P. (1956). *Being and nothingness*. Translated by H.E. Barnes. Washington Square Press.

Sartre, J.-P. (1994). *Sketch for a theory of the emotions*. Translated by Philip Mairet. London: Routledge.

Scanlon, T.M. (1998). *What we owe to each other*. Cambridge, MA: Belknap Press.

Scarantino, A. (2010). Insights and blindspots of the cognitivist theory of emotions. *British Journal for the Philosophy of Science*, 61, 729–768. DOI: 10.1093/bjps/axq011

Scherer, K.R. (2001). Appraisal considered as a process of multilevel sequential checking. In K.R. Scherer, A. Schorr, & T. Johnstone (Eds), *Appraisal processes in emotion* (pp. 92–120). Oxford and New York: Oxford University Press.

Scherer, K.R. (2009). The dynamic architecture of emotion: Evidence for the component process model. *Cognition and Emotion*, 23, 1307–1351. DOI: 10.1080/02699930902928969

Scherer, K.R. (2013). The nature and dynamics of relevance and valence appraisals: Theoretical advances and recent evidence. *Emotion Review*, 5, 150–162. DOI: 10.1177/17540739 12468166

Schorr, A. (2001). Appraisal: The evolution of an idea. In K.R. Scherer, A. Schorr, & T. Johnstone (Eds.), *Appraisal processes in emotion* (pp. 20–34). Oxford and New York: Oxford University Press.

Schwitzgebel, E. (2008). The unreliability of naïve introspection. *Philosophical Review*, 117, 245–273. DOI: 10.1215/00318108-2007-037

Scott, P. A. (2000). Emotion, moral perception, and nursing practice. *Nursing Philosophy*, 1, 123–133. DOI: 10.1046/j.1466-769x.2000.00023.x

Shaver, P.R., Schwartz, J., Kirson, D. & O'Connor, C. (1987). Emotion knowledge: Further exploration of a prototype approach. *Journal of Personality and Social Psychology*, 52, 1061–1086. DOI: 10.1037/0022-3514.52.6.1061

Sherman, N. (1989). *The fabric of character*. Oxford: The Clarendon Press.

Slovic, P., Finucane, M.L., Peters, E., & MacGregor, D.G. (2004). Risk as analysis and risk as feelings. Some thoughts about affect, reason, risk, and rationality. *Risk analysis*, 24, 311–322. DOI: 10.1111/j.0272-4332.2004.00433.x

Smith, C.A. & Ellsworth, P.C. (1985). Patterns of cognitive appraisal in emotion. *Journal of Personality and Social Psychology*, 48, 813–838. DOI: 10.1037/0022-3514.48.4.813

Smith, C.A. & Kirby, L.D. (2001). Towards delivering the promise of appraisal theory. In K.R. Scherer, A. Schorr, & T. Johnstone (Eds), *Appraisal processes in emotion* (pp. 121–138). Oxford and New York: Oxford University Press.

Smith, C.A. & Lazarus, R.S. (1990). Emotion and adaptation. In L.A. Pervin (Ed.), *Handbook of personality: Theory and research* (pp. 609–637). New York: Guilford.

Smith. E.R. & Neumann, R. (2005). Emotion processes considered from the perspective of dual-process models. In L.F. Barrett, P. Niedenthal, & P. Winkielman (Eds.), *Emotion and Consciousness* (pp. 287–311). New York: The Guilford Press.

Smith, P. (1992). *The emotional labour of nursing*. Basingstoke: Palgrave Macmillan.

Solomon. R.C. (1980) Emotions and choice. In A. Oksenberg Rorty (ed.), *Explaining Emotions* (pp. 251–282). Los Angeles: Universtiy of California Press.

Solomon, R.C. (1988). On emotions as judgments. *American Philosophical Quarterly*, 25, 183–191.

Solomon, R. C. (1993). *The passions. Emotions and the meaning of life.* Indianapolis/Cambridge: Hackett Publishing.

Solomon, R.C. (2004). Emotions, thoughts, and feelings: Emotions as engagements with the world. In R.C. Solomon (Ed.), *Thinking about feeling* (pp. 76–88). Oxford & New York: Oxford University Press.

Sorabji, R. (2000). *Emotion and peace of mind.* Oxford: Oxford University Press.

de Sousa, R. (1987). *The rationality of emotion.* Cambridge, MA: The MIT Press.

de Sousa, R. (2002). Emotional truth. *Proceedings of the Aristotelian Society.* Supplementary volume 76, 247–263. DOI: 10.1111/1467-8349.00098

de Sousa, R. (2004). Emotions: What I know, what I'd like to know, and what I'd like to think. In R. Solomon (Ed.), *Thinking about feeling* (pp. 61–75). Oxford & New York: Oxford University Press.

de Sousa, R. (2007). Truth, authenticity, and rationality. *Dialectica,* 61, 323–345. DOI: 10.1111/j.1746-8361.2007.01104.x

de Sousa, R. (2011). *Emotional truth.* Oxford: Oxford University Press.

Staden, H. (1998). Alertness to the needs of others: A study of the emotional labour of caring. *Journal of Advanced Nursing,* 27, 147–156. DOI: 10.1046/j.1365-2648.1998.00498.x

Stanovich, K.E. (2009). Distinguishing the reflective, algorithmic, and autonomous minds: Is it time for a tri-process theory? In J. St.B. Evans & K. Frankish (Eds.), *In two minds: Dual processes and beyond* (pp. 55–88). Oxford: Oxford University Press. DOI: 10.1093/acprof:oso/9780199230167.003.0003

Steinberg, R.J. & Figart, D.M. (1999). Emotional labour since *The managed heart". Annals of the American Academy of Political and Social Science,* 561, 8–26. DOI: 10.1177/0002716299561001001

Steinfath, H. (2002). Emotionen, Werte, und Moral. In S. Döring & V. Mayer (Hsg), *Die Moralität der Gefühle.* Deutsche Zeitschrift für Philosophie, Sonderband 4 (ss. 105–122). Berlin: Akademie Verlag.

Stevenson, C.L. (1947). *Ethics and language.* New Haven: University of Yale Press.

Stocker, M. (1996) *Valuing emotions.* Cambridge studies in philosophy. Cambridge: Cambridge University Press.

Svensson, D. (2004). The softhearted but hardheaded problem: Sentimentalism, emotive cognitivism and the circularity problem. *Lund Philosophy Reports,* Lund: University of Lund.

Sundararajan, L. (2002). The veil and veracity of passion in Chinese poetics. *Consciousness & Emotion,* 3, 231–262. DOI: 10.1075/ce.3.2.08sun

Tappolet, C. (2011). Values and emotions. Neosentimentalism's prospects. In C. Bagnoli (Ed.), *Morality and the emotions* (pp. 117–134). Oxford: Oxford University Press.

Taylor, C. (1991). *The ethics of authenticity.* Cambridge, MA: Harvard University Press

Taylor, C. (1989). *Sources of the self.* Cambridge: Cambridge University Press.

Teasdale, J.D. (1999). Multi-level theories of cognition-emotion relations. In T. Dalgleish & M. Power (Eds.), *Handbook of cognition and emotion* (pp. 665–682). New York: John Wiley & Sons.

Teasdale, J.D. & Barnard, P. (1993). *Affect, cognition, and change: Remodeling depressive thought.* Hover, UK: Erlbaum.

Teroni, F. (2007). Emotions and formal objects. *Dialectica,* 61, 395–415. DOI: 10.1111/j. 1746-8361.2007.01108.x

Thompson, R. (2011). Emotion and emotion regulation: Two sides of a developing coin. *Emotion Review,* 3, 53–61. DOI: 10.1177/1754073910380969

Tolich, M. (1993). Alienating and liberating emotions at work. *Journal of Contemporary Ethnography*, 22, 361–381. DOI: 10.1177/089124193022003004

Tomkins, S.S. (1962). *Affect, imagery, consciousness. Vol. 1: Positive affects*. New York: Springer.

Tracy, S.J. & Trethewey, A. (2005). Fracturing the real self vs. false self dichotomy: Moving towards crystallized organizational discourses and identities". *Communication Theory*, 15, 168–195.

Trilling, L. (1972). *Sincerity and authenticity*. Cambridge, MA: Harvard University Press.

Tye, M. (1995). *Ten problems of consciousness*, Cambridge: The MIT Press.

Van Maanen, J. & Kunda, G. (1989). Real feelings: Emotional expression and organizational culture. In B.M. Staw & L.L. Cummings (Eds.), *Work in organizations* (pp. 34–103). Greenwich, CT: JAI.

Walden, T.A. & Smith, M.C. (1997). Emotion regulation. *Motivation and Emotion*, 21, 7–25.

Wentworth, W.M. & Ryan, J. (1992). Balancing body, mind, and culture: The place of emotion in social life." In D.D. Franks & V. Gecas (Eds.), *Social perspectives on emotion*, Vol. 1 (pp. 25–46). Greenwich, CT: JAI.

Wharton, A. (1993). The affective consequences of service work. *Work and Occupations*, 20, 205–232. DOI: 10.1177/0730888493020002004

Wiggins, D. (1997). A sensible subjectivism. Reprinted in S. Darwall, A. Gibbard, & P. Railton (Eds.), *Moral discourse and practise* (pp. 229–244). New York & Oxford: Oxford University Press.

Williams, B. (2002). *Truth and truthfulness*. Princeton: Princeton University Press.

Wright, C. (1992). *Truth and objectivity*. Cambridge, MA: Harvard University Press.

Wright, C. (1996). Truth in ethics. In B. Hooker (Ed.), *Truth in ethics* (pp. 1–18). Oxford, UK/ Cambridge, MA: Blackwell.

von Wright, G.H. (1989). A reply to my critics. In P.A. Schilpp & L.E. Hahn (Ed), *The philosophy of Georg Henrik von Wright*. Library of living philosophers, Vol. 19 (pp. 731–887). La Salle: Open Court.

Yanay, N. & Shahar, G. (1998). Professional feelings as emotional labour. *Journal of Contemporary Ethnography*, 27, 346–373. DOI: 10.1177/089124198027003003

Young, J.E., Klosko, J.K., & Weishaar, M.E. (2003). *Schema therapy: A practitioner's guide*, New York & London: The Guilford Press.

Zajonc, R.B. (1980). Feeling and thinking: Preferences need no inferences. *American Psychologist*, 25, 151–175. DOI: 10.1037/0003-066X.35.2.151

Zajonc, R.B. (1984). On the primacy of affect. *American Psychologist*, 39, 117–123. DOI: 10.1037/0003-066X.39.2.117

Zapf, D. (2002). Emotion work and psychological well-being. A review of the literature and some conceptual considerations. *Human Resource Management Review*, 12, 237–268. DOI: 10.1016/S1053-4822(02)00048-7

Index names

Index terms